D0846836

Organizational Change for Corporate Sustainability

The sustainability of business, both economically and ecologically, is one of this century's key debates. In this fully revised and updated edition of their ground-breaking study of organizational change and corporate sustainability, Dexter Dunphy, Andrew Griffiths and Suzanne Benn argue that there are important benefits to the corporation in making changes for sustainability, and that a sustainable world is only possible with the formation of creative alliances between corporations, citizens and governments.

Bringing together global issues of ecological sustainability, strategic human resource management, organizational change, corporate social responsibility, leadership and community renewal, this book develops a unified approach to corporate sustainability and sets out a fully integrated plan of action to bring about corporate change. Drawing on the most recent field research, and including detailed examples of incremental and transformational changes, it represents an invaluable, practical introduction for leaders, managers and policy makers, and for all students of management, sustainability, environmental studies or organizational studies.

Dexter Dunphy is Distinguished Professor, University of Technology, Sydney. His research interests include corporate sustainability, the management of organizational change and human resource management. His publications include *Corporate Governance and Sustainability: Challenges for Theory and Practice* (2006, edited with Suzanne Benn).

Andrew Griffiths is an Associate Professor in Strategy and Sustainability at the University of Queensland. His areas of research include the impact of climate change on corporate strategy, management of corporate change and innovation, and strategic issues relating to the pursuit of corporate sustainability. His publications include *Sustainability: The Corporate Challenge of the Twenty-first Century* (2000, co-edited).

Suzanne Benn is Associate Professor in the School of Management, Faculty of Business, University of Technology (UTS), Sydney. Her research interests include governance, organizational change and partnerships and collaboration for sustainability. Her publications include *Corporate Governance and Sustainability: Challenges for Theory and Practice* (2006, edited with Dexter Dunphy).

Understanding Organizational Change

Series editor:
Dr Bernard Burnes

The management of change is now acknowledged as being one of the most important issues facing management today. By focusing on particular perspectives and approaches to change, particular change situations, and particular types of organization, this series provides a comprehensive overview and an in-depth understanding of the field of organizational change.

Books in the series include:

Organizational Change for Corporate Sustainability
Second edition
A guide for leaders and change agents of the future
Dexter Dunphy, Andrew Griffiths and Suzanne Benn

Reshaping Change
A processual perspective
Patrick Dawson

Agency and Change
Rethinking change agency in organizations
Raymond Caldwell

The Sustainability and Spread of Organizational Change
Modernizing health care
Edited by David A. Buchanan, Louise Fitzgerald and Diane Ketley

Organizational Change for Corporate Sustainability

A guide for leaders and change agents of the future

Second edition

Dexter Dunphy, Andrew Griffiths
and Suzanne Benn

Routledge
Taylor & Francis Group

LONDON AND NEW YORK

First published 2003
by Routledge
Second edition 2007
2 Park Square, Milton Park, Abingdon, Oxon OX14 4RN

Simultaneously published in the USA and Canada
by Routledge
270 Madison Ave, New York, NY 10016

Routledge is an imprint of the Taylor & Francis Group, an informa business

© 2003, 2007 Dexter Dunphy, Andrew Griffiths and Suzanne Benn

Typeset in Times by Keystroke, 28 High Street, Tettenhall, Wolverhampton
Printed and bound in Great Britain by MPG Books Ltd, Bodmin

British Library Cataloguing in Publication Data
A catalogue record for this book is available from the British Library

Library of Congress Cataloging in Publication Data
Dunphy, Dexter C. (Dexter Colboyd), 1934–
Organizational change for corporate sustainability: a guide for leaders and change
agents of the future / Dexter Dunphy, Andrew Griffiths, and Suzanne Benn. – 2nd ed.
p. cm.
Includes bibliographical references and index.
ISBN 0–415–39329–9 (hard cover) – ISBN 0–415–39330–2 (soft cover)
1. Organizational change. 2. Sustainable development. 3. Business planning.
4. Social responsibility of business. I. Griffiths, Andrew, 1969– II. Benn, Suzanne.
III. Title.
HD58.8.D862 2007
658.4′06—dc22   2006028985

ISBN10: 0–415–39329–9 (hbk)
ISBN10: 0–415–39330–2 (pbk)

ISBN13: 978–0–415–39329–4 (hbk)
ISBN13: 978–0–415–39330–0 (pbk)

Contents

List of illustrations and tables

Figures

Tables

The authors

Dexter Dunphy is Distinguished Professor, University of Technology, Sydney, a position he took up in January 2000 after seventeen years as professor at the Australian Graduate School of Management. Dexter holds the degrees of BA(hons), MEd(hons) and DipEd from Sydney University and PhD in Sociology from Harvard University. His main research and consulting interests are in corporate sustainability, the management of organizational change and human resource management. His research is published in over ninety articles and twenty-five books, including *The Sustainable Corporation: Organizational Renewal in Australia* (co-authored with Andrew Griffiths, 1998); *Sustainability: The Corporate Challenge of the Twenty-first Century* (co-edited with others, 2000); *Beyond the Boundaries: Leading and Re-creating the Successful Enterprise* (with Doug Stace, 2001); and *Corporate Governance and Sustainability* (co-edited with Suzanne Benn, 2007).

Andrew Griffiths is an Associate Professor at the UQ Business School, at the University of Queensland. His areas of research include the strategic management of sustainability issues and corporate responses to climate change. Andrew's doctorate from the University of New South Wales, Sydney, examined the relationship between organizational strategies and industry responses to competitive threats. He has co-authored *The Sustainable Corporation: Organizational Renewal in Australia*(with Dexter Dunphy, 1998) and *Sustainability: The Corporate Challenge of the Twenty-first Century* (co-edited with others, 2000) and has published extensively in leading international management journals, including *Academy of Management Review* and *Journal of Management Studies*.

Suzanne Benn is Associate Professor at the University of Technology (UTS), Sydney. She co-ordinates the MBA programmes at UTS in managing for sustainability and change management. She is the author of a number of publications on sustainability, and is the co-editor of *Corporate Governance and Sustainability*, also published by Routledge. Suzanne holds a bachelor's degree in chemistry from the University of Sydney and postgraduate qualifications in education. She also holds a master's degree in science and society and a doctorate in science and technology studies from the University of New South Wales, Sydney.

Series editor's preface to the second edition

It is with real pleasure that I welcome this second edition of *Organizational Change for Corporate Sustainability*. When Dunphy, Griffiths and Benn launched the first edition of this book in 2003, it was clear that environmental sustainability would be one of the major challenges of the twenty-first century. In the first edition, the authors argued that corporate 'greening' was central to achieving a sustainable world. The book also showed how corporations could begin to change themselves to achieve sustainability. The first edition was warmly welcomed and quickly became a leading text in the field. This new, updated and fully-revised edition of the book further develops the arguments for and approaches to sustainability. I am sure that, like the first edition, it will establish itself as the leading book on change and sustainability.

As well as making a considerable contribution to the sustainability debate, the new edition also makes significant contribution to the Routledge book series on *Understanding Organizational Change*. It is an accepted tenet of modern life that change is constant, of greater magnitude and far less predictable than ever before. For this reason, managing change is acknowledged as being one of the most important and difficult issues facing organizations today. This is why both practitioners and academics, in ever-growing numbers, are seeking to understand organizational change. This is why the range of competing theories and advice has never been greater and never more puzzling.

Over the past 100 years, there have been many theories and prescriptions put forward for understanding and managing change. In the 1940s, Kurt Lewin created perhaps the most influential approach to managing change. His planned approach, encapsulated in his three-step model, became the inspiration for a generation of researchers and practitioners, mainly –

though not exclusively – in the USA. Throughout the 1950s, Lewin's work was expanded beyond his focus on small groups and conflict resolution to create the Organization Development (OD) movement. From the 1960s to the early 1980s, OD established itself as the dominant Western approach to organizational change.

However, by the early 1980s more and more Western organizations found themselves having to change rapidly and dramatically, and sometimes brutally, in the face of the might of corporate Japan. In such circumstances, many judged the consensus-based and incrementally-focussed OD approach as having little to offer. Instead a plethora of approaches began to emerge that, whilst not easy to classify, could best be described as anti OD. These newer approaches to change were less wary than OD in embracing issues of power and politics in organizations; they did not necessarily see organizational change as clean, linear and finite. Instead they saw change as messy, contentious, context-dependent and open-ended. In addition, unlike OD, which drew its inspiration and insights mainly from psychology, the newer approaches drew on an eclectic mix of sociology, anthropology, economics, psychotherapy and the natural sciences, not to mention the ubiquitous post-modernism. This has produced a range of approaches to change, with suffixes and appellations such as emergent, processual, political, institutional, cultural, contingency, complexity, chaos, and many more.

It is impossible to conceive of an approach which is suitable for all types of change, all types of situations and all types of organizations. The aim of this series is to provide both a comprehensive overview of the main perspectives on organizational change, and an in-depth guide to key issues and controversies. The series will investigate the main approaches to change, and the various contexts in which change is applied. The underlying rationale for the series is that we cannot understand organizational change sufficiently, nor implement it effectively, unless we can map the range of approaches and evaluate what they seek to achieve, how and where they can be applied, and, crucially, the evidence which underpins them.

Series editor
Bernard Burnes
Professor of Organizational Change
Manchester Business School
The University of Manchester

Acknowledgements

This book is the culmination of four years of collaborative work between the three authors. However, it builds on more years of their collective experiences in consulting, research and teaching about organizational change, human resource management, social responsibility and ecological sustainability. Each of the authors was involved in undertaking case studies, interviewing managers and change agents, supervising and co-ordinating research students, presenting conference papers and publishing journal articles. All these activities provided a rich set of resources that we have drawn on in the book. In particular, however, we acknowledge the special contribution played by Phyllis Agius and Gabriela Pulczynski in tracking down, synthesizing and organizing much of the research material which appears in various chapters.

In writing this second edition, the three authors undertook different tasks. Because so much has changed in the four years since the first edition in terms of the forces and incentives for change and the implications of sustainability for corporate governance, Suzanne made major revisions to Chapter 2 and Chapter 3. She also took responsibility for adding considerable amounts of new case material concerning leadership to Chapter 9 and revised Chapter 1. Andrew undertook revisions of Chapters 4–8. In each chapter new case material, literature and theoretical insights were integrated into the existing themes and content. Dexter read all the revised chapters, added additional material and made further revisions where appropriate.

Consequently the end product in the case of each chapter was the result of the work of all three authors and of a handful of selected reviewers. We express our particular gratitude to all those in the organizations we studied. We thank them for the interview time and research material they so generously provided and hope that we have given a fair and balanced view of their contribution to sustainability. We also thank other researchers whose published work we have accessed and summarized where relevant.

The following people gave us valuable feedback on drafts of particular chapters: Gabriela Pulczynski, Phyllis Agius, Lino Caccavo, Graham Cavanagh-Downs, Dr Renato Orsatto, Professor Ian Palmer, Stuart Smith and Professor Doug Stace. We also wish to acknowledge the contribution of Jodie Benveniste and Philip Sutton to the original Sustainability Phase Model that we have modified for use in this book. We are also indebted to Philip Sutton for providing us with the term 'sustaining corporation' to describe our 'ideal' sustainable corporation. We sincerely thank Frank Hubbard of Worthwhile Projects Pty Ltd for permission to quote from his Sustainability SMART© system.

We are also deeply indebted to our families. Dexter would like to thank his partner, Francine, for her interest and enthusiasm for the project and his children, Mark, Kristen and Roger for their good humour in accepting that 'Dad's writing another book'.

Andrew would like to thank Jenine for her patience and understanding of the consuming focus involved in writing the manuscript and for the late-night debates on creating better societies. He would like to dedicate these efforts to Jenine and his children, Meg, Liam and Dominic, in the prospect of creating sustainable futures.

Suzanne would once more like to thank her partner, Andrew Martin, for his ongoing advice and support and for the inspiration of his own continuing commitment to the Australian environment. As always, she dedicates her efforts to her three sons, Steven, Andrew and Thomas.

This book outlines critical challenges facing corporations in the new millennium. We hope that the ideas we present here provoke readers to take up the challenge of creating sustainable corporations that support human welfare and a viable future for all life on the planet.

D.D.
A.G.
S.B.

Part I
Towards third wave corporations

1   Setting the agenda for corporate sustainability

- Why corporate sustainability?
- Redesigning the corporation
- Phase models of sustainability
- Change agent roles and the phase model
- Appendix 1.1: Phases in the development of corporate sustainability

Why corporate sustainability?

Since the first edition of this book was published in 2003 there has been a dramatic increase in interest in the fields of corporate sustainability and corporate social responsibility. Corporate managers, government agencies and regulators as well as academics and change practitioners are now engaged in the debate on the 'why' and 'how' of sustainability and social responsibility.[1] In 2006 we are still faced with an extraordinary situation. Never before in the history of the world has the viability of much of the life on this planet been under threat from humanity; never before have so many of the world's people experienced such material wealth and so many others lived in abject poverty; never before have so many had such interesting and fulfilling work and so many others such degrading work or no work at all. If we are to live healthy, fulfilling lives on this planet in the future, we must find new life-affirming values and forge new patterns of living and working together.

The critical situation in which we find ourselves has been brought about by multiple causes but one important contributing factor is the rise of the corporation. Corporations are the fundamental cells of modern economic life and their phenomenal success in transforming the earth's resources into wealth has shaped the physical and social world in which we live. The powerful dynamism of modern organizations has transformed nature and society. The central question to be answered in this century is whether the current model of the corporation needs to be modified to contribute to the continuing health of the planet, the survival of humans and other species, the development of a just and humane society, and the creation of work that brings dignity and self-fulfilment to those undertaking it. And if so, how?

In this book we argue that some traditional organizational values and forms are not sustainable and, unless significantly reshaped, will continue to undermine the sustainability of society and the planet. Corporations have contributed to the problems outlined above and they must therefore be part of the answer. Fortunately their transformation is already under way, driven in part by the changing demands of modern society and also by the leadership of far-sighted and responsible people within and outside corporations who see the need for change. However, for the transformation to be successful, many more change agents are needed. Some of the most important changes in history have been created by people of vision and imagination who were not content simply to react to events about them but could envisage the possibility of a different world and initiate action to bring the new reality into being. They were often regarded as deluded or heretical at the time but later celebrated for their foresight and courage.[2] Today senior executives from some of the world's largest and most profitable corporations – Ford, BP, Toyota, Honda, Du Pont, Swiss Re, Shell, Hewlett-Packard, Unilever – are actively seeking to transform their businesses to respond to sustainability issues. In their minds there is no doubt that we face serious issues such as climate change, resource scarcity, vulnerable ecosystems and poverty. These depleted services provided by nature to humankind require a shift in how corporations think about and deal with sustainability. There is a compelling business case for sustainability as well as an ethical responsibility to find ways forward on these issues.

This book is written to assist change agents to drive the necessary changes faster and farther while there is time. We discuss key issues in the debate around the nature of sustainability but not at great length. For those interested in taking this further we provide references to some of the key books and articles which are the focus of this theoretical debate. Our view is that this debate will now be most fruitfully engaged through the process of reconstructing organizations so they support a sustainable world. The current crisis is too urgent to wait for consensus; we need to start out on the path towards sustainability by generating new models of organizational action that support social relationships and the natural world. The time to debate abstract theories is past; what we need now is to embed our theories in action and to engage in dialogue around working models.

In our view, many corporations need to change significantly the way they do business. However, we are not arguing that corporations are the enemy. We are arguing that new circumstances require new responses. The crises faced by humanity can be resolved only by the use of concerted corporate action. Corporations are instruments of social purpose, formed within society to accomplish useful social objectives. If they do this, they have a right to a continued existence, a licence to use resources and a responsibility to produce socially beneficial products and services. However, if they debase human life, act with contempt for the community of which they are part, plunder and pollute the planet, and produce 'bads' as well as 'goods', they forfeit their right to exist. They become unsustainable because they are unsustaining. The single-minded pursuit of short-term profitability for shareholders or owners does not justify a 'couldn't care less' approach to people and the planet. The prevailing economic value of unlimited and unending growth is the ideology of the cancer cell. Living within the natural limits of the earth's resources and exercising responsible resource stewardship are a universal requirement for all of us, individually and collectively.

This book examines the transition to the organization of the future that functions as an instrument for the fulfilment of human needs and the renewal of the biosphere. We define key steps along the way and indicate how to make an incremental transition from step to step or, in some cases, a transformative leap to the fully sustainable and sustaining corporation. This is therefore a guidebook for corporate change agents – executives, managers and members of the work force, external consultants, community activists – who are dissatisfied with the *status quo* in organizational life and who dream of a new organizational world where individuals are cherished, the community is supported and the natural environment nourished as a matter of course as the organization goes about its core business. Nothing less than this is worthy of our humanity, our intelligence and our ingenuity.

The distinctive contribution of this book is that it concentrates on how to implement the changes that make organizations more sustainable themselves and also more sustaining of the environment and society. In doing this, we draw on leading-edge change theory from management and the social sciences. So this book is a practical and informed tool for creating sustainable corporations that are part of the solution to keeping a world fit to live in. It is an invitation to you to be part of the future solution – a responsible agent of creative change.

For those who are prepared to act with purpose and direction in reshaping the organizational world this is perhaps the most exciting period in human history. Each generation faces its challenges. But this and the next two or three generations will be decisive in determining whether more humans than have ever lived on this planet can create the collaborative institutional forms needed for our survival and the survival of those other precious life forms who share this planet with us. And beyond survival, to create innovative institutional forms to provide us all, and those who come after us, with a quality of economic, social and cultural life that nurtures and develops our human capabilities.

That is the challenge we deal with in this book. In meeting this challenge we must redesign many of our organizations. So we begin here with a short discussion of the evolution of the institution which is the focus of our book: the corporation. Because corporations share so many common features and are so pervasive, we can easily assume that the corporation is an immutable social form. But it is not – it has already undergone substantial redefinitions over time. The question we address here is how can we redesign the corporation for human and ecological sustainability?

Redesigning the corporation

Corporate scandals such as James Hardie, Enron and Anvil Mining have highlighted the extent to which powerful corporate entities can write their own rules for action regardless of the consequences for others. As a result there is increased public pressure for corporations to be made more accountable. The difficulties associated with holding organizations accountable for compliance with legal requirements and legitimate community expectations will be discussed in Chapter 3.

The rise of the multinational corporation and the internationalization of financial markets have taken the power of the modern corporation to the point where it can represent a formidable challenge to the authority of the nation state, let alone small groups of citizens. Global corporations operate across political boundaries and so escape overall surveillance by particular nation states. The wealth of the largest global companies exceeds that of most nations and this has given them unprecedented power. The existence of large-scale power discrepancies does not in itself guarantee that the power will be used irresponsibly but it does create the potential for the misuse of power. Throughout corporate history many corporate chieftains have used their power rapaciously and irresponsibly. For example, a coalition of oil companies and large construction firms in the United States planned and efficiently brought about the demise of the US railroad system to favour the construction of a vast network of interstate highways.

But of course, there are also plenty of instances of corporate leaders exercising social and environmental responsibility. In fact there is a growing divide between those corporate leaders who have embraced the responsibilities and opportunities of corporate citizenship and those who, through ignorance or design, continue to exploit natural and human resources. The tide is turning in favour of the former group – for instance, a recent survey of bankers carried out by the IFC found that '65 per cent reported tangible benefits from sustainable policies, including developing business in new areas and obtaining first mover advantage in areas such as energy efficiency'.[3]

Are corporations evil?

It is a naive and simplistic view that portrays corporations as evil by their very nature. Almost everything we depend on in our modern world is the product of corporations – from the food we eat, the clothes we wear to the phones and computers we use to communicate with each other. We cannot do without corporations. What is important, however, is that we exercise sufficient collective control over the way in which they operate to ensure they support rather than destroy the ecological and social fabric we depend on.

Throughout the history of corporations there has been a continuing debate over how the corporation should be defined, including its legal constitution, its social responsibilities, its role in environmental protection and the constituency to which it is accountable. The core of this debate can be summarized as the argument about whether the role of the corporation is simply to create financial wealth for its owners or to contribute to the well-being of a wider range of stakeholders, including the community, the environment and future generations.

This debate has gone on for as long as 'modern' corporations have existed and its history is too long and complex to trace here. The debate has included, for example, fierce critiques of the legitimacy of the slave trade; sabotage of the 'dark satanic mills' that blighted the lives of workers and devastated England's 'green and pleasant land'; large-scale demonstrations against nuclear power plants; experiments in 'industrial democracy'; the rise of 'green' political parties; organizational innovations such as the 'triple bottom line'; demonstrations against globalization. Since corporations came into being each generation has engaged with and continued this debate which has shaped corporations as we know them today.

Most recently a critical issue in the debate has been the relative virtues of the prevailing neo-liberal economics ('economic rationalism') versus 'stakeholder capitalism'. Neo-liberal economics, led by the economist Milton Friedman, argues that the role of the corporation is simply to maximize short-term returns to shareholders. The widespread acceptance of this point of view, especially by economic advisers to governments, has been influential in shifting considerable power from the public to the private sector, the ongoing privatization of government services, the deregulation of major industries and markets and the creation of international competitive 'free trade' markets. Critics of this viewpoint argue that these changes have had destructive consequences for other important stakeholders – employees, customers, suppliers, governments, local communities, future generations, other species of planetary life, and the environment. A shot across the bows of the neo-liberal economists was fired by Allen Kennedy in his book *The End of Shareholder Value* which argues vehemently against what he sees as the legitimation of 'pure greed'.[4] At least some of the destructive consequences of corporate activity result from the relentless drive for short-term profitability at the expense of longer-term sustainability – an issue we shall return to later in this book. Kennedy suggests reforms to create genuinely sustainable wealth for all the corporation's stakeholder groups, not only its shareholders.

The nature of the modern corporation, and the philosophy of economic neo-liberalism that supports it, has been strongly influenced by the success of the US economy and the history of leading US corporations. The culture of modern capitalism has evolved from the experiences of a multitude of corporations developing on a continent with enormous unexploited and virtually free natural resources. For example, at the time of European settlement, the number of bison on the North American continent was estimated at between 30 million and 60 million. They were the most economically valuable wild animals that ever inhabited the American continent. When a halt was called to their slaughter in the late 1800s only 600 survived. The passenger pigeon, once the most numerous bird in North America and on the planet, did not survive the onslaught of the hunters' guns – they were completely exterminated.[5] Despite depredations of this magnitude, the size of the continent ensured that, for the formative two centuries of US capitalism, the torrent of ecological destruction and the increasing waste and pollution emitted in converting resources into wealth could be absorbed by nature. The wealth that was generated enabled the United States to become the most powerful nation on earth, with a business culture dominating the late twentieth and early twenty-first centuries.

As a result, most corporations today operate under accounting rules and cultural assumptions that reward them for disregarding many of the social and environmental consequences of their activities. They 'externalize' many costs of ongoing operations to the community, the environment and future generations. Neo-classical economics, based on the experience of environmental plenty, still assumes that many inputs from the natural and social environments, like air and parenting, are free goods because there are no financial charges for them. In addition, the goods and services produced by the firm are given value but the 'bads' and 'disservices' created at the same time are often neither identified nor costed and charged back to the corporation. The discourse of business and economics largely defines our ecological and community issues. Hence in the most significant business decisions these issues are ignored because they are invisible – the decision makers have no cultural categories for them – or, if perceived, the issues are regarded as irrelevant or of marginal importance. In fact they are of increasing importance for survival of life on this planet and for social justice and they must become central to strategic decision making. We need a new economics that redefines economic capital to include nature and people.[6]

So we face a situation where corporate decision makers, many of whom are well intentioned, community-minded citizens, make decisions which cumulatively are having a catastrophic impact on the planet and on the global community. And they are supported in this pattern of decision making by consumers (us) who reward them by purchasing goods and services they produce. We are all captives of a culture of capitalism that, over 200 years, produced enormous wealth and an increased standard of living for large numbers of people. But the costs of continuing on this path, using the same methods, are now threatening to destroy our ability to use the wealth in the creation of healthy, satisfying lives and also threatening the viability of such a life for future generations. We have become, in the words of Tim Flannery, 'future eaters'.[7] Most of us have a stake in our current culture and are threatened by any substantial critique of it. We sense that we must, at least for the sake of our children and future generations, start to do some things differently. But the size and the complexity of the issues are daunting and we are caught in a spider web of cultural categories that constrain our effective action. Change must begin with us – but where can we begin?

> Like it or not, the responsibility for ensuring a sustainable world falls largely on the shoulders of the world's enterprises, the economic engines of the future.
>
> (Stuart Hart, Kenan Flagler Business School)[8]

Making a start

Wherever we are in society and the world of work, we can engage in the debate about the social role of the corporation. All of us can contribute to a redefinition of corporations to ensure they become major contributors to sustainability rather than social and environmental predators undermining a world fit to live in. There is a huge opportunity here to ensure that all corporations are instruments of a broader social purpose than the generation of short-term wealth for shareholders. Of course shareholders deserve a return on their investment. As we shall show, in most cases this return is enhanced rather than reduced by sustainable practices. We think it is vital that corporations make profits – but not at the cost of destroying the future viability of society and the planet.

Many well informed scientists and social philosophers are warning that humanity is facing a potential environmental catastrophe of our own making and that we cannot continue to use up the earth's resources at an ever increasing rate. Three examples:

> because we are advancing along this non sustainable course, the world's environmental problems *will* get resolved, in one way or another within the lifetimes of the children and young adults today. The only question is whether they will become resolved in pleasant ways of our own choice, or in the unpleasant ways not of our choice, such as warfare, genocide, starvation, disease epidemics, and the collapse of societies.[9]

> The life of nature demands a revolution in the way we live. And we have no time to lose.[10]

> Now is our last chance to get the future right.[11]

There is an urgent need to act intelligently now to protect ourselves and the unique ecology of this planet that supports us.

The sustainability debate is currently being engaged in three ways: first, at the intellectual level as the immensity of current unsustainable practices is documented and we all become aware of the considerable challenges of changing these practices; second, at the level of corporate action as hundreds of thousands of members of boards of management, executives, managers, supervisors, members of the work force, external consultants, non-government organizations and community groups take a multitude of actions on a daily basis that impact on issues of social and environmental sustainability; third, at the level of consumption, as we collectively create the powerful patterns of financial rewards that shape the economy. If we continue to purchase products that strew our world with waste and poison our environment we cannot blame the captains of industry for the resulting destruction. If we are to make corporations instruments of renewal the debate must be engaged at these three levels: through forging a powerful new ideology that creates a compelling vision of a future world fit to live in, and implementing the practical actions in the workplace and in our consumption patterns that will bring the vision into being.

A new approach to economics has developed in recent years to deal with the fact that traditional economics has largely taken the ecological and social environment for granted. This approach recognizes that economics must take 'natural capital' (ecosystems) and 'social capital' (relations between people) into account. Neoclassical economics treats the economy as a closed system, with negative results, such as pollution, treated as 'externalities' which can be ignored in economic terms. Similarly some of the world's most critical resources are treated as 'free' inputs and accorded no value unless they acquire economic worth in the process of production. Ecological economics, by contrast, makes such externalities an integral part of the economic system. Ecological economics is a new field of study which integrates principles from ecology and economics. As a result of the increasing importance of these new approaches, economists are recognizing the implications of ecological functioning and resilience for human welfare. For instance, biological resources such as trees and fish and ecological services such as erosion control and climate stabilization depend on maintaining certain levels of ecosystem functioning.[12]

The depletion of natural and social resources and the accumulation of toxic wastes or rising crime rates can be consequences of economic decisions that seem 'rational' in traditional economic terms. But in the new economic models their social and economic effects are included rather than excluded. It is fair to say that in these new models some 'rational' decisions begin to look insane. For instance, the decision to build bigger, more technologically efficient fishing fleets to maximize harvests of fish from the world's oceans looks rational – but only on the assumption that the supply of fish is inexhaustible.

This book makes a contribution at all three levels: to the intellectual agenda for change; to the strategies for corporate action; and to changing consumption patterns. We outline the need for sustainability, identifying the gap between where we are now and where we need to be, and then we provide a detailed discussion of the kinds of strategic actions that are needed to carry us forward.

In accomplishing this, we outline developmental phases that lead to the fully sustainable organization, that is, an organization that is itself sustainable because its stakeholders including its employees will continue to support it. But it is also a sustaining organization because it is sustaining the wider society and the ecological environment. Since 1992, when the leaders of the world's governments gathered in Rio to endorse the principles of sustainable development, they have struggled with the challenge of integrating the social, environmental and economic principles that sustainability requires. Corporations which develop according to our integrated model will make a major contribution to ensuring that the world progresses along this path.

Phase models of sustainability

Various authors have described the historical processes by which corporations have moved towards supporting ecological sustainability.[13] Studies of historical stages underlying moves towards corporate social responsibility (or, as we refer to it here, human sustainability) are more rare. An exception is a model proposed by Austin. Austin proposed that corporations develop relationships with other non-profit organizations according to a 'collaboration continuum'. In this continuum the relationship can develop from the philanthropic phase through a transactional relationship, such as sponsorship, to an integrated phase. In this stage profit and non-profit share a common aim.[14] Our interest in phase theories such as this is not primarily to develop historical understanding, although that is useful, but more important to understand the paths corporations must travel to reach a full commitment to a comprehensive model of sustainability that covers both human and ecological issues. If we are to move corporations towards full sustainability we must be able to identify the stage where they are now so we can determine how to move forward.

Much can be learned by examining the history of moves towards sustainability in particular industries. For example, Hoffman has made a detailed analysis of the movement towards ecological sustainability in the chemical industry in the United States.[15] He distinguishes four stages, from 1962, when environmental issues were rarely discussed, to 1993, when the chemical industry and its key stakeholders increasingly adopted a proactive stance, viewing the environment as offering a set of strategic opportunities. In between, the chemical corporations reacted defensively and were met by tough governmental regulations; the initiative then moved from government to environmental activists. Finally the leading US chemical companies absorbed what they had seen as 'heretical' ideas, acted more responsibly and found that the result was actually beneficial in business terms.

There is a great deal of overlap in models such as this, despite differences in the names given to the various phases and different numbers of phases. Clearly any generalized phase model is a high-level abstraction from the bewildering diversity of corporate life. Nevertheless, ideal type models of this kind have a long history in the sciences – without such a model it is difficult to compare and contrast individuals, organizations, communities.[16]

In writing this book we reviewed current models in the ecological and management literature and also drew on our own organizational experience and research. We also reviewed the parallel but unrelated literature on the developmental phases of the movement towards human sustainability in corporations.[17] The result is a comprehensive model of the developmental phases through which corporations progress towards both human and ecological sustainability. This model is central to the approach to change outlined in this book; we summarize it here and explain it in more detail in subsequent chapters.

The sustainability phase model

The phase model is designed as a tool for making meaningful comparisons between organizations to assess their current commitment to and practice of behaviours relevant to two kinds of sustainability: human and ecological. The phases outline a set of distinct steps organizations take in progressing to sustainability. There is a progression from active antagonism,[18] through indifference, to a strong commitment to actively furthering sustainability values, not only within the organization but within industry and society as a whole.

We can use the phases to characterize an organization's characteristic way of treating the human and natural resources it employs. We can also use them to trace the historical trajectory that the organization has taken in getting to where it is and to chart possible paths forward. The phases we distinguish are:

- Rejection.
- Non-responsiveness.
- Compliance.
- Efficiency.
- Strategic proactivity.
- The sustaining corporation.

We do not assume that a firm necessarily progresses through the phases step by step on an 'improving' trajectory. To the contrary, an organization may leapfrog phases or regress by abandoning previously established sustainability practices. Significant shifts are often triggered by changes such as the appointment of a new CEO, stakeholder pressure, new legislation, economic fluctuations or the loss of committed enthusiasts.

What are the distinguishing characteristics of each of these phases?

Rejection involves an attitude on the part of the corporation's dominant elite that all resources – employees, community infrastructure and the ecological environment – are there to be exploited by the firm for immediate economic gain. On the human side, employees are regarded simply as industrial 'cannon fodder': there is no commitment to developing them, and health and safety measures are ignored or paid 'lip service'. There is a strong belief that the firm simply exists to maximize profit and any other claims by the community are dismissed as illegitimate. The firm disregards the destructive environmental impacts of its activities and actively opposes any attempts by governments and 'green' activists to place constraints on its activities.

Non-responsiveness usually results from lack of awareness or ignorance rather than from active opposition to a corporate ethic broader than financial gain. Many of the corporations in this category embody the culture of the past century, concentrating on 'business as usual', operating in conventional ways that do not incorporate sustainability issues into corporate decision making. The firm's human resource strategies, if they exist, are focused mainly on creating and maintaining a compliant workforce. Community issues are ignored where possible and the environmental consequences of the firm's activities are taken for granted and, if negative, disregarded.

Compliance focuses on reducing the risk of sanctions for failing to meet minimum standards as an employer or producer. In organizations at this stage the dominant elite emphasizes being a 'decent employer and corporate citizen' by ensuring a safe, healthy workplace and avoiding environmental abuses that could lead to litigation or strong community action directed towards the firm. However, they are primarily reactive to growing legal requirements and community expectations for more sustainable practices. A recent shift has seen the development of co-regulatory practices. Instead of the traditional 'command and control' approach of governmental regulation, industry, NGOs and governments are collaborating to develop new systems of voluntary compliance. This shift represents a transition from compliance towards later phases.

Efficiency reflects a growing awareness on the part of the dominant elite in the corporation that there are real advantages to be gained by proactively instituting sustainable practices. In particular, human resource and environmental policies and practices are used to reduce costs and increase efficiency. There is, for example, growing awareness in many firms that what is defined as 'waste' derived from the production process may be a valuable resource to another firm. (For example, the spent hops from a brewery may be valuable as cattle feed and therefore sold rather than dumped.) Similarly, investment in training may involve expense but result in compensating added value through increased quality of products and services. While moves towards sustainability may involve additional expense, they can also have significant pay-offs in terms of generating income directly or indirectly. This is the beginning of the process of incorporating sustainability as an integral part of the business.

Strategic proactivity moves the firm further along the sustainability path by making sustainability an important part of the firm's business strategy. The firm's strategic elite views sustainability as providing a potential competitive advantage. Consequently they try to position the organization as a leader in sustainable business practices: with advanced human resource strategies that help make the organization an 'employer of choice', with 'corporate citizenship' initiatives that build stakeholder support and with innovative, quality products that are environmentally safe and healthy. The commitment to sustainability, however, is strongly embedded in the quest for maximizing longer-term corporate profitability, that is, it is motivated by intelligent corporate self-interest.

The sustaining corporation, the final phase, is one where the strategic elite has strongly internalized the ideology of working for a sustainable world. If it is a 'for profit' company the organization still pursues the traditional business objective of providing an excellent return to investors, but voluntarily goes beyond this by actively promoting ecological sustainability values and practices in the industry and society generally. Its fundamental commitment is to facilitate the emergence of a society that supports the ecological viability of the planet and its species and contributes to just, equitable social practices and human fulfilment.

These are only broad summaries of these categories. For the sake of simplicity of presentation our summaries assume consistency in an organization's sustainability stance across the human and ecological areas. This is an oversimplification. In reality an organization can have quite different philosophies in each area. The organization as a whole, for instance, may have relatively enlightened human resource and social responsibility strategies that place it in Phase 5 for human sustainability (HS5) yet be simultaneously pursuing an unsustainable ecological strategy and so be in Phase 2 in ecological sustainability (ES2). For example a mining company may invest strongly in the training and development of its employees and subcontractors and also in local community development (HS5) but it may operate environmentally polluting mining operations (ES2).

A fuller version of the model, which allows for differences of this kind, is given in the appendix at the end of this chapter. We suggest that, on finishing this chapter, you skim-read this, and identify where the organization you are involved in would be appropriately placed on these two important dimensions. As we mentioned above, we shall be dealing with each of these phases in much more detail later in the book and you can check out the specific implications of our argument for your particular organizational situation.

We have categorized the phases of sustainability according to three waves. These waves are set out in relation to the six phases of our phase model in Figure 1.1.[19] Figure 1.1, modified from Kemp *et al.*'s diagrammatic version of our original phase model, shows an 'ideal type' model of the

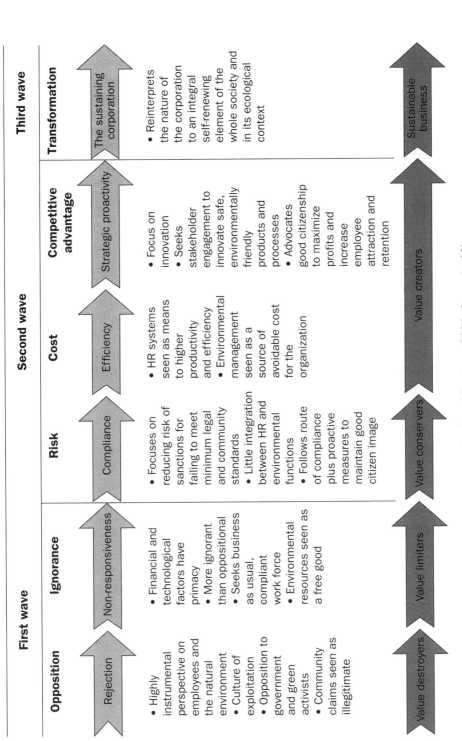

Figure 1.1 Waves of sustainability (modified from Kemp, Stark and Tantrum, 2004. See note 19)

First wave		Second wave		Third wave
Opposition	**Ignorance**	**Risk**	**Cost**	**Third wave**

First wave		Second wave			Third wave
Opposition	**Ignorance**	**Risk**	**Cost**	**Competitive advantage**	**Transformation**
Rejection	Non-responsiveness	Compliance	Efficiency	Strategic proactivity	The sustaining corporation
• Highly instrumental perspective on employees and the natural environment • Culture of exploitation • Opposition to government and green activists • Community claims seen as illegitimate	• Financial and technological factors have primacy • More ignorant than oppositional • Seeks business as usual, compliant work force • Environmental resources seen as a free good	• Focuses on reducing risk of sanctions for failing to meet minimum legal and community standards • Little integration between HR and environmental functions • Follows route of compliance plus proactive measures to maintain good citizen image	• HR systems seen as means to higher productivity and efficiency • Environmental management seen as a source of avoidable cost for the organization	• Focus on innovation • Seeks stakeholder engagement to innovate safe, environmentally friendly products and processes • Advocates good citizenship to maximize profits and increase employee attraction and retention	• Reinterprets the nature of the corporation to an integral self-renewing element of the whole society and in its ecological context
Value destroyers	Value limiters	Value conservers		Value creators	Sustainable business

phases through which an organization that begins by exploiting the ecological and social environment might progress to eventually become a sustaining organization. The phases of our model are shown in the top line of arrows. The diagram shows (above the arrows) how the various phases fit into each of the 'waves' of corporate change. (The first wave, for example, is made up of organizations still in the phases of rejection and non-responsiveness.) The second line provides a single word which characterizes the predominant attitudinal focus of senior executives at each phase. So, for example, in the rejection phase senior executives are focused on rejection of the relevance of sustainability attitudes to their business while, by contrast, at the strategic proactivity phase their predominant focus is on achieving strategic advantage. The dot points summarize some key characteristics of organizations at each phase – more detail is given in the relevant chapters in this book. Finally the arrows at the foot of the diagram how each phase affects the value of the organization. Rejection of sustainability, for example, actually destroys the value of the firm, as it increases risk; non-responsiveness limits value; compliance conserves value by reducing risk, and efficiency and strategic proactivity create value; finally the sustaining corporation represents a transformation of the corporation into a truly sustainable business that is adding value for the business itself and also adding value to society as a whole and for the environment.

Change agent roles and the phase model

The phase model represents the path forward to corporate sustainability. Progress on that path can take place only through the action of various change agents. In Chapter 9 we review the kinds of change agents who can impel the corporation forward on this trajectory and briefly outline their particular roles in the process. In that final chapter we discuss these roles in more detail. Different change agent roles are critical in different phases. Nevertheless at this point you may wish to identify which kind of change agent you are so that, as you read on, you can take particular note of how you can contribute to the progressive redefinition of those organizations you can influence. This will help clarify how you can contribute to creating a more sustainable world.

The range of potential change agents includes those who work in corporations and those outside who wish to influence them. Internal change agents are board members, CEOs, executives, managers, supervisors, professionals in staff roles and other members of the work force. External change agents include politicians and bureaucrats, investors, consultants, suppliers and subcontractors, financial analysts, social and ecological activists and other key stakeholders such as community groups, regulators and consumers. Throughout this book we shall argue that all have legitimate roles to play and that concerted action among different kinds of change agents will be needed to create the significant changes we are advocating.

The way these change agents exert influence varies – we shall take these up in more detail in Chapter 9, but some examples are useful here. Executives may exert influence through the exercise of authority: for example, through interpersonal influence in informal networks or through ensuring that their organization markets only sustainable products. Consumers may help dramatize a key environmental issue or organize a boycott of company goods if they do not meet acceptable environmental standards. Concerted action between internal and external change agents can be particularly powerful in bringing about significant change and we shall be illustrating how this can be orchestrated. Leadership in corporate change is not exercised only by senior executives; in our final chapter we show how the most powerful force for shaping the sustainable corporation of the future will be the collaborative initiatives of a variety of change agents. We emphasize the importance of employees as change agents for sustainability and the importance of leadership which encourages diversity as a way not only to develop human sustainability but to increase the innovative capacity of the organization to progress towards ecological sustainability.

We hope that you now have an understanding of the exciting task we have set ourselves in this book and have begun to see where you can contribute to the significant social shift on which our collective future depends. The rest of the book will help you deepen your understanding of your potential role and maximize your influence in this change process. To guide your path through the book, we give below a brief overview of the contents of each chapter. You may wish to read the chapters in a linear fashion or identify where you think your organization lies on the path to sustainability and leap ahead to read that first. This chapter outline will help assist you to decide which way to go.

However, we do suggest that you start by reading Chapter 2, 'The drivers of change'. Chapter 2 develops a broad overview of the political, economic and social environment in which we as change agents will be operating. We all need a realistic description and assessment of the forces that will restrain our attempts to influence corporate strategic action as well as those drivers of change that we can draw on to support what we are doing.

The story is told of a young emperor in ancient China who was exploring the labyrinthine interior of his palace. In his wanderings he came upon a room in which the palace butcher was carving carcasses. He watched the butcher at work for some time and was surprised to find that he didn't stop to sharpen his carving knife. The emperor enquired: 'My good man, I am surprised to see that you do not sharpen your knife. Surely with such work it must frequently become blunt?' The butcher replied: 'Your Highness is correct in perceiving that for this work the sharpest of knives is necessary. However, I seldom need to resharpen my knife as I cut where there is least resistance.' As change agents we too need to learn how to work with the grain rather than against it, to act with skill and sure timing to ensure that our limited energy has maximum impact in bringing about movement towards the fully sustainable corporation.

Chapter 2 is designed to provide a basis for understanding the context of political and social forces in which our action is a small but potentially powerful part. If we understand the major forces that are transforming the world, we can align our energy with those forces already moving society in the direction we support. In this way even small actions may be amplified to create transformational change rather than neutralized and dissipated by countervailing forces. Chapter 2 presents the context for change while later chapters describe the goals for change and the means for achieving these goals. In Chapter 2 we highlight some of the major shifts that have occurred in the appreciation of the importance of sustainability and intangible value by individual organizations and across industry sectors since the first edition.

Chapters 3–6 then discuss the major steps organizations typically take as they move beyond the phases of rejection and non-responsiveness. Organizations in the first two phases are what we refer to as 'first wave corporations' in contrast to what we have termed the more progressive and forward-thinking 'second' and 'third wave' organizations. Their attitudes of antagonism or indifference to the compelling need to create a more sustainable world reflect the lingering persistence of a collapsing corporate model. In this 'first wave' model the corporation simply exists to exploit human and natural resources for profit, regardless of the impact on the current world or the world of the future.

Chapter 3 deals with Phase 3 of our sustainability development model – compliance. In this phase, organizations seek to minimize the risk of ignoring the increasing demand, from governments, communities and activist organizations, for environmental protection and social justice. The chapter outlines the issues to be addressed at this stage in complying with relevant environmental and social legislation and in meeting the demands of key stakeholders. It places particular emphasis on the values, culture and learning characteristics that can enable organizations to move towards and beyond compliance. The chapter also points to the benefits for the corporation in going to 'compliance-plus', that is, voluntarily exceeding legislative requirements and stakeholder expectations by playing a more proactive role in launching further sustainability initiatives.

This sets the scene for Chapter 4, 'Achieving sustainable efficiencies', which deals with Phase 4 of our model, efficiency. In this stage, organizations start to reap the positive rewards of concerted action on environmental and social issues. Chapter 4 discusses the nature of efficiency, enlarging the concept well beyond cost-cutting exercises. In particular it shows how the sustainability perspective creates a new mind set that can reveal three successive and cumulative cycles of efficiency-oriented measures. Each of these cycles brings important business benefits as well as contributing to the well-being of the community and the natural environment. At this point organizations often discover how wasteful are many of the traditional production or service processes they have used. Redesign of products, production flows and service systems generates significant returns. For example, recycling carpets (Interface) or remanufacturing office machine components (Xerox; Fuji-Xerox) can save millions of dollars as well as benefiting the community and environment by eliminating toxic waste from landfill.

Chapter 5, 'The strategic advantage', moves on to Phase 5: strategic proactivity. At this phase, sustainability becomes important in the organization's strategic repositioning. New competitive advantages can be gained, for example, by moving into rapidly expanding markets for alternative energy (BP) or becoming involved in projects designed to help regenerate communities. An example of the latter was Lend Lease Corporation's successful Bluewater retail shopping complex near the UK end of the Channel tunnel. This massive infrastructure project took place in a community with high unemployment. Lend Lease built a training centre on site to train local unemployed people for jobs in building and, later, as the completed complex came on line, in retail skills. Its effective example of contributing to community renewal led to further substantial construction projects for Lend Lease in Europe – its development arm, Bovis, was selected as the preferred tenderer to build a £200 million hospital at Romford on the outskirts of London.[20]

Strategic proactivity is an exercise in enlightened self-interest on the part of the corporation. However, Phase 6, the sustaining corporation, represents a move beyond enlightened self-interest to a reinterpretation of the nature of the corporation itself – its redefinition as an integral, self-renewing element of the whole society in its ecological context which also actively seeks to sustain and renew the context in which it operates.

Chapters 4 and 5 deal with what we regard as 'second wave' corporations. Second wave corporations represent the dominant business ideology in today's world, particularly the world of large corporations. Second wave corporations at least accept the rhetoric of adopting a view of enlightened self-interest, that is, promising policies that bring wider benefits than short-term financial returns to shareholders. Second wave corporations often fall short of these ideals for various reasons which we shall discuss later. What we are seeking in this book is to assist the transition of first wave corporations into second wave corporations; to find ways to turn the rhetoric of second wave corporations into the reality of realistic action and, where possible, to support the move of more second wave organizations into third wave organizations that are truly sustainable and sustaining.

The characteristics of our ideal organization of the future – the Sustaining Corporation – are discussed in Chapter 6. The sustaining corporation goes beyond self interest to work actively for a fully sustainable world. If we are to lead change, we must have a view of what the ideal organization will be like. Sustaining corporations represent the third wave – the organizations of the future that act as constituent cells in a fully self-renewing world.

The final part of the book takes up the issue of the implementation of change. Corporate change is a theme that permeates the entire book but in Part IV we concentrate on defining pathways towards sustainability, that is, on making corporate change that moves organizations towards sustainability.

Many organizations will prefer to make changes slowly, systematically building on the achievements of one phase as they move into the next. So in Chapter 7 we discuss how to progress incremental change. For example, BP spent most of the 1990s transforming the global company from a rigid, slow-moving, hierarchical organization to a networked, fast-moving, agile company. This was a long-term, substantial and sustained investment in the work force worldwide. This significant investment in renewing the corporate culture and building corporate capabilities proved its worth, for example, in meeting the crisis of the terrorist attack on the United States of 11 September 2001. Within hours of the attack the global executive team knew exactly how each country BP operates in was reacting to the unfolding crisis. Within days they had formulated and launched a comprehensive response. According to Greg Bourne, then regional president, BP Asia/Pacific Holdings, this would have been impossible in the old BP. The change programme did transform the organization 'but in an incremental fashion over a nine-year period'.[21]

Other organizations will want to make widespread, rapid and quite radical alterations to the business they are in, the way they do business, their structure, their corporate culture (or all of these). The choice of a transformative path is often driven by a desire to seize new strategic opportunities or it may come from the organization facing a major threat to its viability. Chapter 8 outlines how this can be done and provides examples such as DuPont which has had several periods of transformative change, its most recent being in search of sustainability practices.

Finally, Chapter 9 takes up the issue of how corporate change can be led. We discuss how a variety of change agents, occupying different kinds of roles and acting individually or collectively, can create the momentum needed to create more sustainable organizations. All of us can exercise leadership where we are. If you already are or wish to be a leader in creating this new social reality, the sustainable and sustaining organization, we dedicate this book to you. You will find it useful in the challenging task that lies ahead.

Appendix 1.1

Phases in the development of corporate sustainability

 ### Phase 1: rejection

Human sustainability (HS1)

Employees and subcontractors are regarded as a resource to be exploited Health and safety features are ignored or paid 'lip service'. Disadvantages stemming from ethnicity, gender, social class, intellectual ability and language proficiency are systematically exploited to advantage the organization and further disadvantage employees and sub-contractors. Force, threats of force and abuse are used to maintain compliance and workforce subjection. Training costs are kept to a minimum necessary to operate the business; expenditure on personal and professional development is avoided. The organization does not take responsibility for the health, welfare and future career prospects of its employees nor for the community of which it is a part. Community concerns are rejected outright.

Ecological sustainability (ES1)

The environment is regarded as a 'free good' to be exploited. Owners/managers are hostile to environmental activists and to pressures from government, other corporations, or community groups aimed at achieving ecological sustainability. Pro-environmental action is seen as a threat to the organization. Physical resource extraction and production processes are used which directly destroy future productive capacity and/or damage the ecosystem. Polluting by-products are discharged into the biosphere, causing damage and threatening living processes. The organization does not take responsibility for the environmental impact of its ongoing operations nor does it modify its operations to lessen future ecological degradation.

 ### Phase 2: non-responsiveness

Human sustainability (HS2)

Financial and technological factors dominate business strategies to the exclusion of most aspects of human resource management. 'Industrial

Ecological sustainability (ES2)

The ecological environment is not considered to be a relevant factor in strategic or operational decisions. Financial and technological factors relations' (IR) or 'employee relations' (ER) strategies dominate the human agenda, with 'labour' viewed as a cost to be minimized. Apart from cost minimization, IR/ER strategies are directed at developing a compliant work force responsive to managerial control. The training agenda, if there is one, centres on technical and supervisory training. Broader human resource strategies and policies are ignored, as are issues of wider social responsibility and community concern.

dominate business strategies to the exclusion of environmental concerns. Traditional approaches to efficiency dominate the production process and the environment is taken for granted. Environmental resources which are free or subsidized (air, water and so on) are wasted and little regard is given to environmental degradation resulting from the organization's activities. Environmental risks, costs, opportunities and imperatives are seen as irrelevant or are not perceived at all.

 ## Phase 3: compliance

Human sustainability (HS3)

Financial and technological factors still dominate business strategies but senior management views the firm as a 'decent employer'. The emphasis is on compliance with legal requirements in industrial relations, safety, workplace standards and so on. Human resource functions such as training, IR, organization development, total quality management (TQM) are instituted but there is little integration between them. Basically the organization pursues a policy of benevolent paternalism with the expectation of employee loyalty in response. Community concerns are addressed only when the company faces the risk of prosecution or where negative publicity may have a damaging impact on the company's financial bottom line. Compliance is undertaken mainly as a risk-reduction exercise.

Ecological sustainability (ES3)

Financial and technological factors still dominate business strategies but senior management seeks to comply with environmental laws and to minimize the firm's potential liabilities from actions that might have an adverse impact on the environment. The most obvious environmental abuses are eliminated, particularly those which could lead to litigation or strong community action directed against the firm. Other environmental issues, which are unlikely to attract litigation or strong community action, are ignored.

Phase 4: efficiency

Human sustainability (HS4)

There is a systematic attempt to integrate human resource functions into a coherent HR system to reduce costs and increase efficiency. People are viewed as a significant source of expenditure to be used as productively as possible. Technical and supervisory training is augmented with human relations (interpersonal skills) training. The organization may institute programmes of teamwork around significant business functions and generally pursues a value-adding rather than an exclusively cost reduction strategy. There is careful calculation of cost–benefit ratios for human resource expenditure to ensure that efficiencies are achieved. Community projects are undertaken where funds are available and where a cost benefit to the company can be demonstrated.

Ecological sustainability (ES4)

Poor environmental practice is seen as an important source of avoidable cost. Ecological issues that generate costs are systematically reviewed in an attempt to reduce costs and increase efficiencies by eliminating waste and by reviewing the procurement, production and distribution process. There may be active involvement in some systematic approach such as Total Quality Environmental Management (ISO 14001). Environmental issues are ignored if they are not seen as generating avoidable costs or increasing efficiencies.

 ## Phase 5: strategic proactivity

Human sustainability (HS5)

The workforce skills mix and diversity are seen as integral and vitally important aspects of corporate and business strategies. Intellectual and social capital are used to develop strategic advantage through innovation in products/services. Programmes are instituted to recruit the best talent to the organization and to develop high levels of competence in individuals and groups. In addition,

Ecological sustainability (ES5)

Proactive environmental strategies supporting ecological sustainability are seen as a source of strategic business opportunities to provide competitive advantage. Product redesign is used to reduce material throughput and to use materials that can be recycled. New products and processes are developed that substitute for or displace existing environmentally damaging products and skills are systematized to form the basis of corporate competences so that the organization is less vulnerable to the loss of key individuals. Emphasis is placed on product and service innovation and speed of response to emerging market demands. Flexible workplace practices are strong features of workplace culture and contribute to the work force leading more balanced lives. Communities affected by the organization's operations are taken into account and initiatives to address adverse impacts on communities are integrated into corporate strategy. Furthermore, the corporation views itself as a member of the community and as a result contributes to community betterment by offering sponsorship or employee time to participate in projects aimed at promoting community cohesion and well-being.

processes or satisfy emerging community needs around sustainable issues (reforestation; treatment of toxic waste). The organization seeks competitive leadership through spearheading environmentally friendly products and processes.

 ## Phase 6: the sustaining corporation

Human sustainability (HS6)

The organization accepts responsibility for contributing to the process of renewing and upgrading human knowledge and skill formation in the community and society generally and is a strong promoter of equal opportunity, workplace diversity and work–life balance as workplace principles. It adopts a strong and clearly defined corporate ethical position based on multiple stakeholder perspectives and seeks to exert influence on the key participants in the industry and in

Ecological sustainability (ES6)

The organization becomes an active promoter of ecological sustainability values and seeks to influence key participants in the industry and society in general. Environmental best practice is espoused and enacted because it is the responsible thing to do. The organization tries to assist society to be ecologically sustainable and uses its entire range of products and services to this end. The organization is prepared to use its influence to promote positive sustainability policies on the part society in general to pursue human welfare, equitable and just social practices and the fulfilment of human potential of all. People are seen as valuable in their own right.

of governments, the restructuring of markets and the development of community values to facilitate the emergence of a sustainable society. Nature is valued for its own sake.

Notes

1　We note for instance that the number of abstracts for refereed journal articles that refer to corporate social responsibility has increased by 280 per cent since 2002, while the total number of refereed articles has increased by 120 per cent.
2　D. Dunphy and A. Griffiths, *The Sustainable Corporation: Organizational Renewal in Australia*, Sydney: Allen & Unwin, 1998.
3　Quoted in *Financial Times* Special Report 'FT Sustainable Banking', Monday 12 June 2006, pp. 1–2, this quote p. 1.
4　A. Kennedy, *The End of Shareholder Value: Corporations at the Crossroads*, London: Orion Business, 2000.
5　T. Flannery, 'The lonesome prairie', *Good Weekend, Saturday Herald*, Sydney, 3 March 2001, 35–41; T. Flannery, *The Eternal Frontier: An Ecological History of North America and its Peoples*, Melbourne: Text Publishing Company, 2001.
6　P. Hawkins, A. Lovins and H. Lovins, *Natural Capitalism: Creating the Next Industrial Revolution*, London: Earthscan, 1999.
7　T. F. Flannery, *The Future Eaters: An Ecological History of the Australasian Lands and People*, Port Melbourne: Reed Books, 1994.
8　S. Hart, 'Beyond greening: strategies for a sustainable world', *Harvard Business Review*, January–February 1997, 67–76. This quote p. 76.
9　J. Diamond, *Collapse: How Societies Choose to Fail or Survive*, New York: Allen Lane Penguin, 2005, p. 499.
10　R. Sheldrake, *The Rebirth of Nature*, London: Random Century Group, 1990, p. xv.
11　R. Wright, *A Short History of Progress*, Melbourne: Text Publishing, 2004, p. 132.
12　D. Pearce and E. Barbier, *Blueprint for a Sustainable Economy*, London: Earthscan, 2000.
13　C. B. Hunt and E. R. Auster, 'Proactive environmental management: avoiding the toxic trap', *Sloan Management Review*, 1990, 31, 7–18.
14　J. Austin, 'Strategic Collaboration between Non-profits and Businesses', Working Paper, Harvard University, 1999.
15　A. J. Hoffman, 'Institutional evolution and change: environmentalism and the US chemical industry', *Academy of Management Journal*, 1999, 42(4), 351–7.

16 For a recent discussion and analysis of the stage model approach, see A. Kolk and A. Mauser, 'The evolution of environmental management: from stage models to performance evaluation', *Business, Strategy and the Environment*, 2002, 11, 14–31.

17 Dunphy and Griffiths, *The Sustainable Corporation*.

18 We do not imply here, of course, that all organizations start the journey from a position of active antagonism to sustainability. Some organizations are actually founded on strong ethical commitments (Phase 6) – they are, however, the exception, rather than the rule.

19 Our original phase model has been represented diagrammatically in V. Kemp, A. Stark and J. Tantrum, *To whose Profit: Evolution*, London: WWF-UK, 2004. We have modified this diagram.

20 C. Cummins, *Sydney Morning Herald*, 1 March 2002, Business Section, 23; 'Case example 12: Lend Lease Bluewater', in B. Hirsch and P. Sheldrake, *Inclusive Leadership*, Melbourne: Information Australia, 2000, pp. 141–2.

21 Personal communication in an interview with Dexter Dunphy undertaken as part of PriceWaterhouseCooper's CEO *Snapshot on Culture*, Sydney, January 2002.

2 The drivers of change

- Issues of global survival
- Social and environmental impacts of 'business as usual'
- The business case for sustainability
- Conclusion

Issues of global survival

On 6 February 2006, UN Secretary General Kofi Annan remarked:

> The world remains locked into short-term thinking, from election
> cycles in politics to profit-taking in the business world. Sustainable
> development cries out for a long-term perspective. The world remains
> captive to the old idea that we face a choice between economic growth
> and conservation. In fact, growth cannot be sustained without
> conservation. One of two jobs worldwide – in agriculture, forestry and
> fisheries – depends on the sustainability of ecosystems.[1]

Sustainability is now widely held to be the desirable path forward for
organizations. The notion has an increasing purchase on legitimacy.
Yet there is still little agreement on what sustainability means or how
we can achieve it. Consequently, governments and corporations are
struggling with issues of survival and renewal – for themselves, for
the human community and for the ecosphere.

We see five key issues pressuring corporations to become more
responsible global citizens:

- The first issue is poverty. There are still 1.2 billion poor people in the
  world.[2]
- Second, much of the material wealth is owned by the major
  corporations of the developed world.
- Third, the negative effects of globalization and industrialization are
  largely impacting on the developing world and are linked with the

loss of traditional localized cultures and community life.[3] There has been a pattern of special pleading and avoidance on the part of some self-interested nations and corporations which has both limited the ability of international agreements to address these inequities and increased the social pressure on corporations to be more responsible citizens.

- Fourth, the failure of the international community of nations and individual corporations to address these concerns is now a subject of intense interest to an increasingly aware and communicative global audience. Society is less willing to take lack of scientific evidence as a reason for inaction in the cause of environmental and social well-being. A wider range of stakeholders is demanding much more from the corporation, particularly those stakeholders who have come together under the broad banner of sustainability.
- Finally, national governments are experimenting with ways to use market and legislative mechanisms to encourage change toward more corporate accountability and innovation for sustainability.

The findings of the 2004 *Living Planet Report* clearly indicate that existing policies have failed to deal with the planetary impacts of industrialization and globalization. Figure 2.1 for instance shows the trends in population of terrestrial, freshwater and marine species worldwide. These declined by 20 per cent between 1970 and 2000. Figure 2.2 shows the use of renewable natural resources by humans measured in number of planets. It shows that the human demands on the biosphere are two and a half times larger in 2001 than in 1961, exceeding the biocapacity by 20 per cent. This depletion is not reversible.

The benefits of raising more people out of poverty than ever before in human history are manifest. Even the sceptics agree we should be able to do better than create a world where 800 million people are actually starving[4] and where the number of people living in extreme poverty is still 1.2 billion (a figure little changed since 1990).[5]

It is true that the positive effects of industrial development in East and South East Asia are striking in terms of literacy rates and life span, for example the average life span in China has gone from thirty-five to seventy years in two decades. But these landmark achievements have come at an environmental cost so large that China's leadership publicly recognizes it will impede the continuing economic development of that country. Shi Guangsheng is chairman of the Chinese Association of Enterprises with Foreign Investment and a former head of foreign trade.

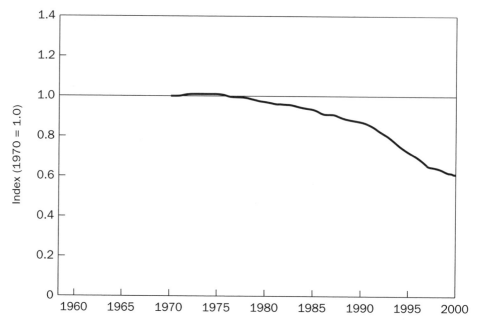

Figure 2.1 *Living Planet index, 1970–2000*

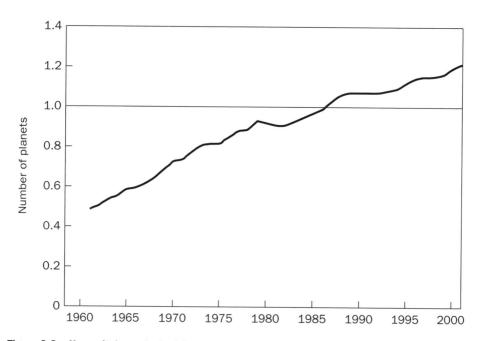

Figure 2.2 *Humanity's ecological footprint, 1961–2001 (taken from WWF,* Living Planet Report, *2004)*

He called for foreign companies to help China with problems of growing income disparity and environmental pollution. He stated that one-seventh of the country suffers from acid rain, half the country's rivers are seriously polluted and one-fourth of Chinese citizens do not have clean drinking water. He added that China represents a huge consumer market for foreign firms, who should therefore help China address such issues.[6] The Chinese environmental watchdog acknowledges that mass protests over pollution in China have been mushrooming, increasing at the rate of 30 per cent per year. There has been an environmental incident every other day in China since the disastrous spill of benzene and nitrobenzene on the Songhua river in 2005 which forced authorities to turn off the water supplies for millions of people.[7] Chinese meteorologists say that crippling dust storms are occurring as a result of increased temperatures, poor construction practices, overgrazing and high emission levels from transport. They are now frequent in north and north-western China, including the capital Beijing.[8]

The destructive environmental and social side effects of the combination of population growth and increased consumption have contributed to these issues of global survival. How do we address these issues? What role should corporations, governments and individuals play in creating a more desirable future? Central to the resolution of these issues is the need for all sectors of society to co-operate in changes designed to promote human and ecological sustainability. In this book we support the position that the health of the natural environment does not have to be traded for the sake of human and economic development. If corporations integrate human and ecological sustainability into their business planning, then community, marketplace and workplace concerns can be addressed alongside those of the planet.

Emerging forces driving sustainability

The Earth Summit in 1992 endorsed the need for a positive relationship between the environment and business and introduced the concept of 'sustainable development'. Sustainable development is generally understood to mean development which meets the needs of the present generation without compromising the ability of future generations to meet theirs. Since then, integrating the social, environmental and economic dimensions of sustainability into a holistic process has proven a major challenge to business managers, community activists, politicians, bureaucrats and theoreticians.

This chapter examines the pressures on corporations to meet the challenge of adopting a more socially and responsible position rather than continuing to disregard the social and environmental impacts of 'the business as usual' approach to economic development. The public is becoming increasingly aware of the potentially catastrophic impact of climate change which is only one result of industrialization. These pressures come from stakeholders vital to the corporation's prosperity such as governments, community members, consumers, customers, other corporations, industry associations, and other non-government organizations. Other driving forces are corporate leaders and change agents who see sustainability as a competitive advantage for the firm. Marketing, human resource and operations managers are now making decisions influenced by sustainability factors.[9] Employees, shareholders and investment companies are assessing the firm's performance against sustainability criteria such as the maintenance of intellectual, knowledge and social capital, commitment and values, risk management and, increasingly, an innovative corporate culture. These are all factors supporting the long-term survival of the firm in the new economy.[10]

Many corporate leaders are also driven by a sense of moral purpose that goes beyond rational utility and business advantage. They have an increasing sense of responsibility: to future generations and to the health of the planet. Leading writers talk of new models for corporations that will dictate a novel way of doing business. For these writers, the firm, like any other 'cell' of society, is a living organism in an interconnected ecological community, where caring for others and for the biosphere is the ongoing function of each community member.[11]

Social and environmental impacts of 'business as usual'

Climate change

A 2006 report[12] prepared for the Australian government by the Australian National University (ANU) shows that climate changes could be much more drastic than previously expected. Climate change science has made important advances even since the most recent report by the Intergovernmental Panel on Climate Change's (IPCC) Third Assessment Report (TAR). Among the factors which scientists now believe add more urgency are: the effects of aerosols which act in opposition to greenhouse gases and whose concentration is likely to decrease; the decrease in albedo or the reflectivity of ice and snow where it has melted because of global warming, and a range of other organic processes, such as the oxidation of organic matter previously buried under the snow. The overall impact of these factors has led many climate scientists to revise upward the speed and degree of global warming due to the release of more carbon into the atmosphere.

According to the ANU report:

> Although much uncertainty still surrounds the timing, rate and magnitude of these effects, they all operate to amplify the initial greenhouse warming. Thus, there is now perceived to be a greater risk that the upper end of the well known IPCC Third Assessment Report (TAR) estimate that a 1.4 to 5.8°C temperature rise will be reached or exceeded by 2100.

In developed countries there are expected to be major impacts in three major industry sectors: water and primary industries, tourism and infrastructure and insurance. In Australia, for instance, Table 2.1 shows examples of negative expected effects in the three sectors for temperature rises 1–4 °C.[13]

Table 2.1 *Effects of climate change on selected industry sectors in Australia (modified from Preston and Jones. See note 13)*

Temperature rise	Tourism	Water and primary industries	Infrastructure and insurance
4 °C	Most vertebrates lose 90%–100% of core habitat	Extreme rainfall in some states increases by 25%	180 days a year above 35 °C in some states
3 °C	Distribution of Great Barrier Reef shrinks by 95%	55% loss of eucalyptus core habitat[a]	Temperature-related deaths of people over 65 rise by 144%–200%
2 °C	80% of World Heritage Kakadu freshwater wetlands lost	Pasture growth slows by 31%	Road maintenance costs in Australia rise by 17%
>1 °C	Vertebrates in World Heritage wet tropics lose 90% of their habitat	40% loss of eucalyptus core habitat	Double the number of people exposed to flooding in Australia and New Zealand
<1 °C	Vertebrates in World Heritage wet tropics lose half their habitat	Droughts in state of New South Wales 70% more frequent and more widespread	18% more days above 35 °C in state of South Australia

Note (a) While some areas of Australia will show increased timber yields of 25%–50% other areas are expected to show similarly decreased yields.

The weather-related damage associated with global warming has the most disastrous effects on the poorer, uninsured nations. In the floods of 1998, for instance, two-thirds of Bangladesh was submerged.[14] Even critics of the Kyoto Protocol on Climate Change agree that global warming has massive costs and that the 'developing countries will be hit much harder' by the rises in temperature.[15]

An assessment by the Intergovernmental Panel on Climate Change

- *Overall, climate change is projected to increase threats to human health, particularly in lower-income populations, predominantly in tropical/subtropical countries.*
- *Populations that inhabit small islands and/or low-lying coastal areas are at particular risk of severe social and economic effects from sea-level rise and storm surges.* Many human settlements will face increased risk of coastal flooding and erosion, and tens of millions of people living in deltas, in low-lying coastal areas and on small islands will face the risk of displacement. Resources critical to island and coastal populations such as beaches, fresh water, fisheries, coral reefs and atolls and wildlife habitat would also be at risk.
- *The impacts of climate change will fall disproportionately upon developing countries and the poor persons within all countries, and thereby exacerbate inequities in health status and access to adequate food, clean water and other resources.* Populations in developing countries are generally exposed to relatively high risks of adverse impacts from climate change. In addition, poverty and other factors create conditions of low adaptive capacity in most developing countries.
- *Ecological productivity and biodiversity will be altered by climate change and sea level rise, with an increased risk of extinction of some vulnerable species (high to medium confidence).* Significant disruption of ecosystems from disturbances such as fire, drought, pest infestation, invasion of species, storms, and coral bleaching events is expected to increase. The stresses caused by climate change, when added to other stresses on ecological systems, threaten substantial damage to, or complete loss of, some unique systems and extinction of some endangered species.[16]

Christian Aid has calculated, on the basis of statistics from the United Nations, the insurance industry and other sources, that between 2000 and 2020:

- Half the world's population, most of them living in poor countries, could be at risk of drought or flood.

- The world could face a bill of £6,500 billion (£6.5 trillion) for climate-related disasters – equivalent to the cost of 6,000 space shuttles or 8,600 Millennium Domes.
- There could be as many as 245 climate-related catastrophes.[17]

In its report Christian Aid estimated that as many as 182 million people in sub-Saharan Africa could die of diseases related directly to climate change.[18] A World Bank publication also emphasizes the inequitable effects of climate change, pointing to other effects such as the spread of tropical diseases, more frequent and more intense droughts in Asia and Africa and the large number of people likely to be displaced by a rise in the sea level – including tens of millions in Bangladesh alone, as well as entire nations inhabiting low-lying islands such as those in the Caribbean Sea and the Pacific Ocean. But according to The World Bank:

> Most threatening is the fact that, according to current understanding, the global climate is a finely tuned mechanism that can be pushed out of balance and irreversibly set on a course toward catastrophic consequences that scientists can't even fully predict. These risks are hard to evaluate, but they appear credible enough to demand urgent attention.[19]

There is some good news that change is happening in response to public concern and a rapidly developing consensus particularly on the realities of climate change and the damaging effects of chlorofluorocarbons (CFCs) on the protective ozone layer. The UN recently reported that more than 120 climate change mitigation projects implemented since 1991 have avoided an estimated 1.2 billion tonnes of carbon dioxide and that developed countries have reduced their consumption of CFCs by 99 per cent since 1987.

In a number of countries, corporations, state and local governments are addressing the lack of action by national governments on climate change. In the United States, for instance, the mayors of more than 200 cities have signed the US Mayors' Climate Protection Agreement, and nine eastern states have established the Regional Greenhouse Gas Initiative, while California, in a landmark initiative, has passed tough automobile emission controls.[20] Emission trading aimed at achieving environmental outcomes via the international financial markets has been estimated to be worth $US10 billion-plus in 2005. Table 2.2 shows examples of carbon trading schemes around the world:[21]

More firms are taking initiatives to meet these challenges. One example of a corporate initiative comes from the major consulting firm

Table 2.2 Examples of carbon trading schemes

International mandated schemes	Intra-national schemes	Voluntary schemes
Kyoto Protocol	Australia-NSW Greenhouse Gas Abatement Scheme	California Climate Action Registry
European Union Greenhouse Gas Emissions Allowance Trading Scheme	Regional Greenhouse Gas Initiative (RGGI) – north-east states of the US	Chicago Climate Exchange

PricewaterhouseCooper (PWC). It has made a global commitment to reduce its greenhouse gas emissions because it makes environmental and business sense, according to the firm's Australian infrastructure director. The Australian office alone has spent A$1 million over six months to upgrade the lighting in its 32,000 m^2 of office space in Sydney, where 2,400 staff work. Installation of a new lighting system means that each day, when the first staff member walks out of the lift and to his or her desk, sensors pick up the movement and turn on the lights. When no movement has been detected for more than twenty minutes the lights go out. The lighting redesign for this office alone will save 630 tonnes of carbon dioxide a year, equivalent to the greenhouse gas emissions generated by 140 cars. Estimates are that it will take PWC five years to recoup the A$1 million spent on the system, but in the four months since its installation the firm has already cut its energy use by 15 per cent.[22]

In another example of enlightened business leading government, we report in Chapter 9 on the Australian Business Roundtable on Climate Change, made up of the CEOs of six leading Australian companies. The group has commissioned its own research into the effects of cutting emissions on economic growth. It has concluded that Australia could cut its emissions by 60 per cent from 2000 levels by 2050 and still have strong economic growth. At the launch of the round table, David Morgan, CEO of Westpac Banking Corporation, recounted an anecdote concerning his recent conversation with the head of the General Electric Company in the United States, Jeff Immelt. According to Morgan:

> He [Immelt] said to me he was virtually certain that the first action
> of the next President of the United States would be to initiate urgent
> action on climate change. And he wasn't saying that as a casual
> political statement . . . he is [allocating] billions of dollars' worth
> of investment in the confidence of that development.[23]

Globalization

Globalization has opened markets, dispersed capital and grown investment and has been endorsed by most leaders of developing and developed countries. The UN figures show that international trade has increased from 35 per cent in 1974 to almost 50 per cent in 2002. Increases are in all regions but strongest in East Asia.[24]

But globalization is also reinforcing and extending inequities in human living standards and exacerbating climate change. Sub-Saharan Africa is expected to see further industrial decline as a result of the ending of the textile quota system.[25] Global activity, such as increased trade, movement of skilled workers and financial flows, disproportionately benefits the richer countries. For example, the expansion in the British health service in recent years has been possible only with the migration of foreign-trained workers from, among other countries, Malawi, Zambia, Sierra Leone, Botswana and Ghana, and 12 per cent of all doctors in United Kingdom have been trained in India.[26]

The globalization of food

Figures from the New Economics Foundation illustrate the extent to which food products move back and forth across international boundaries and highlight the possible environmental impacts. In 2004:

- UK imported 465 tonnes of gingerbread and exported almost the same volume, 460 tonnes
- UK sent 1,500 tonnes of fresh potatoes to Germany and brought in 1,500 tonnes of fresh potatoes back from the same place
- UK imported 44,000 tonnes of frozen boneless chicken cuts and exported 51,000 tonnes of fresh boneless chicken
- UK sent 10,200 tonnes of milk and cream to France and imported 9,900 tonnes from France
- UK imported 391,432 tonnes of chocolate and exported 170,652 tonnes[27]

In another example of the negative impacts of globalization, the United States receives two-thirds of all international investment while most developing countries receive little.[28]

Inequities of this magnitude feed social unrest, which in turn exacerbates social inequities and wreaks more environmental destruction. As the

Executive Director of the United Nations Environment Program (UNEP), Klaus Toepfer, has pointed out: 'Fifty percent of the world's peoples now live in cities and often the most toxic element in the environment is poverty.'[29] The implication for corporations becomes only too apparent. Do they defend and take part in this system that contributes to these social and environmental problems or do they shift their mind set and activities to become part of the solution?

'Globalization from above'

Two sets of actors have emerged on the global stage in reaction to these adverse social and environmental effects of globalization and industrialization. From above, government representatives are negotiating international agreements, such as the response to diminishing world oil reserves, the nuclear non-proliferation treaties, GATT, the World Economic Forum, the World Trade Organization and the inter-governmental agreements on the environment.[30] However, national governments experience difficulty in co-operating in the implementation of the intergovernmental agreements concerning sustainability for various reasons, including unemployment, economic conditions and the activities of various interest groups. Some governments, like that of the United States under President George W. Bush, refuse to co-operate or work to actively undermine these developments. This puts the onus on multinational corporations to take more responsibility for their actions.

The World Commission on Environment and Development (WCED) was established by the United Nations in 1983 and was chaired by Gro Harlem Brundtland. The WCED report *Our Common Future* was the first attempt by an intergovernmental body to promote global dialogue on sustainability.[31] The report takes appropriate sustainable development or progress to be development which 'meets the needs of the present without compromising the ability of future generations to meet their own needs'.[32]

This view of appropriate development was promoted at the Second United Nations Conference on the Environment and Development (UNCED), held in 1992 in Rio de Janiero. It was the largest ever heads of government meeting, with more than 170 countries represented. The conference endorsed the major action plan Agenda 21. The 400 page Agenda 21 has been widely taken as a blueprint for the implementation of sustainable development and the integration of economic growth with environmental responsibility. Since then the international community has developed a range of treaties and agreements, which are designed to monitor 'progress' largely according to this definition. Ten global treaties and hundreds of regional and bilateral agreements have been negotiated.[33]

Responses to 'globalization from above'

In actual fact some of these treaties do not result in effective action and often preserve existing inequities that favour the interests of the already privileged nations. Corporate and government irresponsibility and equity issues in the development of treaties and agreements are putting business under pressure to implement voluntary sustainability measures to supplement the international agreements.[34]

In Chapters 3 and 9 we discuss some of the voluntary codes that industry organizations, multi-stakeholder arrangements and individual organizations have developed to restore their credibility. They include the *Valdez* Principles, the US Business Principles for Human Rights of Workers in China and the Business Charter for Sustainable Development. Other corporations have taken part in the creation of measurement and reporting systems. For instance, the ISO 14000 series for systems of environmental management was created by the collaboration of ninety standard-setting groups from 100 different countries. Figure 2.3 shows the rate of increase in ISO 14000 registered sites in the United States. Another group, the Coalition for Environmentally Responsible Economies (CERES), in partnership with the United Nations Environment Programme (UNEP), has convened the Global Reporting Initiative (GRI) to develop indicators to assess corporations in terms of their economic, environmental and social performance.

A precautionary model for development

The difficulty encountered so far in ensuring social and environmental health in the face of global capitalism is also putting pressure on the United Nations to take on broader and more binding responsibilities. At the World Economic Forum in Davos in 1999 UN Secretary General Kofi Annan challenged business to support a Global Compact he called 'Globalization with a Human Face'.[35] The compact is intended to promote human rights, just labour standards and good environmental practices and

Figure 2.3 *Rates of registration under ISO 14001 in the United States*
Source: 'Environmental Systems Update', www.qsuonline.com/Submission
Instructions/ESUjuly04.pdf (accessed 18 June 2006), provided by Capaccio Environmental
Engineering, 31 January 2004.

marks an attempt by the United Nations to lead both the private and
public spheres in the direction of a more equitable and ecologically
sustainable model of development. In 2006 there are many hundreds of
companies throughout the world which have signed the Compact.
Although the 'globalization from above' movement has to date
demonstrated a limited capacity to implement sustainability,[36] there is
evidence of corporations co-operating proactively to lend more support to
the sustainability movement. Some world and corporate leaders are
showing that they are willing to push for development which is more
cautious and self-reflective. As well, an equally powerful force is welling
up from below.

'Globalization from below'

Organized by transnational NGOs and spread largely on the internet,
'globalization from below' is an initiative directed against the perceived
self-seeking manipulations of elite nation states and transnationals
driving 'globalization from above'.[37] The aims of 'globalization from
below' are diffuse and the vision of the future is not clearly specified.
But the message is clear on two counts. The 'globalization from below'
movement, and the criticism of Western 'imperialism' surrounding the

events of September 2001, indicate the extent to which some constituent groups in society are opposed to Western developmentalism. Second, influential environmentalists, such as Paul Hawken and Dr Vandana Shiva, whose books and articles have a worldwide audience, are leading anti-globalization protesters in support of decentralized decision making on human and ecological sustainability issues.[38] In this debate, many multinationals have been targeted by demands to deliver more sustainable outcomes.

According to Vandana Shiva:

> Food hazards have increased with industrialisation of food production and processing. On a global scale, new diseases are emerging and more virulent forms of old diseases are growing as globalisation spreads across factory farming and industrial processing and agriculture.[39]

Organizations such as OXFAM have considerable influence in the world media. The 2006 Oxfam *Offside! Labor Rights and Sportswear Production in Asia* report, for instance, has been well publicized. The report raises questions concerning the large sums paid to sports stars to market sports brands compared with the tiny wages paid to workers in developing countries. This report cites numerous cases whereby it is common practice for abuse, violence and instant dismissal to be exercised on workers who attempt to organize or negotiate for better work conditions, higher pay and their employee entitlements under domestic law.

Offside! Labor Rights and Sportswear Production in Asia[40]

In this report Oxfam examines the steps twelve international sports brands – Adidas, ASICS, FILA, Kappa, Lotto, Mizuno, New Balance, Nike, Puma, Reebok, Speedo and Umbro – have taken to ensure their suppliers in Asia allow workers to organize in trade unions and bargain collectively for better wages and conditions. It concludes that all sportswear companies need to take a more serious approach to workers' right to freedom of association – although some companies such as Nike and Adidas have made major advances through developing transparency measures and codes of practice for their many suppliers. The report finds that sportswear manufacturer FILA, owned by Sports Brands International (SBI), has taken the least action to improve respect for trade union rights in its Asian supplier factories. It concludes that 'FILA has failed to adequately

continued

address serious labor rights abuses when they have been brought to the company's attention and since February 2005 has ignored multiple attempts by labor rights groups and trade unions to communicate with the company about labor issues'. Research conducted by Oxfam in 2004 into one of FILA's Indonesian factories, PT Tae Hwa, found that there was a denial of trade union rights, high levels of sexual harassment and intrusive procedures for women wishing to claim their legally entitled menstrual leave. One female worker reported to Oxfam that when she attempted to organize a strike against the requirement that they work through the night when orders are high, the factory hired violent thugs to break up the protest. Women who work in the sewing department in PT Tae Hwa reported that management threw production materials at them and called them names like 'pig' and 'donkey'. The report also highlights shifts of production by sportswear producers away from countries which have ratified International Labour Organization Conventions recognizing core labour standards fundamental to the rights of human beings at work. For example, Nike has subtly shifted its sourcing to countries where trade union and workers' rights don't have legal force – whilst in 1998 52 per cent of its shoe production was in countries which gave force to worker freedom of association, that figure has fallen to 38 per cent in 2005. The report concludes that only limited progress has been made to adequately undertake effective programmes which will address the issue of human rights and workers' rights abuses in Asian sportswear factories.

The business case for sustainability

The networked society

'Globalization from below' highlights two important points for corporations. First, globalization and the information revolution have also given the general public the means for self-critique and self-transformation. As awareness of the limitations of our traditional institutions spreads, we are moving towards what Hazel Henderson has termed 'the networked society'. Henderson argues that the most noticeable current political trend has been the advance of citizen organizations and movements. They are now a distinct third sector in the world, holding the private and public sectors more accountable. More access to information has helped empower citizens, consumer choice, employees and socially responsible investors. 'The information society has created new winners – and morphed into the "age of truth"'.[41]

Second, increased public awareness of sustainability issues and diminishing public trust in both corporations and governments are

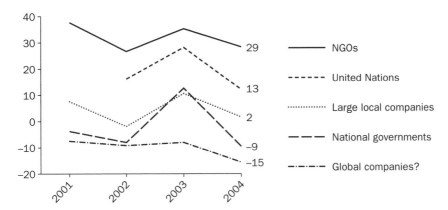

Figure 2.4 *Overall changes in trust, 2001–05 (average of fourteen tracking countries)*
Source: GlobeScan survey of trust in governments, corporations and global institutions. Reprinted with permission of GlobeScan® Incorporated.
Note The fourteen countries that were tracked are: Argentina, Brazil, Canada, Germany, Great Britain, India, Indonesia, Italy, Mexico, Nigeria, Russia, Spain, Turkey and the USA.

creating market expectations of more responsible corporate behaviour and sustainable products and services. The 2005 survey by GlobeScan carried out for the World Economic Forum in twenty countries, interviewing more than 20,000 citizens, indicates the extent to which trust is declining. It shows that trust in a range of institutions has dropped significantly since January 2004 to levels not seen since the months following the 11 September 2001 terrorist attacks.[42]

Alliances for sustainability

Another force driving the corporate shift to sustainability is the formation of new alliances in the name of sustainability. In this new global reality, alliances and networks are forming between social and natural scientists, business, local government, community and other social actors whose allegiances cross established boundaries. The media, information systems and *ad hoc* 'coalitions of opposites', such as those between NGOs and business organizations, are increasingly influential in all aspects of society. The Global Reporting Initiative, for instance, gathers input from environmental, human rights and industry association NGOs. Consumer action and mass boycotts and protests are forcing corporations to defend their actions. The open-ended nature of the sustainability ethic gives it the power to bring together, at least to the discussion table, people and groups with very different political and ideological perspectives. Some supporters advocate greening of business models which work within the current model of capitalism and democracy and support continuing technological innovation and economic growth.[43] Others argue that this approach merely encourages the continuing exploitation of ecological resources, rather than guiding us towards a more harmonious relationship with nature.[44] Other critics argue that reliance on technical solutions for sustainable development and their diffusion to the countries of the South represents just another exploitative, special-interest-based relationship between North and South.[45] Still others take the long-term value of life on earth to be the crucial component of the sustainability ethic; an approach incompatible with the standard approach from economics of discounting the future.[46] 'Social ecologists', on the other hand, argue that human beings will continue to exploit nature if they continue to exploit each other, as in current conditions of global capitalism.[47]

Because of the capacity of sustainability to bring together different factions of society, a wide range of environmental and human rights organizations have emerged as a powerful force for corporate change, operating at both national and international levels in co-operation with corporations. Some have become heavily involved as gatekeepers of national deregulatory reforms and in co-operative arrangements at the international level.[48]

Dynamic partnerships between these newly recognized stakeholders are bringing about major shifts in corporate attitudes and practices. The Global Reporting Initiative, as mentioned, is one. In another instance, the NGO Global Forest Watch provides maps indicating the whereabouts of old growth forests and other data for the Ikea corporation to enable purchasing of forest products according to sustainable criteria. Another example is the partnership formed between the World Wide Fund for Nature (WWF) and the Unilever corporation, at the time the world's largest supplier of frozen fish, with the aim of developing incentives to support sustainable fishing. The Marine Stewardship Council was developed as a result of this alliance.[49] The community-based Landcare movement in Australia, which aims to foster sustainable natural resource management, has formed many partnership arrangements with corporate supporters such as the major mining firm Rio Tinto, the resources company BHP and Fuji Xerox. Sponsorship agreements can influence corporate support for sustainability. Examples include more precautionary labelling on paint tins for safe disposal and the development of an approved environment policy by the manufacturer of own-brand paints.[50]

The Play Fair Alliance

The Play Fair Alliance – a network of organizations including the Clean Clothes Campaign, the International Confederation of Free Trade Unions and the International Textile, Garment and Leather Workers' Federation (ITGLWF) and eleven Oxfams – proposed in 2004 that the World Federation of Sporting Goods Industries (WFSGI) and sports companies co-operate in a programme of work to improve respect for labour rights in the industry. Major recommendations include:

● Confidential and accessible means for workers to report exploitation and abuse.
● Independent education and training for workers concerning their rights at work.
● Transparency regarding company supply chains and efforts to improve conditions.
● Purchasing practices which allow suppliers to respect labour standards (including stable business relationships and reasonable prices and delivery times).
● A framework agreement between the ITGLWF and the WFSGI to facilitate freedom of association and collective bargaining.

In addition, this report recommends that sports brands should:

● Prioritize retaining unionized factories in the companies' supply chain.
● Ban, or severely restrict, the employment of workers on short-term contracts.[51]

Corporations are learning from relations with other sectors. They are learning to be mission- and board-led, and their employees are learning the value of social cohesiveness and a shared sense of responsibility. They can gain in legitimacy while keeping to their central business focus.[52] They are recognizing the growing demand from across society for more participatory decision making and accountability.[53] In the process they have learnt the value of strategic alliances and of sustainability.

The mining industry faces new challenges

A new and independent study group, Mining, Minerals and Sustainable Development (MMSD), has been established with the aim of assisting the mining industry to solve the problem of how to satisfy demand for minerals while addressing the social, environmental and community impact of their industry. MMSD has established an assurance group comprising twenty-five representatives from the mining industry, the union movement, investment houses and NGOs, including environmental activists,

continued

who will evaluate the integrity of the project. So far, the group has established eight areas of priority attention. These include environmental and land management issues, national economic development, sustainable markets and consumption patterns.[54] The International Council of Mining and Minerals has now developed a set of ten guiding principles of sustainable development designed to assist mining companies and their employees to operate in accordance with sustainability principles and practices.[55]

The dangers of 'greenwash'

The UK Turnbull report emphasized the need to build reputational capital, pointing out that 'a company's social, ethical and environmental working practices can make or break a brand name and affect share prices'.[56] The implications for share price, and thus for investment decisions by large investment funds, and for employee perceptions of corporate trustworthiness and values make reputation a powerful driver of change. Shareholders are increasingly concerned at the loss in value of their stocks in cases of failure to meet government regulations or community expectations. The Asian financial crisis, the Nike child labour issues, the Lockheed bribery scandal and the alleged involvement of Shell in the internal political situation in Nigeria have all contributed to corporate leaders shifting their attitude to sustainability away from a narrow focus on technical aspects of environmental problem solving to a more holistic approach which includes social concerns such as human rights and community impacts. In the emerging discourse of corporate citizenship, sustainability, reputation and performance are inextricably linked. The big corporate brands are particularly vulnerable.

Coca-Cola under pressure

Coca-Cola's Indian operations have put its famous brand in the spotlight for neglecting the concerns of local communities and the sustainability of the natural resources upon which they depend. Bottling plants in India have been in world news because of accusations that the company's use of powerful pumps that reach down into deep-water aquifers through large-bore wells within its premises. Local villages, angered at the lowering of the water table at a time of extreme drought, have drawn in environmental activists and government experts to support and broadcast their case.[57] As well, the

Kerala State Pollution Board shut down the $US25 million dollar Coca-Cola bottling plant in the remote Kerala village of Plachimada. Chairman of the KSPCB, G. Rajmohan, said the closure was ordered because the plant 'does not have adequate waste treatment systems and toxic products from the plant were affecting drinking water in nearby villages' and that the plant 'has also not provided drinking water in a satisfying manner to local residents'.[58] Even before the ruling, Coca-Cola sales had already dropped 14 per cent in the April–June 2005 quarter. Much publicity had surrounded the case, with Indian NGOs and politicians as well as global environmental groups drawn in to the high-profile investigation and exposure of the presence of pesticides in colas manufactured in India. Plachimada is likely to be seen as a signpost struggle on the role that local communities and NGO action can have in protecting natural resources.

Pressure from investors

More informed shareholders are demanding a role in corporate decision making. Not only can shareholder activism be extremely damaging to the reputation of the corporation, but shareholders are now using sustainability as a measure of financial success. Sustainability indices such as the Dow Jones Sustainability Index are outperforming other indices.[59] The financial markets are generally requiring more information on standards of accountability, and the financial services industry is now under considerable pressure to provide for ethical investment.[60] Currently, the ethical investment sector in the United States represents 13 per cent of all dollars under management, with more than US$13 trillion invested.[61] The socially responsible investment (SRI) industry is a major growth sector of the financial services industry, growing by a factor twelve times that of the broader managed funds sector.[62]

In April 2006 UN Secretary General Kofi Annan was joined by the heads of leading institutional investors managing combined assets worth more than US$2 trillion to launch Principles of Responsible Investment. Many of these are public pension funds accounting for 35 per cent of total global investment.[63]

The UK government has passed legislation to regulate pension funds so that they have to take account of the environmental, social and ethical impact of their investments. The funds are evidently prepared to take a strong stance on these issues. In a survey of the twenty-five largest UK pension funds, around 70 per cent of the funds said that they would implement SRI principles through active engagement rather than simply boycotting specific industry sectors such as tobacco and alcohol.[64] According to former US Vice-President Al Gore, the cult of short-termism is leaving investors, businesses and society short-changed. The argument of Gore and others involved in the growing sustainable investment market is that sustainable investing is really about examining a company's ability to survive through protection of revenues in the longer term and securing sustainable competitive advantage. Issues that influence the sustainability of the firm from this perspective range from macro issues such as demographic change, global warming and geopolitical tensions to more micro issues such as how companies attract and retain employees, corporate governance and community relations.[65]

National governments: new approaches to change

Since the Brundtland report and the Rio conference, business has been drawn into a system of co-regulation, where government, business and community are all expected to play a part in sustainable development and pollution prevention. Many members of the public, and increasing numbers of industry and government leaders, recognize that government alone cannot bear the responsibility for decisions taken by industry. Corporate capture has remained an issue[66] but is increasingly challenged.

During the 1990s co-regulation also meant the development of new forms of legislation designed to integrate sustainability principles into business decision making. Many governments are examining incentives to prompt business recognition of the new reality that moral and ethical responsibility can coexist with financial success. The 'user pays' principle has emerged as a key driver of corporate change. In essence, governments are now working towards ensuring that those who create the risks pay for them.[67] Taxes such as consumer fees for the disposal of appliances (applied in Japan), legislation on producer responsibility (in Sweden and the Netherlands) and pollution taxes in many countries are examples.[68] In the United States, Superfund represents an early attempt by government to force corporations to internalize environmental costs.

Incentives-based and 'polluter pays' strategies include load-based licensing and tradable permits to encourage reduction of pollution. In load-based licensing, companies are charged licence fees which vary according to the amount of pollution they discharge. Other economic policy tools include tradable rights to natural resources to encourage efficient resource management, innovative design and cleaner production.

Examples of such incentives include vehicle emission quotas, landfill taxes and 'green taxes', such as carbon taxes (as in Denmark), congestion taxes (as in Singapore) and vehicle return bonuses.

New reporting requirements and concepts

The 'Porter hypothesis' is that better designed regulation can lead to greater innovation, reduce uncertainty, raise corporate awareness and signal areas of potential resource inefficiency. Because this argument was advanced by a person widely regarded as the leading thinker in corporate strategy, it has been influential in the debate during the late 1990s concerning the framing of the environment–competitiveness relationship.[69] Although many writers have taken issue with Porter's perspective on the government–corporate relationship, the debate overall has created support for the idea that a properly designed and strictly regulated framework can prod managers to abandon ingrained ways and static models of thinking and operate for a more innovative approach to sustainability.

Accompanying the push for greater regulation is increased pressure on corporations to employ better assessment and measurement techniques in activities relevant to sustainability.[70] Accordingly, governments have become involved in the setting of sustainability targets, indicators, reporting requirements, standards and a variety of other initiatives designed to effect change in corporate behaviour. Research indicates that government initiatives have been responsible for an increased rate of publishing of health and safety and environmental reports in all countries except the United States. Bigger companies, with a higher public profile or under regulatory pressure from a number of countries, are also more likely to report. Further pressure is also placed on organizations to report by voluntary sector-specific agreements such as the Responsible Care programme of the chemicals sector.[71]

Ecological modernization

Porter's argument that regulation can force or 'enlighten' corporations to employ the environment as a 'competitive opportunity' has been taken up by some governments in northern Europe and Japan.[72] These governments have initiated policies geared to encourage the emergence of a specific sector, which focuses on the development of green technology, or environmental services. This powerful approach, termed 'ecological modernization' by academic writers, sees scientific and technological advances as an answer to the dilemma of how to provide for continued economic growth without negative impact on the environment. The basic argument is that we do not have to create a new political economy to achieve sustainability. It is enough to ensure that innovative environmental goods and services become a source of profit.[73] This approach is also co-regulatory, its proponents arguing that market, government and NGOs all have a role to play in industrial transformation incorporating more ecologically friendly principles.[74] Indeed, many of the governments, such as Japan, Sweden, Norway and Germany, which have been most successful in shifting the economy away from dependence on unsustainable production technology towards green production technology have a tradition of close associative relations between industry, business and government.[75]

As a result of applying these strategies, the eco-industry sector in Europe now provides up to 3.5 million jobs. Currently, the core eco-industries in the European Union, not including renewable energy and energy efficiency equipment and services, supply around half the world market of €300 billion per year. With massive expansion forecast for regions such as China, South America and South East Asia, the world market is expected to increase to €740 billion by 2010.[76]

Globalization and the information society, informed consumers and shareholders, and new roles and policy making on the part of NGOs and national governments are major external pressures on corporations to take a more ethical stance in their business dealings in terms of respect for the rights of current and future generations. The traditional distinction between external and internal drivers is useful to highlight another set of pressures, to do with efficiency, risk management and business advantage. We can think of these pressures as the internal drivers of sustainability.

Increased pressure from consumers is evident in the Ethical Consumer Report, which acts as a barometer of ethical spending in the United Kingdom, shows that in 2004 UK consumers spent a total of £25.8 billion in line with their values, an increase of 15 per cent on the previous year. Over the same period, UK household expenditure increased by only 3.7 per cent.[77]

According to Professor Richard Welford, director of the corporate environmental governance programme at the University of Hong Kong, many companies in Asia are taking up CSR principles. According to Welford these companies are often relatively unknown suppliers of the large brand-name companies, and so the shift may not be so publicly recognized. In addition, because of the migrant labour shortage in China, Chinese companies are adopting CSR strategies in order to attract workers. In this recent interview, Welford quoted the following examples of companies following CSR principles in Asia.

- Unilever's engagement with its own farmers down the supply chain in Indonesia has helped farmers produce more, guaranteed them better incomes and at the same time has generated a secure quality product for Unilever itself – it is a win–win situation.
- The Mass Transit Railway in Hong Kong has a long history of being proactive on environmental issues. It has been rated Hong Kong's most respected company and has won many awards for its sustainability reports.
- The Tata conglomerate in India has seen its reputation increase because of its commitment to CSR and that company now provides an example to others in India.[78]

Traditionally government and other external actors have been the major forces for corporate sustainability. More recently, internal factors are putting pressure on companies to reconsider their product design, human resource development, marketing and operations management strategies in light of business ethics and environmental and social responsibility. Each of these internal factors can be analysed in terms of business value. In a 1998 survey of 481 companies, the consulting firm Arthur D. Little found that 83 per cent of these companies saw business value in implementing sustainable initiatives.[79]

The costs of non-compliance

The most obvious internal pressure on managers in this context is cost avoidance. But the firm now needs to consider potential costs to its reputation in the eyes of its employees as well as external stakeholders such as shareholders, suppliers and consumers. The costs of non-compliance can be devastating for corporations, a point emphasized by a survey which showed that 85 per cent of US manufacturers have a corporate policy requiring compliance with the environmental standards in the country with which they do business.[80]

Being competitive means reducing costs. As we have indicated, governments are still experimenting with measures to ensure increased sustainability. As we have shown above, most governments impose penalty measures for non-compliance. Corporations which do not address social and environmental requirements face fines, workers' compensation cases, criminal convictions and payment of clean-up costs. The potential for damage liability can make non-compliance a significant business risk. Some examples:

- In the United States, the total corporate liability costs for asbestos-related diseases has been estimated at US$30 billion, far more than the product ever earned its manufacturers. In a court decision in South Africa, more than 300 workers in an asbestos mine were awarded damages. Claims by the multinational company that it could not be held accountable for the actions of subsidiary companies were discounted. A major concern of the workers' lawyers was that if larger settlements were won, there appeared a strong likelihood that the company would be bankrupted.[81]
- The Swiss pharmaceutical firm Roche put 8,000 of its workers through training programmes to ensure they follow national and international laws, as a result of some of the world's largest pharmaceutical companies being fined more than US$700 million for operating an illegal price-fixing cartel.[82]

The *Exxon Valdez*

Most managers would have a broad recollection of the 1989 *Exxon Valdez* spill of 10.8 million gallons of crude oil into Prince William Sound and along 2,000 km of beach in south central Alaska. They could probably recall the sad scenes of the deaths of 250,000 birds, 2,800 sea otters and 300 harbour seals. They may remember that the following investigation revealed that the supertanker's captain was inebriated. They may not realize the extent of the fines and damage claims faced by Exxon, some of which are still being resolved. Exxon was fined $150 million, the largest fine ever imposed for an environmental crime in the United States. Although the court forgave $125 million of that fine in recognition of Exxon's co-operation in cleaning up the spill and paying certain private claims, Exxon has argued that the clean-up cost to the firm exceeded $2 billion. The clean-up involved 10,000 workers, 1,000 boats and 100 planes and helicopters. As restitution for the injuries caused to the fish, wildlife and land of the spill region Exxon agreed to pay $100 million. This money was divided evenly between the federal and state governments. The civil settlement took the form of an agreement for Exxon to pay $900 million with annual payments stretched over a ten-year period.[83] The US Justice Department and Alaska in reaching this agreement with Exxon agreed that the state and federal governments had fifteen years to ask for more money. With that time period nearly up, federal and state lawyers are arguing that the remaining oil is still interfering with the ecology of the shore and ocean although the extent of the impact is impossible to calculate. To address residual impacts of the oil, the lawyers are requesting another $92 million from Exxon.[84]

Developing and measuring intangible value

Performance measurement and the management of intangibles are emerging as a key driver of organizational sustainability. The Sustainability Balanced Scorecard, for instance, is an instrument that builds on the well established Balanced Scorecard, adding social and environmental perspectives to the existing financial, customer, business process and learning and development perspectives and linking the perspectives with cause and effect chains.[85]

Westpac Banking Corporation is an example of a leading organization now including intangibles such as CSR, environmental performance and reputation into its strategizing. Figures 2.5 and 2.6 illustrate Westpac's view on the values linkages for customers and employees of these intangibles.

Leadership and risk management

Key trends in risk management now include:

- The need for public trust.
- The need for a partnership approach.
- The role of personal leadership and workforce involvement.
- The use of the law as a lever for safety management.
- The public demand for a risk-free world.[86]

Public opinion often appears to be only the opinion of a few activist NGOs, but it is now also the opinion of many employees and shareholders. It has become very costly to operate companies which are not socially responsible.

Maintaining awareness of the precautionary principle and consultation with a wide range of stakeholders when assessing environmental risk

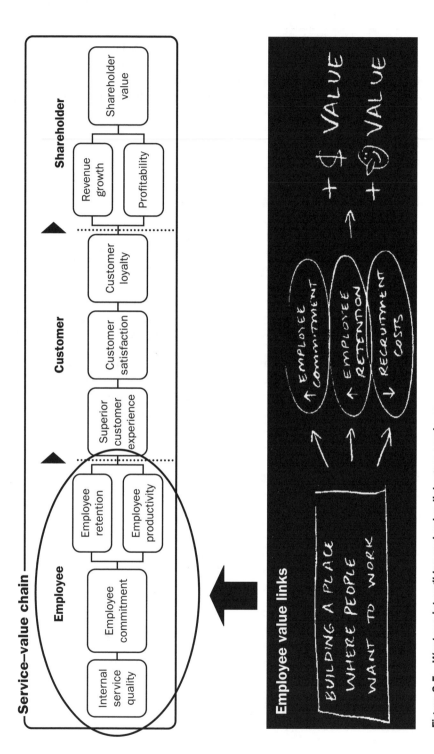

Figure 2.5 *Westpac intangibles and value linkages: employees*
Source: Reprinted with permission of Westpac Banking Corporation.

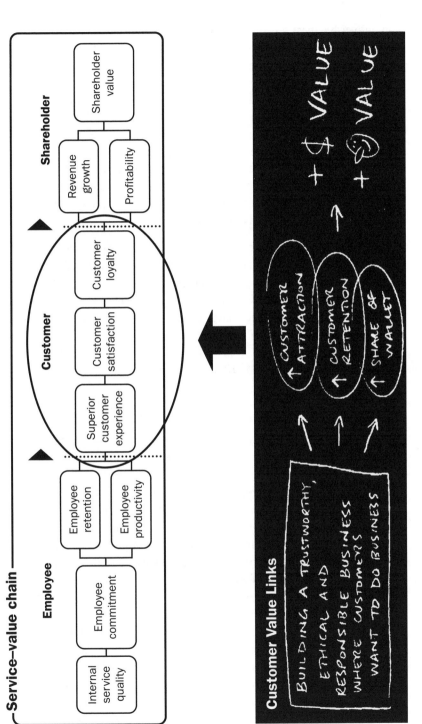

Figure 2.6 *Westpac intangibles and value linkages: customers*
Source: Reprinted with permission of Westpac Banking Corporation.

can deliver business advantages. Reinhardt, for instance, describes a situation where plans for timber harvesting and the building of a pulp mill using chlorine bleaching in the forest areas of northern Alberta were modified according to demands made by local farmers, aboriginal residents and environmental activists. The modified plans, which included forest management plans and reduced pollution levels, cost little compared with the gains in the long-term stability of the project. Reinhardt argues that the 'environmental goods' traded were well worth it in return for 'an insurance policy against regulatory difficulties, sour community relations, business interruptions and related cost shocks'.[87] This issue highlights the importance of leadership in taking a strategic view of shifting corporations towards sustainability.

The costly effects of climate change are increasingly being recognized as an aspect of company value. However, the potential risks and opportunities associated with environmental impacts are not straightforward and differ markedly from sector to sector, as illustrated in Table 2.3 showing the sector-related effects of climate change.

The knowledge-based organization

In the information-based economy, corporations are looking to long-term survival through the development of knowledge systems, stores of social capital and a culture of innovation. These aspects of human sustainability in turn enable the firm to take a position of more environmental responsibility. A position of corporate sustainability requires a firm both to be responsible to employees and to look to its own needs for long-term survival. In this context, managers are being influenced by a significant body of research which indicates that organizations last longer if they have clearly identified their values and goals.[88] The work of Collins and Porras is particularly notable in this regard. In their study of a number of visionary companies, these writers found that, compared with non-visionaries, these companies had an ideology which was made up of core values and purpose. It is this sense of core values which employees identified with and to which they developed commitment. Profit was important but it was not the defining feature of these visionary companies.[89] According to this research, an organization which has a clear sense of its mission for sustainability will more than survive – it can become a visionary organization and thrive in the long term.

Table 2.3 *Effects of climate change on various sectors*

Sector	Weather-related risk	Regulatory related risk	Potential opportunities	
	Short-term			Long-term
Property and Construction	Higher insurance costs	Higher insurance costs or inability to get insurance Decrease in asset value due to changes in flood levels or poor energy performance Increased construction costs due to changes in building codes	Minimum energy performance standards Inclusion of energy intensive construction materials into ETS	Growth market for energy efficiency/ management products and services Growth market for energy efficient construction materials Property energy performance used as differentiation to attract key clients
Transport and infrastructure	Increased maintenance and insurance costs due to increased storms and flooding Increased variability in water supply	Increased construction costs due to changes in civil engineering standards	Minimum energy transport performance standards Inclusion of aviation in fuel and airline industry in ETS	New water infrastructure Alternative fuels
Tourism and tourism related	Destruction of major tourist attractions	Destruction of major tourist attractions Increase in tropical diseases impacting attractiveness as destination		

continued

Table 2.3 *(continued)*

Sector	Weather-related risk	Regulatory related risk	Potential opportunities	
	Short-term			*Long-term*
Retail and consumer discretionary	Increased volatility in earnings of weather exposed or season-dependent products due to increased weather variability	As for short-term	Compulsory energy performance standards for consumer	Growth in demand for energy-efficient consumer goods
General	Increased business interruption due to extreme weather events	As for short-term	Need to include ETS related assets and liabilities in financial accounts Increased electricity price	

Source: I. Woods and M. Wilder, *Climate Change and Company Value*, Sydney: AMP Capital Investors and Baker McKenzie, 2005.

Knowledge management is also drawing attention to the value of an organization's human resources.[90] Motivation, qualifications and commitment, when combined with a significant store of 'corporate memory', are a major asset to the corporation. Companies are increasingly dependent on employees who can work co-operatively and contribute to the social capital of the organization.[91] Social capital is fundamental to the successful working of the new organizational forms such as the network organization and communities of practice.

As prized employees hunt for the firm with a strong sense of values, there are real rewards in becoming an employer of choice. Firms need employees who can give high levels of customer service and 'who are sufficiently motivated by the company's mission and prospects to stay and aspire to higher levels of productivity. The importance of teamwork, loyalty and skills is becoming doctrine in almost every industry.'[92]

Recent work also indicates a relationship between human resource policies, the successful implementation of the environmental management system (EMS) and its maintenance as a strategic business and risk management tool. This research concludes that EMS programmes are more successful if factors such as training, empowerment, teamwork and rewards are addressed.[93]

Natural capitalism: the business advantage

The perspective of 'natural capitalism' has been much publicized. If firms persist with the win–win business logic of 'natural capitalism', profiting from increasing the productivity of natural resources, closing materials loops and eliminating waste, shifting to biologically inspired production models, providing their customers with efficient solutions, and reinvesting in natural capital, they can gain a commanding competitive advantage.[94]

Business advantage is also offered through the organizational restructuring required by following the principles of industrial ecology. Tracking material and energy flows over the whole producer/consumer cycle reduces the likelihood of 'suboptimal solutions' and 'unintended consequences'.[95]

At Hewlett-Packard, for example, their Environmental Strategies and Solutions programme 'confirmed that sustainability does offer companies a strategic competitive advantage'.[96] This conclusion was based on the premise that the planet is a closed system which will eventually face limits. In these circumstances, the firm would be in a new social and economic situation, and would have to deal with the challenges of a new business environment. According to Hewlett-Packard, incorporating sustainability into its core business strategies would 'enable HP to transform potential environmental liabilities such as climate change, resource exhaustion and the energy crisis into strategic business opportunities and competitive advantage'.[97]

A culture of innovation

Managers are also recognizing the links between an organizational culture of innovation and one designed to deliver sustainability. Practices designed to enhance human sustainability and social capital within the organization (such as empowerment, teamwork and continuous learning) are linked with the capacity to innovate and escape from rigid models of operation and production. Arguably, implementing more sustainable practices creates an organizational culture that facilitates both resource productivity and product differentiation.[98]

A number of companies have been successful in employing a strategy of environmental product differentiation. Reinhardt points out that such a strategy will be successful if consumers are prepared to pay more, if the benefits can be communicated readily and if the innovation is unique long enough for a profit to be made.[99] Corporations face an accelerating rate of change and an increasingly complex society. For these business conditions, innovation depends on cultural and structural characteristics of the organization. Both sets of characteristics are linked with the organization's capacity to engage with sustainability. Cultural factors such as those associated with the learning organization also underpin a culture of precaution. Structural factors such as an internal network culture, employee participation and the ability to develop community partnerships also support human sustainability. In other words, innovation, business concept redesign and sustainability can be readily linked in a dynamic relationship aimed at delivering long-term business advantage.

Importantly, such qualities enable the corporation to be more responsive to the external drivers of change. An organization geared to innovation is ready to take up government incentives for 'ecological modernization'; that is, it can readily translate social and moral issues into market issues and can exploit the potentially huge market that ecological sustainability, in particular, represents. But more than that, such an organization can more critically reflect on the possibilities of new relationships between nature, society and technology that will mark a new, more sustainable age.[100]

Conclusion

This chapter began by asking why managers are moving to address the challenges of human and ecological sustainability. In large part, the answer is that the new reality for managers is that business success and sustainability are inextricably linked. Social and environmental health are essential aspects of corporate survival. Some managers are reacting primarily to the reputational and litigious risks associated with the increasingly global reach of corporations, to the actions of internationally mobilized human rights and environmental activists and to international and national agreements and regulations concerning environmental protection and social and environmental justice. International and national governments are experimenting with a variety of policy incentives and models of governance to ensure corporate accountability.

But many other managers are also taking proactive measures in the struggle to conserve resources, minimize waste and contribute to social and ecological renewal. More companies are moving beyond compliance with government regulations to accreditation under voluntary schemes such as ISO 14001. This delivers benefits from recognition by the community, customers and other stakeholders. Importantly, corporations are increasingly influenced by new alliances being formed across the range of corporate stakeholders. Community representatives and NGOs are working with firms to develop the knowledge and social capital required for the shift to sustainable products and processes.

Shareholders and investors are also looking to more than financial success in the assessment of performance. Their selection of investments increasingly takes into account reputation and performance on the longer-term factors of social and ecological sustainability. Investors are also placing more value on the human abilities and commitment that the organization has built. In the new economy the building of knowledge systems, social capital and other strategies designed to increase and sustain human capability are vital to corporate performance.

More and more employees have strong expectations of workplace safety and heightened environmental awareness; they are searching for more meaningful work, particularly for work that makes a social and ecological contribution as well as providing an income.

In this context, the principles of industrial ecology, of community, interconnectedness and co-operation can be seen as a model for the way forward for corporations wishing to move towards sustainability. They provide a framework for new levels of resource productivity and generate new strategic directions. More important, they serve as a way of understanding the corporation as a moral entity.[101]

The following chapters take us along the spectrum of corporate sustainability stances. However, it is in the next chapter that we outline our vision for the corporation of the future – the sustaining corporation.

Notes

1   K. Annan (2006), 'The Secretary-General's Remarks on receiving the Global Leadership Award of the Zayed International Prize for the Environment', 6 February 2006, Dubai: United Nations Environment Programme. Online. Available www.unep.org/Documents.Multilingual/ (accessed 31 May 2006).

2   B. Lomborg, *The Skeptical Environmentalist*, Cambridge: Cambridge University Press, 2001, pp. 48–9.

3   A. Giddens, *Beyond Left and Right*, Cambridge: Polity Press, 1994, p. 206.

4   Lomborg, *Skeptical Environmentalist*, p. 330.

5   C. Flavin and K. Topfer, 'Foreword', in Worldwatch Institute, *Vital Signs, 2001–2002*, London: Earthscan Publications, 2001, pp. 11–13.

6   Yin Ping, 'Plea for social responsibility', *China Daily Shanghai and Delta*, 28 March 2006, 3.

7   Anonymous, 'Shape up or pay price, says pollution watchdog', *Shanghai Daily*, 20 April 2006, A2.

8   Li Fangchao, 'More dusty conditions forecast for northern China', *China Daily*.

9   A. Wilkinson, M. Hill and P. Gollan, 'The sustainability debate', *International Journal of Operations and Production Management*, 2001, 21 (12), 1492–502.

10 Ibid., D. Dunphy and A. Griffiths, *The Sustainable Corporation*, Sydney: Allen & Unwin, 1998.

11 Ibid., J. Ehrenfield, 'Industrial ecology: paradigm shift or normal science', *American Behavioural Scientist*, 2000, 44 (2), 229–41; R. Starkey and R. Welford, 'Conclusion. Win–win revisited: a Buddhist perspective', in R. Starkey and R. Welford (eds) *Business and Sustainable Development*, London: Earthscan Publications, 2001, pp. 353–7.

12 W. Steffan, 'Stronger Evidence but New Challenges: Climate Change Science 2001–2005', Australian National University Report, prepared for Australian government Department of Environment and Heritage, p. 4. Online. Available www.greenhouse.gov.au/science/publications/pubs/science2001-05.pdf (accessed 28 May 2006).

13 B. Preston and R. Jones, CSIRO Marine and Atmospheric Research, quoted in Australian Roundtable on Climate Change, *The Business Case for Early Action*, p. 13. Online. Available www.businessroundtable.com.au>(accessed 10 May 2006).

14 L. Brown, 'Overview: the acceleration of change', in L. Brown, M. Renner and B. Halwiel, *Vital Signs, 2000–2001*, London: Worldwatch Institute and Earthscan Publications, 2001.

15 Lomborg, *Skeptical Environmentalist*, p. 301.

16 Intergovernmental Panel on Climate Change, 'Climate Change 2001: Synthesis Report', p. 12. Online. Available www.ipcc.ch/pub/un/syreng/spm.pdf (accessed 5 June 2006)

17 Christian Aid, 'Global Warming, Natural Disasters and the World's Poor', Online. Available www.christianaid.co.uk/indepth/0011glob/globwarm.htm (accessed 1 June 2006).

18 J. Vidal, 'African climate change "could kill millions", says charity', *Guardian Weekly*, 26 May–1 June 2006.

19 World Bank Group, 'Beyond Economic Growth: The Risk of Global Climate Change'. Online. Available www.worldbank.org/depweb/english/beyond/global/chapter14.html (accessed 5 June 2006).

20 D. Bjerklie, A. Dorfman, D. Cray, G. Fulton, A. Gerlin, R. Healy and E. Roston, 'By any measure Earth is at the tipping point', *Time*, 3 April 2006, 28.

21 EasyBeingGreen, 'A Brief Profile of Carbon Trading in NSW and Beyond'. Online. Available www.easybeinggreen.com.au (accessed 2 June 2006).

22 W. Frew, 'Company puts out lights and gives switches the flick', *Sydney Morning Herald*, 2 June 2006. Online. Available www.smh.com.au (accessed 2 June 2006).

23 D. Snow, 'Business warms to change', *Sydney Morning Herald*, 10 April 2006, 10.

24 UN Department of Economic and Social Affairs, 'Trends in Sustainable Development'. Online. Available www.un.org/esa/sustdev/ (accessed 31 May 2006).

25 J. Vidal, 'The long road from Rio', World in the Balance, *Guardian Weekly*, 28 April–4 May 2006, 3.

26 New Economics Foundation, 'Britain Starts Eating the Planet on 16 April 2006'. Online. Available www.neweconomics.org/gen/Britainstartseatingtheplanet160406.aspx (accessed 31 May 2006).

27 UN Department of Economic and Social Affairs, 'Trends in Sustainable Development'. Online. Available www.un.org/esa/sustdev/ (accessed 31 May 2006).

28 J. Langmore, 'A callous snub to the world's poor', *Sydney Morning Herald*, 27 June 2000, 15.

29 K. Toepfer, UNEP executive director, address to the third Global Forum of Parliamentarians on Habitat, 28 July 2000.

30 Falk, quoted in U. Beck, *World Risk Society*, Cambridge: Polity Press, 1999, p. 38.

31 World Commission on Environment and Development, *Our Common Future*, Oxford: Oxford University Press, 1987.

32 Ibid., p. 8.

33 H. French, 'Environmental treaties gain ground', in Brown *et al.*, *Vital Signs: 2000–2001*, pp. 134–5.

34 G. Bourne, 'A complete health check', in *Social and Environmental Australian Location Report*, BP Australia, 2000.

35 'The United Nations and Business' at http://www.un.org/partners/business/ (accessed 23 January 2002).

36 Ehrenfeld, 'Industrial ecology'.

37 U. Beck, *World Risk Society*, Cambridge: Polity Press, 1999, p. 37; R. Falk, 'The making of global citizenship', in B. van Steenbergen (ed.) *The Conditions of Citizenship*, London: Sage Publications, 1994.

38 J. Palmer, 'Vandana Shiva', in J. Palmer (ed.) *Fifty Key Thinkers on the Environment*, London: Routledge, 2001, pp. 313–21.

39 V. Shiva, quoted in anon., 'Flying in the face of nature', *Guardian Weekly*, 31 March–6 April 2006, 20.

40 Oxfam International, 'Offside, Labor Rights and Sportswear Production in Asia'. Online. Available www.oxfam.org/en/policy/briefingnotes/offside_labor_report (accessed 1 June 2006).

41 H. Henderson, *Beyond Globalization: Shaping a Sustainable Global Economy*, West Hartford CT: Kumarian Press, 1999.

42 World Economic Forum, 'Global survey ahead of world economic forum annual meeting in Davos shows "trust deficit" deepening', Media Release 15 December 2005. Online. Available www.weforum.org/ (accessed 1 May 2006).

43 E. von Weizsacker, A. B. and L. Lovins, *Factor 4: Doubling Wealth: Halving Resource Use*, London: Earthscan Publications, 1997.

44 Ehrenfeld, 'Industrial ecology'; B. Szerszynski, S. Lash and B. Wynne, 'Introduction', in S. Lash, B. Szerszynski and B. Wynne (eds), *Risk, Environment and Modernity*, London: Sage Publications, 1996, pp. 1–26.

45 W. Sachs, 'Global ecology and the shadow of development', in Sachs (ed.) *Global Ecology*; Shiva, 'Greening of the global reach'.

46 R. Goodin, *Green Political Theory*, Cambridge: Polity Press, 1992.

47 A. Dobson, 'Ecologism', in R. Eatwell and A. Wright, *Contemporary Political Ideologies*, London: Pinter, 1999, pp. 231–54.

48 Murphy and Bendell, 'Getting engaged'.

49 Ibid.

50 S. Benn, interview with B. Scarsbrick, CEO, Landcare Australia Ltd, Chatswood, Sydney, 23 May 2001.

51 Oxfam International, Offside, Labor Rights and Sportswear Production in Asia'. Online. Available www.oxfam.org/en/policy/briefingnotes/offside_labor_report (accessed 1 June 2006).

52 S. Sagawa and E. Segal, 'Common interest, common good: creating value through business and social sector relationships', *California Management Review*, 2000, 42 (2), 105–23.

53 B. Beuermann and B. Burdick, 'The German response to the sustainability transition', in T. O'Riordan and H. Voisey (eds) *The Transition to Sustainability*, London: Earthscan Publications, 1998.

54 Planet Ark Environmental News, interview, 'Sustainable Development Group aims to aid Miners', at http://planetark.org/dailynewsstory.cfm/newsid/12485/story.htm (accessed 25 September 2001).

55 Minerals Council of Australia, 'Enduring Value', Online. Available www.minerals.org.au/enduringvalue (accessed 6 June 2006).

56 *Financial Times*, 2 June 2000, quoted in L. Preston, 'Sustainability at Hewlett-Packard'.

57 Ranjit Devaraj, 'India: Coca-Cola accused of water-guzzling in a desert state', 22 June 2004, Inter Press Service, 2004 Global Information Network, accessed through Factiva 31 May 2006.

58 D. Rajeev, Inter Press Service, 'Everything gets worse with Coca-Cola', 21 August 2005. Online. Available www.corpwatch.org/article.php?id=12590 (accessed 31 May 2006).

59 F. Grey, *Sustainable Business Forum*, at www.csp.uts.edu.au/csn/sbfjuly01.html (accessed 18 January 2002).

60 T. Clarke, 'Balancing the triple bottom line', *Journal of General Management*, 2001, 26 (4), 16–27.

61 T. Wallace, 'A quiet move to ethical investment', *Australian Financial Review*, 27 February 2002.

62 Ibid.

63 'United Nations Global Compact, 'United Nations Secretary General launches 'Principles for Responsible Investment'. Online. Available www.unglobalcompact.org/docs/news_events/9.1_news_archives/2006_04_2 7/pri.pdf (accessed 6 June 2006).

64 S. Benn, 'The EHCA 1985 (NSW): a historical perspective on issues arising in the control of toxic chemicals', *Australian Journal of Political Science*, 1997, 32, 49–64.

65 A. Sampson, 'Gore sounds alarm over short-term vision', *Sydney Morning Herald*, p. 2, Online. Available www.smh.com.au/news/money/gore-sounds-alarm-over-shortterm-vision/2005/11/11/1131578230974.html?page=2 (accessed 28 May 2006).

66 Benn, 'The EHCA 1985 (NSW): a historical perspective on issues arising in the control of toxic chemicals'.

67 U. Beck, *Risk Society: Towards a New Modernity*, London: Sage Publications, 1992.

68 O'Riordan and Voisey, *Transition to Sustainability*.

69 M. Porter and C. van der Linde, 'Towards a new conception of the environment–competitiveness relationship', *Journal of Economic Perspectives*, 1995, 9 (4), 97–118.

70 Ibid.

71 Institute for Environmental Management (WIMM), *KPMG International Survey of Environmental Reporting 1999*, Amsterdam: KPMG Netherlands, 1999.

72 Porter and van der Linde, 'Towards a new conception of the environment–competitiveness relationship', p. 114.

73 J. Dryzek, *The Politics of the Earth*, Oxford: Oxford University Press, 1997.

74 A. Mol, 'Ecological modernisation: industrial transformations and environmental reform', in M. Redclift and G. Woodgate (eds) *The International Handbook of Environmental Sociology*, Cheltenham: Edward Elgar, 1997, pp. 138–49.

75 M. Mason, *Environmental Democracy*, London: Earthscan Publications, 1999.

76 M. Wallstrom, European Commissioner for the Environment, 'Database on Eco-industries in the European Union', at http://europe.eu.int/comm/environment/ecoindus/intro.htm (accessed 19 January 2002).

77 Co-operative Bank, 'Ethical Consumerism'. Online. Available www.co-operativebank.co.uk/servlet/Satellite?pagename=CoopBank/Page/tplPageStandard&cid=1077610044424&c=Page (accessed 2 June 2006).

78 O. C. Phang, 'Case of CSR in Asia', *The Edge Financial Daily*, 8 August 2005.

79 A. D. Little & Associates, 1998, quoted in A. B. and L. Lovins and P. Hawken, 'A road map for natural capitalism', in R. Starkey and R. Welford (eds) *Business and Sustainable Development*, London: Earthscan Publications, 2001, pp. 288–312.

80 Manufacturers' Alliance and National Association of Manufacturers' Joint Survey, at www.nam.org/DOCS/ResourcesEnvironmental (accessed 24 May 2001).

81 www.abc.net/news (accessed on 19 February 2002).

82 A. Osborn, 'Vitamin Inc. fined $1.4 bn for price-fix', *Sydney Morning Herald*, 23 November 2001, 14.

83 L. Brown, *The Rise and Fall of the Global Climate Coalition*, Worldwatch Institute Report, Alert 2000–6, 25 July 2000, Washington, DC: Worldwatch Institute.

84 F. Barranger, 'Call for more cash to clean up *Exxon Valdez* oil spill', *Sydney Morning Herald*, Weekend Edition, News, 3–4 June 2006, p. 23.

85 M. Wagner and S. Schaltegger, 'Mapping the links of corporate sustainability', in *Managing the Business Case for Sustainability*, Sheffield: Greenleaf Publishing, pp. 108–27.

86 M. Brinded, 'Perception versus Analysis: How to handle Risk', speech to the Royal Academy of Engineering, London, 31 May 2000.

87 F. Reinhardt, 'Bringing the environment down to earth', in R. Starkey and R. Welford (eds) *Business and Sustainable Development*, London: Earthscan Publications, 2000, pp. 53–64, at p. 62.

88 J. Collins and J. Porras, *Built to Last: Successful Habits of Visionary Companies*, New York: HarperCollins, 1997; B. Hirsh and P. Sheldrake, *Inclusive Leadership*, Melbourne: Information Australia, 2000.

89 Collins and Porras, *Built to Last*.

90 Wilkinson *et al.*, 'The sustainability debate'.

91 Sagawa and Segal, 'Common interest, common good'.

92 Ibid., p. 106.

93 Daily and Huang, 'Achieving sustainability . . .'.

94 A. B. and L. Lovins and Hawken, 'Road map for natural capitalism'.

95 Ehrenfeld, 'Industrial ecology', p. 226.

96 Preston, 'Sustainability at Hewlett-Packard'.

97 Ibid., p. 29.

98 R. Orssatto, 'The Ecological Competence of Organizations: Competing for Sustainability', paper presented to the XVI EGOS Colloquium, Helsinki, 1–4 July 2000.

99 Reinhardt, 'Bringing the environment down to earth'.

100 M. Hajer, 'Ecological modernisation in cultural politics', in Lash *et al.* (eds), *Risk, Environment and Modernity*.

101 Ehrenfield, 'Industrial ecology'.

Part II
Managing the persistent past: dealing with first wave corporations

3 Corporate pre-compliance and compliance

What is compliance?

Compliance is doing what you are required or expected to do. There is, however, a difference between the spirit and the letter of the law. The considerable debate around compliance in accordance with CSR or sustainability hinges on this difference. The compliance approach to corporate sustainability or CSR is that even if shareholder gain or corporate profit is reduced, companies should abide by the letter of the law. According to the American Law Institute, in that way a corporation is no different from a 'natural person'.[1] But compliance with the spirit of the law is a much more vexed question.

The James Hardie case

James Hardie is a leading international building materials company and a global leader in fibre cement, one of the world's fastest-growing building products. The firm employs 2,500 people who generate revenue of more than A$1.55 billion a year in operations located in Australia, New Zealand, the Philippines and the United States.[2]

continued

Between 1937 and 1986 asbestos products were manufactured by two subsidiaries of James Hardie Industries Ltd (JHIL): Amaca and Amaba. In 1990 the board of directors of James Hardie (JHL) began to reassess and reduce the amount of assets which would be available to fund the claims of asbestos victims. Between 1996 and 2001 the assets of Amaca and Amaba were transferred to JHIL (now 'ABN 60'), then to a Netherlands-based company – James Hardie Industries NV (JHI NV). In February 2001 ownership of Amaca and Amaba was transferred to a new body, the Medical Research and Compensation Foundation ('the Foundation'), which was given US$293 million to fund asbestos injury claims. The directors of James Hardie claimed to have relied on reports by management to arrive at this figure, which, as it now turns out, represents only a fifth of what the company will have to pay in asbestos claims. Until June 2004 the company denied that it had any legal obligation to pay any compensation to asbestos victims, arguing that it was following its legal obligations under Part 2D.1 of the Corporations Act 2001 (Cth) which states that the directors owe a duty to shareholders to act in the best interests of the corporation, and consequently that this obligation precluded greater consideration for stakeholders and asbestos victims.

A special commission of inquiry into James Hardie held in 2004 found that whilst there was no legal obligation to fund the long tail liabilities (liability for injuries that arise many years after the events or transactions that gave rise to them) which will arise from exposure to asbestos, there was a moral obligation to do so. The inquiry also reported that senior executives engaged in misleading and deceptive conduct, and that claims the company made to the Australian stock exchange about the sufficiency of the fund were 'seriously misleading'. The directors finally responded to threats of union boycotts and government pressure and agreed to fund a more realistic estimate of the liabilities. The resolution will see James Hardie make contributions into a government-administered scheme which will resolve claims by future asbestos victims.[3]

Changing understandings of governance

The James Hardie case has served to highlight the socially and environmentally destructive aspects associated with the 'corporate veil' of limited liability.[4] In Australia, in response to concerns raised by the case, the Corporate Law Economic Reform Programme (Audit Reform and Corporate Disclosure) Bill 2003 (Cth) (CLERP 9) was introduced into Parliament in October 2003 and came into effect in 2004. The CLERP 9 reforms require publicly listed companies to report on all significant environmental and social matters that could affect their prospects. Financial services, telecommunications and mining are increasingly embracing the principles. Commenting on the James Hardie case, other corporates and a number of legal experts argue that the traditional view on directors' (or fund managers') fiduciary responsibilities is now dated and that directors have ample latitude to consider stakeholders other than shareholders.[5]

James Hardie is not alone in liability for asbestos-related diseases. Estimates of Australia's total liability for future asbestos claims start around A$6 billion. Prompted by the Hardie scandal, and the scale of these potential liabilities, in 2005 the Australian Government Corporations and Markets Advisory Committee (CEMAC) produced a report on the subject of whether directors' duties should include CSR and whether companies should be forced to adopt socially and environmentally responsible business practices. The report notes that while corporations are not required to comply with the spirit of the law, increasingly a company doing so may be perceived as implementing good risk management.[6] This fact marks an international trend towards companies being perceived as 'morally liable', with negative commercial associations, if they comply only with the letter of the law and not the spirit.

In the United States a number of legislatures have implemented corporate constituency statutes which can incorporate CSR and sustainability into the letter of the law. While a number of these statutes are specifically designed to deal with hostile take-overs, others permit directors to take into account the effect that their decision making may have on employees, suppliers and local communities. What is in the 'best interests' of the corporation may now take other factors than those of the shareholders into account. These statutes represent the pluralist approach to whether directors can or should take the concerns of other stakeholders such as the natural environment, employees and communities into account. The alternative 'enlightened shareholder value' approach, incorporated into the US 2005 Company Law Reform Bill, explicitly states the duty of the directors is to advance the financial interests of shareholders specifically, but puts this requirement in a wider context. For instance, Clause 156 requires the directors to promote the success of the company for the benefit of its members, but in fulfilling this duty, directors are required to consider factors such as long-term impacts, effects on the natural environment and other stakeholders.[7] The media focus in recent years on irresponsible or 'sociopathic' corporate behaviour (in the movie and book *The Corporation*) has also contributed to the debate on whether the corporation can legally address a wider social or environmental agenda unless it is of direct financial benefit to the shareholders.[8]

New requirements on reporting

The debate on corporate governance has taken a useful turn in direction to focus on transparency issues. The question is the extent to which the corporation can or should be required to reveal information about practices such as those that relate to CSR or sustainability.

In 2005 the UK government issued regulations on the Operating and Financial Review and Directors' Review (OFR). The OFR requires UK listed companies to report on non-financial aspects of the firm's operations, such as risks associated with environmental impacts or social, community and employee issues. This new reporting requirement is aimed at giving shareholders fuller information on the company, enabling better risk management of share portfolios. Company directors are ultimately responsible for the OFR content. It is they who have to consider these non-financial aspects and decide whether they are likely to influence shareholder return. Similarly, the Accounts Modernisation Directive requires similar information to be reported by large unlisted companies across the European Union in their directors' report.[9]

One effect has been that multinationals such as GE and Nike, once vilified by environmental and anti-globalization activists at their lack of responsibility to the environment, employees and other stakeholders, are leading the way in improving their reporting and sustainability strategies. In the past, for example, GE has been in trouble with regulators over the dumping of chemicals in the Hudson river in New York state. GE, at that time either in the non-responsive or rejection phase, is now commiting to an 'eco-imagination plan'. Under the plan, GE will more than double its research and development into clean technology for its customers, double its sales of new technologies and products that conserve water, and reduce its own greenhouse gas emissions by 1 per cent over the next seven years.[10] Likewise Nike's 2005 report published a complete list identifying all its suppliers, reversing its previous position of rejection concerning public disclosure of its supply chain.

As expected, the shift is influenced by the characteristics of national politics and of industry sectors as well as by the size of the enterprise itself. For instance, according to PricewaterhouseCooper's (PwC's) inaugural Retail and Consumer Outlook report, compared with international companies such as Marks & Spencer, Tesco, Johnson & Johnson and Nike, Australian retail and consumer-product companies are dragging the chain on corporate social responsibility (CSR) and risking their relationships with consumers, suppliers, employees and regulators in the process. Only three of Australia's retail and consumer companies produced reports on the issues in 2004.[11] Paul Hohnen, a former Australian diplomat to the Organization for Economic Co-operation and Development and the European Union, deputy high commissioner to Sri Lanka, Greenpeace director and now chief executive of a European sustainability consultancy, argues that a 'culture of complacency' in Australia has prevented Australian companies being at the global forefront of sustainability initiatives. Where Australians previously were world leaders in solar power and renewable energy, other countries, including China, Spain and Denmark, are now far ahead.[12]

Overall, however, it seems international convergence to the market-based Anglo-American model of corporate governance now seems less likely.[13] New forms of governance are emerging as the boundaries between corporations, other firms and their stakeholders dissolve. Network-based governance, for instance, where relations between firms and other organizations are co-ordinated according to a range of social contracts, is increasingly important in sectors such as biotechnology and financial services. As well, the growing influence of concepts of stakeholder management in business education and consultancies points to corporate governance becoming concerned with a 'set of relationships' rather than a 'set of transactions',[14] while the emergence of compacts between regulators and corporates points to the emergence of a very different understanding of governance and regulation.

Changing attitudes to compliance

In accordance with the shift to more social forms of governance, industry representatives have generally shifted their position on regulation and compliance over the last decade. Where the pace of regulatory change is particularly slow, as occurs with toxic chemicals because of the intensive testing required before chemicals can be banned and taken off the market, government agencies are now seeking partnerships and voluntary agreements with chemical companies in order to reduce more rapidly the use of chemicals with suspected toxic effects. For example, the US EPA called together a group of chemical companies and environmentalists to discuss how to control perfluorooctanoic acid (usually called PFOA), a chemical used in waterproof clothing and non-stick cookware. As a result, each company voluntarily agreed to curtail its use of the substance.

As *The New York Times* put it, companies and environmentalists both think that rules on issues like greenhouse gases, endangered forests and genetically modified crops are inevitable, and they want a hand in setting them. DuPont, for instance, includes environmentalists on its internal biotechnology advisory panel. 'Our ability to get product to market is moving faster than the EPA's ability to get rules out, and we want to agree in advance on what the rules of the road should be,' said Linda J. Fisher, DuPont's chief sustainability officer.[15]

In Australia, the Victorian state government has initiated an Accredited Licensee Scheme under which organizations with good environmental performance in the past are allowed increased flexibility in managing their future environmental performance within the legislation. 'Benefits include lower licence fees, capability to determine their own environmental works, and no approval needed for certain new works.'[16]

The managers of many companies actively contribute to government rule making and are shifting to more proactive strategies. They pre-empt policy changes and adopt precautionary measures before being required to do so. In this way, compliance can become enabling for organizations such as Hewlett-Packard. They can progress human and ecological sustainability measures, enhance their reputation and take leadership in order to increase competitiveness.

Hewlett-Packard Australia Compact with Department of Environment and Conservation (NSW)

This Compact, signed in 2005, emphasizes joint implementation of sustainability projects according to agreed upon targets and timelines. Commitments include:

- Development of a community take-back programme for all HP computers.
- Achieving a better rate of return of printer cartridges and recycling.
- Development of 'buy green' guidelines for environmentally preferable IT purchasing.
- Evaluation of other national programmes of IT recycling and take-back.
- Enhanced resource efficiency of HP sites and operations, including energy efficiency and waste avoidance and recovery.
- Publication of annual HP Sustainability Report.
- Advocacy and awareness raising concerning sustainability principles to HP staff and the IT industry.[17]

According to Annukka Sairanen, Environmental Manager, Hewlett-Packard, South Pacific, collaborating with government agencies through the signing of voluntary agreements and compacts not only demonstrates HP's leadership in sustainability but is a risk management measure: the closer relationship with regulators enables the company to more accurate prediction of likely legislative change. For instance, the company needs a long lead time to modify its products around legislative changes that affect product design, such as the European RoHS (Restriction of the use of certain Hazardous Substances in electrical and electronic equipment).[18]

Global watchdogs for human rights and ecological sustainability

The events of 11 September 2001 have been a harsh reminder to governments and multinationals that many in the developing world associate global deregulated capitalism with corporate aggression, colonization and greed. In the developed countries themselves, the massive expansion of information technology has led to a growing awareness of corporate irresponsibility and antagonism to the idea that multinational corporations can somehow act autonomously, accountable only to shareholders.

More informed consumers have pushed corporations into a new arena of competing for reputation and for access to the benefits of social capital, such as relationship building with other corporations, suppliers, clients and NGOs. NGOs such as Amnesty International, Greenpeace, WWF and Human Rights Watch act as monitors of environmental and social standards across the world and have had a major impact on how corporations perceive compliance. Corporations failing to comply with standards set by these alert watchdogs can be targeted and their transgressions given huge publicity. As the Human Rights Watch executive director Kenneth Roth has said: 'I think there is broad recognition that no business concerned with its brand name can afford to be indifferent to social issues.'[19]

Global principles in action

The scandal associated with the financial collapse of Enron in the United States shows that reputation, communications, disclosure, transparency and trust are interconnected issues for organizations. If any one of these factors fails, all others are affected and the path back to rebuilding them is a long one at the very least. Nike's experience also shows this: after a series of reputational problems, Nike has endorsed the Environmental Code of Conduct of the Coalition for Environmentally Responsible Economics (CERES). While this does not mean that CERES endorses Nike's practices, it does mean that Nike will communicate with CERES members. Drafted by the Coalition for Environmentally Responsible Economies in response to the *Exxon Valdez* oil spill, the code requires companies to adopt environmentally-friendly policies and perform annual self-audits.[20]

Sets of principles and codes such as CERES which provide a formal statement of business practices and values have proliferated since the late 1990s. They differ in author organization and in code content. All are directed at improvement in social and environmental company behaviour according to principles of self-regulation.[21]

We argue that company codes can play a major role in facilitating the organizational learning required for the transition to compliance and beyond. However, we need to recognize their drawbacks. The overwhelming majority of codes have no implementation methods. In particular, there are four major drawbacks of company codes. They can be:

- *Vaguely defined*. Corporate codes often do not specify precisely the limits of their responsibility.
- *Incomplete*. Many company codes exclude the right to organize, refer only to a specific issue such as child labour or are incomplete in other ways.
- *Not implemented*. An important flaw in company codes of conduct is the lack of information on whether or how these codes are being implemented or monitored.
- *Not independently monitored*. Internal monitoring assumes a public willingness to take the company at its own word but the public is often distrustful.
- *Subject to personal bias* of senior managers.[22]

Table 3.1 *Classification of global codes of conduct*

Code type	Criteria used	Example
Author organization	Company trade association	Responsible Care (chemical industry)
	Company	Nike code of conduct, Levi Strauss code of conduct
	Intergovernmental	OECD guidelines for multinational enterprises
	NGO, Multi-stakeholder	CERES principles, Global Compact, Global Compact, SA 8000, Global Reporting Initiative, Forest Stewardship Council, ISO 14000
Code content	Philosophical	Vodafone code of ethics
	Social responsibilities	ILO
	Management philosophy	GlaxoSmithkline code of conduct,
Code function	Model or guide to self-regulate or influence corporate behaviour	All codes

Source: K. Bondy, D. Matten and J, Moon, 'Codes of conduct as a tool for sustainable governance in MNCs', in S. Benn and D. Dunphy (eds), *Corporate Governance and Sustainability*, London: Routledge, 2007.

The case for moving to compliance

The previous sections outlined a broad case for corporations to adopt a proactive approach to compliance. In summary, the reasons are:

- The emergence of more widespread and increasingly sophisticated forms of government regulation.
- Increasing scrutiny by NGOs.
- Public access to information technology and the risks to corporate reputation of public perception of poor corporate citizenship.
- The opportunities compliance can provide to improve the firm's competitive situation.
- The benefits of building a co-operative relationship with regulators.

- The risks associated with delays in achieving compliance. While rejection or non-responsiveness to regulation may delay costs and assessments, they can end up resulting in much higher costs being paid for non-compliance and in more negative assessments by the law and the public – James Hardie is an example.

As we noted in Chapter 2, the relationship between risk management and climate change is sensitizing the insurance industry and indeed the financial services industry as a whole to sustainability. In many ways this industry sector is driving change toward giving stronger support to corporate sustainability.[23] For example, companies such as Swiss Re and Insurance Australia Group are leaders in both corporate governance and sustainability. Swiss Re assesses the sustainability performance of its corporate clients before issuing property or casualty insurance. According to a Swiss Re spokesperson, Swiss Re risk engineers comprehensively screen about 20 per cent of their corporate clients, with environmental, social and governance as part of that screening.[24]

In the remainder of this chapter we take up issues relating to the move to compliance and 'compliance-plus'. We concentrate on substantive issues in the move, that is, what to do. In Chapters 7 and 8 issues of process (how to do it) will be addressed in more detail.

Limitations of current organizational change and development models

Many of the change strategies recommended throughout this book derive from the classic Organization Development (OD) approach. For instance, we emphasize teams and groups as the locus of attitude change leading to incremental change. We also argue for the importance of top leadership support and of values such as openness, social justice and self-realization – the typical value sets associated with the OD movement.[25] Other change tactics we recommend relate more to the Change Management approach adopted by change leaders engaged in large-scale transformational change.

However, neither of these approaches can address the changes needed to move an organization from rejection or non-responsive phases to compliance and beyond unless sustainability principles are integrated into the change process and set as a specific target to be achieved. For example, the Home Depot, one of the largest home improvement retailers in the world, moved towards sustainability by implementing the Natural Step principles into its business model. The Natural Step principles are:

- Substances from the earth's crust cannot systematically increase in the biosphere.
- Substances produced by society cannot systematically increase in the biosphere.
- The physical basis of the productivity and diversity of nature must not be systematically deteriorated.
- There must be fair and efficient use of resources to meet human needs.[26]

At the Home Depot the change programme for sustainability began in 1998 when these principles were integrated into an intensive training programme for senior management which included systems mapping of the organization so that managers could develop an awareness of the sustainability impacts of its operations and its 40,000 products. Top-to-bottom commitment to sustainability is the target – to be achieved by ongoing education and awareness programmes at all levels of the organization. The firm has now progressed to developing a sustainable procurement policy, and selecting vendors which themselves have sustainability policies in place.[27] Similarly, McDonald's Sweden has achieved major sustainability outcomes by engaging top leadership support for Natural Step principles, conducting a comprehensive sustainability analysis and educating suppliers into the principles. Achievements include cutting waste by 85 per cent and a major reduction in the heavy metals used in toys and construction.[28]

At Carlton & United Beverages' (CUB) Kent brewery, the implementation of a learning centre associated with a structured and supportive learning programme for all staff facilitated a transformational change in an organization with high levels of employee illiteracy and alcoholism and conflict between different unions as well as between management and their staff.[29] A new culture based around the human sustainability principles of shared knowledge and learning enabled major improvements in environmental performance (Table 3.2).

The case of CUB supports the argument for an integrated perspective on the sustainability change programme whereby environmental sustainability and human sustainability are seen as inextricably linked. If work systems are reconceptualized around humanistic values of fulfilment and skills development, rather than around intensive, deskilled standards, compliance and beyond can be assured. Key aspects of the

Table 3.2 *Changes in ecological sustainability at Kent Brewery*

Culture pre-human sustainability changes	Human sustainability change initiatives	Environmental management outcomes
Centralized engineering department with responsibility for environmental management issues	Engineering and Health, Safety, Environment (HSE) services integrated into ongoing projects and decentralized to cross-functional teams	Environmental management the responsibility of all teams and employees. Shared knowledge and learning culture facilitated of Best Practice People and Processes energy management programme at CUB
Health, Safety, Environment (HSE) seen as a state-based issue of minimal importance	HSE considered a national/international issue	A corporate environmental policy
Little consultation across sites. HSE basically dealt with at site level according to actual risks	Development of the new HSE manual involves cross-site discussion • Groups represent and discuss issues from each plant • Fortnightly video-conferences • Telephone conferencing • Each site has a say in change needs and recommendations	A structured HSE approach across all sites
No consideration beyond compliance	Beyond compliance a consideration on efficiency grounds	Attention given to environmental problems such as disposal options for diatomaceous earth filter material
Limited measurement of environmental factors, e.g. energy/water use comparisons; low levels of technological capability	Better more regular measurement and internal reporting (especially for water and energy)	Water use halved over eight years. Reliable figures still to be obtained on waste
Little emphasis on training	Establishment of Learning Centre; emphasis on learning culture and continuous improvement; systematic skills and competence-based training system	ISO 14000 in place. CUB has introduced energy awareness programmes at other CUB sites. Overall savings of at least A$500,000 per year and 8,000 tonnes of greenhouse gases

Source: Benn, Dunphy and Crittenden, 2005. See note 29.

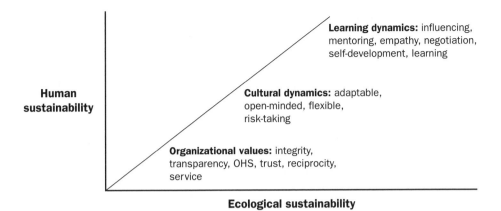

Figure 3.1 *Factors enabling change*

change at CUB, for instance, included fostering teamwork, improving rewards and empowering employees. In Figure 3.1 we summarize the factors enabling organizations to move towards compliance and beyond in terms of sustainability.

Making the structural changes needed for compliance

Making the initial changes

Moving to compliance involves important changes such as an increased emphasis on training, top-level commitment, and guidance from skilled change agents. Moving towards compliance does not necessarily require major restructuring, but it does require management to identify roles and responsibilities more clearly in relation to all legislative requirements. Take, for example, the case of a manufacturing company which has traditionally opposed governmental regulation of its activities and is non-compliant in several key areas such as plant safety and pollution of ground water. A new CEO is appointed and discovers that the firm is non-compliant and in a high-risk situation. What can the CEO do?

In the area of human sustainability, the CEO needs to focus on those compliance aspects which will give the firm the status of a 'decent employer'. How is this achieved? He or she may decide to begin moving, in the area of human sustainability, from the rejection phase towards compliance by selecting change agents who initiate *ad hoc* incremental changes. The place to start is with areas that represent the major risks of non-compliance. These have to be identified first. The culture and vision of the company can then be gradually adjusted by assigning staff the responsibility for more systematic improvement to areas such as industrial relations, worker health and safety, and equal employment opportunities (EEO). Human resource requirements for training, the introduction of Total Quality Management (TQM) and organization development can be addressed while the organization is moving towards a more systematic integration of these measures into an overall plan. New quality standards can also be introduced before an overall strategy is delineated.

In the area of ecological sustainability, 'compliance officers' need to be allocated responsibilities for environmental management. For some manufacturing sectors, firms must also comply with requirements to establish a community liaison committee and an identified member of staff who can communicate readily with community representatives. At the INCO Nickel manufacturing plant in South Wales, UK, for instance, the Environmental Officer has the responsibility of contacting local residents concerning community liaison committee meetings. In keeping with INCO's proactive strategy, not only is the community advised of any expected changes in noise or chemical emissions but the Environmental Officer makes sure he goes to see community members on a regular basis to identify areas of potential complaint.[30]

New technical solutions or programmes may be implemented to enable cleaner production techniques and improved worker health and safety. These often include operating within 'consents' or specified standards, eliminating hazardous operations, waste disposal, water quality and planning requirements for new developments.

Employee empowerment is a key aspect of these initial changes. For instance, if technological developments are to lead to a more sustainable workplace, employees with low standards of qualification must still be able to succeed in the company. The case of CUB illustrates this key principle of change to compliance with sustainability and beyond.

Developing a more systematic approach

There is a limit to what can be achieved by an *ad hoc* approach to compliance. A more systematic approach usually involves making structural changes and developing new co-ordinating mechanisms to create a systematic, integrated compliance framework. An important first step in this is carrying out an environmental impact assessment (EIA), preferably using an outside independent assessor. An introduction to what is involved in carrying out such an assessment can be found in Staub (2005).[31] The usual framework for environmental compliance is an environment management system (EMS), supported by a range of human resource and community development tools or techniques. These techniques focus on two areas: the management and operation of facilities, and the design, manufacture and delivery of products or services.[32]

At this stage, strong adherence to codes of occupational health and safety and well advertised workplace safety precautions are leading areas of change for human sustainability. Progressing this requires an occupational health and safety (OH&S) policy and an OH&S committee with equal representation from employees and managers. A process designed to upgrade safety performance, for example, could commence with a safety audit by a third-party safety professional. Other steps typically include establishing bookkeeping arrangements, such as keeping required records of emissions, or required training to satisfy OH&S regulations, and monitoring the implementation and effectiveness of OH&S programmes. Governments may blacklist firms from receiving government contracts unless they are compliant with human rights, environmental, tax and antitrust standards. Such legislation was passed in the United States under the Clinton administration but later repealed by President Bush. However, it is in force in many other countries.

For multinational organizations, the CSR Starter Pack, developed by the Corporate Social Responsibility Network, has useful suggestions that assist an organization to ensure that the supply chain is moving to compliance with human rights legislation.[33] These include:

- Knowing which issues are likely to be significant in a particular country or sector.
- Requiring suppliers to certify their compliance with environment or employment legislation.
- Using all opportunities to monitor performance.
- Working collaboratively to foster changes.

The next step towards compliance is the implementation of environmental and human resource reviews. The reviews require management to formulate a strategy which anticipates and scopes future issues and the intended impacts of company operations, products and services.[34] A stakeholder analysis which defines roles and responsibilities, including those of senior management, is a key aspect of the review. For instance, the Dutch investment bank ING Group has identified its core stakeholders as employees, clients, shareholders and society. In order to ensure compliance, it has established a Code of Conduct and Business Principles as internal regulations applicable to these stakeholders. A compliance organization has been created within ING and an executive board member serves as Head of Group Compliance.

For compliance to be effective, each organization must develop policies for the environment, for community development and for employee training and development. These can be developed in parallel. Together they give a vision of what management wants to achieve, set out goals, objectives and strategies, and outline how success will be measured. To be comprehensive, the environment policy should align with community relations policies and with human resource policies covering industrial relations, safety and workplace standards and worker protection. Systems such as TQM assist in ensuring that the workplace compliance system, once established, is maintained.

Mobilizing change units and agents

Change units and change agents are business units and staff charged with the specific responsibility for organizational change. Sustainability initiatives are typically taken by change agents who are concerned individuals, but not necessarily privy to a technological overview or part of the senior executive group; for one reason or another, they have the personal or professional capacity to influence a limited area of organizational activity. Initiatives of this kind can provide an initial impetus and a heightened awareness that can be expanded and systematized in the next phase. Managers can encourage such personal initiatives by communicating widely throughout the organization that they welcome sustainability initiatives and will provide resources where appropriate.

Ad hoc initiatives are important but systematic progress needs competent, qualified professional change agents. Developing a specific sustainability change unit and a cadre of change agents enables attitudinal change, the building, managing and accounting for social as well as environmental capital and fosters the innovation needed for significant corporate change.

Simple measures can send powerful signals to employees that corporate behaviour should be modified according to environmental and social responsibilities. Structural reforms that enable organization-wide reforms include:

- Creating functional positions responsible for compliance that report to the CEO and the board of directors.
- Requiring training and experience in the management of environmental, human resource and community relations for 'fast-tracking' careers in management and professional areas.
- Creating audit committees that report to the board or are represented on the board.[35]

While important in many situations, technical solutions are not the basis for ensuring compliance. Organizations are human constructs, and human needs, attitudes and responses are ambiguous more often than they are clearly specified and predictable. Change agents need to develop a tolerance of ambiguous situations. This skill development and the processes of change are dependent upon the firm's human resource function. The resources available need to be adequate to provide training in interactive skills, team building, benchmarking, brainstorming and consensus building.[36]

Within a traditional hierarchical organization, the structural requirements are relatively clear-cut and the 'environmental manager' and HR managers can play separate and effective roles in enabling compliance. But they will achieve the required changes only if strongly supported by senior management. Traditional hierarchical organizations often handle cultural change ineffectively and this may offset the apparent advantage of a command structure in developing corporate compliance.

Assessing and measuring the change

The performance of operational and review systems is critical in the shift to compliance. Auditing is a key tool and can be established at multiple entry points. Audits of the operations of newly acquired plant, other environmental auditing and verification of systems should be conducted at regular intervals. Failures of new initiatives may be due to inappropriate organizational structuring. For instance, creating a new staff function may be seen as the way to achieve an environment management system or to devise a human resources plan. However, if this function has no authority over other staff it will be marginalized and ineffective.

A survey of Australian firms showed that 'cost and resource constraints' and 'additional resources required initially' are the major impediments to companies producing sustainability reports, with 78 per cent of respondents nominating cost as a problem.[37] A number of companies are shifting to sustainability sections in annual reports and Web site reporting as a way of reducing these costs.

The trend towards flatter organizational structures, more participative management styles and the implementation of self-managed teams, task forces and project groups can make compliance monitoring more difficult. Consequently, monitoring by external organizations becomes more important in ensuring that compliance is maintained. Every three years KPMG carries out a survey of over 100 companies. The most recent KPMG survey showed that, of the top 100 companies in the Netherlands, 37 per cent have a non-financial corporate report or a sustainability report. As George Molenkamp, of KPMG Environmental Consulting, puts it: 'The reporting is not greenwash – a lot of energy is required to implement a policy of reporting for complex organizations with thousands of employees. It is a real challenge to get the data and do proper reporting.'[38]

External verification can establish system weaknesses and often results in recommendations to improve reporting procedures. This usually involves the introduction of a systematic environmental auditing system which has the advantage of ensuring that the organization is complying with external legislative and other requirements (such as ISO 14000) and meeting internal sustainability goals.[39]

Multinationals operating across a variety of cultures need to organize external verification locally, due to different expectations and regulations in each locality. As a result, external verification of reporting is increasing. The spate of corporate and auditor self-examination in the wake of the Enron collapse highlighted the need for the audit committee to take a central and more strategic role in the organization. Broad-based reporting on anything questionable not only attests to compliance but facilitates best-practice governance.[40]

The benefits of reporting against the triple bottom line (TBL) of social, environmental and economic performance are twofold: reputation and the information it provides on the strategic priorities and the likely long-term risks and opportunities for the company.[41] Table 3.3 gives examples of indicators that can be used in the TBL reporting system.

Table 3.3 *Examples of TBL performance indicators*

Economic performance indicators	
Direct economic impacts	Customers
	Suppliers
	Employees
	Providers of capital
	Public sector
Environmental performance indicators	
Environmental impacts	Materials
	Energy
	Water
	Biodiversity
	Emissions, effluents and waste
	Suppliers
	Products and services
	Compliance
	Transport
	Overall
Social performance indicators	
Labour practices and decent work	Employment
	Labour management/relations
	Health and safety
	Training and education
	Diversity and opportunity
Human rights	Strategy and management
	Non-discrimination
	Labour/management relations
	Freedom of association and collective bargaining
	Child labour
	Forced and compulsory labour
	Discipline practices
	Security practices
	Indigenous rights
Society	Community
	Bribery and corruption
	Political contributions
	Competition and pricing
Product responsibility	Customer health and safety
	Products and services

Source: Group of 100 Incorporated in Institute of Chartered Accountants in Australia, *Extended Performance Reporting*, report prepared by Wua Fong Chua, 2005. http://www.icca.org.au at p. 6.

In sum, establishing a structured, systematic response to compliance requirements depends on implementing learning strategies and appointing change agents or specific change units, such as compliance committees, environmental management committees, human resource and environmental health and safety units to gatekeep information. But for more effective compliance these responsibilities need to move from the periphery into the core function of the firm.[42] They should be integrated into such departments as marketing and product and process design. Importantly, these reforms will succeed only if employees recognize that they create value for them. Employee ownership of the changes takes us into the area of cultural change.

Moving to 'compliance-plus'

While many managers may argue that 'it could never happen to us', the issue of liability and risk stands out as a powerful leverage point for organizations to change course on sustainability issues before they become the subject of the next crisis of confidence.[43]

Adding further weight to the high-profile cases are other pressures as managers of corporations across the world face consumer boycotts, public scrutiny, regulatory monitoring and even fines over their seemingly casual approach to sustainability issues. It prompts a simple question: is there a better way of doing business that enables organizations to achieve sustainability and economic outcomes?

Corporations are now being called on to meet tougher standards set by industry associations and a range of other internal and external stakeholders. An organization which does not take responsibility for current or future environmental impacts or for the health, welfare and future career prospects of employees, and rejects community concerns, is now under pressure from across society to change. Initiatives such as green taxes on emissions and products, supply chain requirements and consumer pressure all place demands on corporations to move along the sustainability spectrum from rejection and indifference to compliance and to 'compliance-plus'.[44]

Moving to a culture of 'compliance-plus'

Organizational structure, policy formation and technical systems are the 'hard-wired variables' of change. The 'soft' variables are those that involve people and the transformation of meaning. While these are usually labelled 'soft', they are in fact more difficult to manage effectively. An integrated approach to 'compliance-plus' is needed to create the consistent achievement of compliance goals that is only possible with ongoing employee commitment. This normally requires cultural change. Hence moving to compliance from the rejection or non-responsiveness phases is dependent on managing both soft and hard variables of change. The human resource function becomes a critical element in such a transition: a matter we take up in more detail in Chapters 7 and 8.

As surveillance at all levels of the corporation is not possible, compliance requires the internalization of new standards by people at all levels of the organization. Major litigation costs, for example, are often a result of employee carelessness. So attitudinal change is essential to ensure respect for legislative requirements. It is a major cultural shift to move from ignoring issues of wider social responsibility and community concern to meeting even minimal community expectations.

As indicated in Figure 3.1, compliance is not just a matter of changing policies and values: it involves capturing the hearts and minds of all employees and building practical procedures which everyone in the organization can understand. As Udeke Huiskamp, environmental manager of KLM, puts it: 'New ideas need to come from the bottom up. We have developed an awareness-raising course and are thinking of having a regular information day. Some employees see the environment as a technical issue and difficult to understand.'[45]

Values and attitudinal changes are required where employees have not been aware of their legal responsibilities as members of the organization. If the collective assumption within the organization has been that exploitation of community groups, employees or the environment is justified by economic benefits to the corporation, the cultural values of the organization are in need of reformulation. Such cultural change cannot be enforced – it evolves only with leadership and over time. Structural change underpins and provides some of the social organization needed for the shift to compliance. But the enthusiasm and commitment of the work force at all levels have to be generated. In effect, both top-down and bottom-up approaches are needed, neither being sufficient on its own.[46]

The challenge of maintaining a position in the compliance and beyond phases of sustainability applies particularly to multinationals operating in the resources sector. According to Malcolm Brinded, chairman of Shell UK, words alone cannot change the culture. Regular deeds are the answer.[47]

Yet *Failing the Challenge: The Other Shell Report*, issued by Friends of the Earth,[48] argues that Shell committed itself to sustainability in 1995, but 'the reality is a far cry from the green promises in glossy brochures and advertising campaigns'. This point is illustrated by the case of Shell in Nigeria.

Shell in Nigeria

The Federal High Court of Nigeria, in November 2005, issued an order to Shell Oil requiring that the company should immediately stop gas flaring in Nigeria, as it was found that this activity was a 'gross violation' of the right to life and dignity as outlined in Nigeria's constitution. As at May 2006 Shell continues to operate the gas flares. The company has also appealed against a $US1.5 billion fee to the local community to compensate them for environmental damage. It has been reported that local communities suffer abnormally high rates of respiratory diseases, and that they also endure constant noise, light and heat. Crop yields in the area have been damaged by air pollution, and the toxic smoke pumped into the sky by the flares is causing more greenhouse emissions than any other single source in sub-Saharan Africa, according to the World Bank. Shell's continuing operations have resulted in consistent attacks on oil installations by the local Ijaw militants who, since 2000, have been campaigning for compensation for environmental degradation. The attacks and kidnappings of foreign oil workers have increased to the extent that Nigeria's oil output has been affected and cut by 25 per cent. Shell presents no intention of paying the compensation fee ordered by the court and has launched a High Court appeal, stating that it has no legal obligation to halt operations until the appeal is heard.[49]

Ensuring senior managers are committed and that their roles and responsibilities are defined is crucial to the cultural change involved in ongoing and full compliance. At KLM, the first airline to obtain ISO 14000 for all departments, senior managers have remained committed to sustainability, despite the pressures on the airline industry since 11 September. According to KLM's environmental manager:

Since September 11 2001, insurance costs have increased and more money is being spent on IT systems. But the Board has said that we do not want to change ambitions. We have a lot of support from the Board of Directors – it is important to have their leadership.[50]

The role each employee must play in the compliance agenda and the purpose of the compliance initiative should be workshopped and discussed in team meetings and other forms of workplace interaction. Increasingly, compliance also involves participation by the wider community. Community consultative committees can facilitate the internal and external cultural changes required. Placing employees in face-to-face situations with those who will be most affected by their work activity can have a powerful impact on attitudes.

The emergence of newer structural forms such as networks and strategic business units bring new challenges for the implementation of the cultural shift.[51] Employee participation in decision making through work groups or quality circles is commonly used as a strategy to improve organizational performance, motivation and commitment in these situations.[52]

Integrating sustainability agendas

Planning a fully integrated approach to the broad agenda of human and ecological sustainability requires an even more profound change in organizational culture. The change should be set in the context of an overall sustainability plan. The organizational change strategy developed to achieve the sustainability plan must be selected to suit the mission and context of the firm. Too often environmental managers and human resource managers move in different worlds from strategic business managers. The environmental manager is technically focused and often unaware of business objectives, except in the broadest sense. Similarly the human resource manager's interest may be in training and other intra-organizational needs. As a result, sustainability issues may be marginalized or moved off to agendas unrelated to the firm's core business. As a counter to this, human and ecological compliance policies are usually integrated into an overall sustainability policy which is an integral part of the firm's business policy.

Integration is a key concept for both successful business and sustainability. It points to the need for cross-functional relationships and the building of trust between areas of business that have previously been regarded by managers as only loosely connected.[53] Active relationships can be fostered between line managers and sustainability experts, so that the issues of human and ecological sustainability are not perceived by employees as an add-on, irrelevant to the core priorities of management. For instance, at KLM, line managers all have sustainability action points and targets.[54]

Limiting staff training to the technical training required for compliance is an add-on approach, not likely to bring about attitudinal changes or allow the development of a culture capable of adopting self-regulation. Restricting skills development to a few key individuals can also lead to disaster, particularly in some industries where toxic chemicals or dangerous technologies are used by others in the corporation. The global banking, insurance and investment company ING Group has attempted to avoid these problems by developing an e-learning compliance course in order to familiarize its 7,000 employees in eleven countries with compliance principles.

Sharing knowledge across the institution and developing an integrated policy according to the triple bottom line of social, environmental and economic objectives requires more co-ordination between internal elements of the firm.[55] A significant step along this road is the merging of human and ecological sustainability policies through the explicit recognition by management of the need for a comprehensive sustainability strategy.[56] Nuon Energy, for instance, the second largest energy producer and largest producer of green energy in the Netherlands, has an Environmental Knowledge Centre which is part of a larger section, Human Relations Management.[57]

Steps that organizations can take to bring about a more integrated vision include the following.

Step 1: getting started

- Establish sustainability indicators and keep senior management informed on the progressive development of human capabilities, community relations and environmental initiatives. Measures of sustainability have been developed that combine social, economic and environmental indicators and which demonstrate links between and among them. The TBL approach, for instance, requires establishing key performance indicators for social, environmental and economic performance and auditing against these indicators.

- Establish working groups and project teams that can assist in the internalizing of sustainability norms.[58] Liaison roles can be developed within these groups to take the findings of the groups deeper into the organization. These don't need to be authority roles, but rather to act more as information conduits and thus motivators.[59] While these liaison roles may be part-time positions, there may also be a need for a special 'risk communicator' to act as an integrator.
- Develop the informal links across the organization required for the shift to an integrated position on sustainability. This can be achieved by encouraging the development of the informal roles that enable inter-unit collaboration. Examples of these roles include the champion, the gatekeeper, the idea generator and the sponsor.[60] These informal roles can become ineffective if formalized but thrive when those in them are good networkers and strongly committed to the core value of sustainability.

At the INCO nickel plant in South Wales, for example, the company doctor acts as the 'champion' and represents the company at international conferences and forums. The environmental officer acts as the 'idea generator'. He attends meetings of business units on a regular basis, negotiates standards with the regulatory agency and ensures that employees are trained according to ISO 14001 requirements. The role of 'gatekeeper' is played by some senior people who are also trained as auditors for ISO 14001. The 'sponsor' is the plant manager whose idea it was to start the plant down the road to ISO 14000 and who gives 'very decisive leadership'.[61]

Systems thinking is vital, as it provides an impetus to move the organization towards the next phases of efficiency and strategic sustainability. Everything the firm produces should be regarded as an output to society and the environment. Human impacts such as the provision of employment and the social consequences of restructuring are included. When goods and services are increasingly made more environmentally friendly, and any deleterious effects are eliminated, employees become more committed and the company enjoys more community support. At Nuon Energy, for example:

> We regard sustainability as part of our being. It is a strategic long-term vision but also is a policy designed in response to the fact that we have to develop sustainable sources with the end of non-renewable sources of energy. Sustainability is also applied to an understanding of employee priorities – the use of the intranet for education, for instance. In terms of community relations, Nuon has some

partnerships in developing countries such as one concerned with knowledge development and sustainable water use in Mali. Another relationship is with various organizations in Albania, where the staff can use some of the company's time to work on various projects. These projects also try to bring in sustainability, in the sense of helping and developing to achieve more equitable outcomes.[62]

Step 2: winning staff support

Results of a survey of 5,000 employees carried out by a Sydney recruitment agency indicate that worker loyalty is fostered by 'mutual respect' (48 per cent of respondents), 'open and honest communication' (46 per cent of respondents), and by a 'pat on the back' (2 per cent). Only 3.7 per cent said more money would make any difference.[63] As Gollan points out, employee consultation, participation and feedback are crucial if the organization is to move towards an integrated position on sustainability compliance and beyond.[64]

Through the implementation of quality schemes, companies can raise compliance levels and ensure continued compliance with legal requirements such as safety and workplace standards. A more meaningful integrated compliance system develops through the active participation of the work force in developing the documented procedures. A coercive culture and bureaucratic administration are not appropriate for an organization moving to integrate sustainability principles into the organization for the long term. Participative processes may take longer initially but they result in more genuine internalization of the new norms.

Lowering business risk through compliance demands a trained work force. Enabling cultures which concentrate on staff training and ongoing participation have more capacity to achieve and maintain an internalized commitment to compliance than coercive cultures. Performance benefits are more likely if this training is contextual, based on collaborative learning principles and provided by supervisors in an ongoing fashion.[65]

Step 3: assessing for 'compliance-plus'

The 'compliance-plus' stage involves increased disclosure and generally introduces codes of conduct such as ISO 14000. Implementing systems according to the internationally set standards of ISO 14000 and ISO 9000 helps identify priorities for improvement programmes. The Responsible

Care code provides the basis of a broad new ethic for business management in the chemical industry. This code states that every R&D, manufacturing, storage, distribution and waste management site will have an active community awareness and emergency response programme in place. The differences between the old ethic and the new ethic fostered by Responsible Care are summarized in Table 3.4.[66]

The Global Reporting Initiative (GRI) provides an outstanding example of benchmarks for 'compliance-plus' set by external organizations. The GRI consists of three tools: a set of core metrics applicable to all business enterprises; sets of sector-specific metrics customized to specific types of enterprises; and a uniform format for reporting these metrics and related information integral to a company's sustainability performance. The GRI also aims to create a permanent institutional 'home' to monitor, advocate and continually upgrade the practice of standardized reporting worldwide. Institutions which have followed the GRI format for sustainability reporting include Fuji Xerox (Japan), KLM Royal Dutch Airlines (Netherlands), Konica (Japan), Nissan (Japan), Ricoh (Japan), Saint-Gobain (France) and Suncor Energy (Canada).[67]

Table 3.4 *Old and new ethics*

Old ethic	New ethic
Do the minimum the law requires	Do the right thing
Keep a low profile	Show you are doing the right thing
Limit product obligations to the minimum	Exercise life-cycle stewardship
Downplay public concerns	Seek to identify and address public concerns
Make decisions on the bottom line and laws alone	Integrate all the above into decision making
Ignore or fight advocates	Seek advocates' inputs
Act on the belief that it is 'every company for itself'	Work collaboratively with industry associations to set standards; collaborate with stakeholders
Provide hazard information only if necessary	Accept the public and employees' right to be informed of all risks
Assume product 'innocence' unless others produce contrary evidence	Operate according to a risk-based precautionary principle

Source: Adapted from Canadian Chemical Producers Association, *Codes of Practice*.

The Sustainability SMART© tool has been developed by the Sydney-based consultancy Worthwhile Projects to assist organizations in evaluating their progress to sustainability and point to directions for improvement.[68] The tool draws from the internationally recognized Global Reporting Initiative and the Standards of Corporate Social Responsibility developed by the US-based Social Venture Network.

Table 3.5 describes an indicative set of twenty sustainability elements appropriate for, say, a manufacturing company.[69] The sample Sustainability SMART© element shown at Table 3.6 describes the sustainability features for specific business aspects and enables users to select the stage of development or progress relevant to their organization or business unit.[70] The numerical score on sustainability status for each element is then applied using the rating ruler. A weighting can be applied to individual elements if desired – this provides the opportunity to give extra importance to certain sustainability elements as required.

Step 4: risk management through 'compliance-plus'

Instituting a compliance-based management approach avoids the financial risk associated with non-compliance. But achieving compliance does not necessarily foster the continuous improvement required to minimize compliance costs, or reduce or eliminate all penalties. Consequently many firms are now moving to the 'compliance-plus' stage in order to develop this capacity and thus achieve both flexibility and consistency.

Legislation is generally lagging behind leading-edge sustainability thinking and can make some abrupt shifts particularly as governments move in and out of power. Companies which have developed and established a system of voluntary compliance are best prepared for this eventuality and may have already anticipated and acted on the new expectations; if not, they are still in a better position to respond rapidly. Hence the move to 'compliance-plus' also indicates a changing perception of the importance and nature of business risk. Risk management now involves more prediction than control.[71]

The importance of risk management through proactive implementation of sustainability programmes and systems is highlighted by an example from within our own sector of higher education. The Australian Campus Climate Challenge Scorecard Questionnaire is being produced by the Australian Student Environment Network (ASEN), Greenpeace and the Australasian Campuses Towards Sustainability (ACTS). Its purpose is to

Table 3.5 *Sustainability elements*

1	*Corporate and business unit management*
1.1	Scope of commitment
1.2	Management systems
1.3	Accountability
1.4	Risk management
1.5	Compliance review and reporting
1.6	Continuous improvement
1.7	Supply chain and outsourcing
2	*Financial planning*
2.1	Budgeting
2.2	Investor relations
2.3	Cost controls
3	*Human resources*
3.1	Communications
3.2	Employee relations
3.3	Health and safety
4	*Social responsibility*
4.1	Community relations
4.2	Business ethics
5	*Environment*
5.1	Land protection, remediation and rehabilitation
5.2	Environment protection
5.3	Waste management, recycling and reuse
5.4	Energy conservation and climate change
5.5	Water management

rank Australian universities on their climate change mitigation plans. All Australian universities are being sent the questionnaire, which asks for details of energy use and sustainability strategies. The purpose of the scorecard is to provide a resource for prospective university students. The authors of the scorecard claim that institutions' rating on the card will influence student choice of university. In an increasingly competitive sector, such a scorecard could be a potent trigger for change.

Step 5: establishing the learning organization

We have discussed the nature of the shift from (1) achieving compliance with the demands of external regulators to (2) voluntary compliance with

Table 3.6 Sustainability SMART© sample: risk management element

1 Corporate and business management	1.4 Risk management – new business and/or new development, plant, equipment					
Not applicable	Level 1	Level 2	Level 3	Level 4	Importance	Notes
Not applicable	**Regulatory processes are followed** during the development approval/permitting process for new equipment/operations. The company **responds to government or customer pressure** to modify or introduce products, services and/or operations in order to prevent serious impacts on the community or the environment.	Systems are in place to **identify potentially serious or irreversible environmental or community impacts** that may arise from products or operations. Processes are in place to identify feasible alternatives and appropriate changes to practices.	The company actively supports development of improved processes to reduce risk. **Integrated approach to identification, analysis and implementation of improvements** in the way products and services are made, delivered and used. Design and marketing strategies respond to changes in a coordinated manner. Products and services are analysed for long term impacts and decisions taken on a **precautionary principle approach.**	Cross-functional teams co-ordinate efforts to **reduce direct and indirect impacts from products and services** on the environment and communities. System for implementing changes is monitored, evaluated and changed to ensure that **aspects of importance to the community and the environment are not degraded.** Engagement with internal and external sources is co-ordinated and integrated with business units.		
N/A	0 0.5	1 1.5	2 2.5	3 3.5	4	SCORE (Level × Importance)
☐	☐ ☐	☐ ☐	☐ ☐	☐ ☐	☐	☐

internally generated or externally negotiated voluntary standards. This shift requires the whole organization to learn. The development of flexible mental models is the basis of effective organizational change.[72] When a firm makes the move beyond compliance, some 'old ways' may still be appropriate if they help the organization achieve compliance with regulatory standards efficiently and effectively. The processes upon which structured compliance has been built do not necessarily need to be discarded. What must go is the 'machine' metaphor of the closed and highly regulated system. If a structured EMS has been adopted, for instance, it now needs to be reassessed for its value in delivering the negotiated understandings of 'co-regulation'. With the firm now partly responsible for instigating and monitoring compliance, institutionalizing reflection and implementing feedback becomes a priority. The whole organization needs to emerge from a legalistic understanding of regulation and begin to support what may seem less tangible ends, such as the capacity of employees to examine their own attitudes towards change.

For example, many managers are recognizing that learning capacity is the true capital of the firm. Dealing effectively with such issues as risk liability is dependent on this capacity. According to de Geus, the successful company encourages the development of a culture which is sensitive to its general environment.[73] Ongoing compliance is assured because the organization becomes an open system, capable of learning through interaction among employees and between employees and the wide range of stakeholders. These stakeholders include not only customers, competitors and suppliers but the environment and society.[74] In an organization of this kind, compliance simply becomes an integral aspect of the way people conduct business.

Step 6: developing trust

More organizations are moving into the new structural forms which will characterize the third millennium, such as networks, 'spider webs', the 'infinitely flat' organization, alliances and the virtual organization. In this new order, fewer interactions within the organization involve hierarchical relations and more depend on trust. Bureaucratic implementation of procedures will still remain important for some regulatory requirements. But increasingly, managers gain credibility from their ability to put in place voluntary codes for healthy human and ecological relations.

Managers are increasingly required to expand the knowledge base of the work force and institute high performance management practices. Studies demonstrate that these practices (such as reduction of status differences, sharing information and extensive training) can build commitment.[75] In other words, a culture of voluntarism can be developed only through a shared sense of identity. However, this is increasingly difficult to create given that career paths are ill defined and unpredictable and more employment is contractual and part-time rather than permanent and full-time. Managers need high-level skills in team building, empowerment and the development of trust.[76] Because a certain proportion of expert knowledge is tacit, working in self-managed teams requires trust, otherwise the critical knowledge needed to make the new systems work will not be exchanged.[77]

The ongoing challenge

In 1991 a McKinsey survey of 100 business executives confirmed that the environment would be the central corporate issue of the twenty-first century.[78] In the same year a senior official of the US corporation Union Carbide and Director of Occupational Health and Product Safety of the (US) Chemical Manufacturers' Association said: 'We are not just trying to stay with regulation, we are trying to go beyond it.'[79]

A decade and a half later, the major challenge for organizations, as they attempt to systematize compliance requirements and move towards 'compliance-plus', is organizational learning. What will be the role of knowledge management, including both tacit and expert systems? How can managers look beyond the quick technical fix and create effective learning systems that combine compliance with innovation and flexibility?

A strong human resource-based approach to an integrated concept of sustainability facilitates learning of this kind. This approach accords with current perspectives on corporate behaviour. Rather than doctrinaire systems or constant surveillance, commitment to a clearly articulated sustainability policy is the key element in a system of compliance that can be sustained.

Sustained compliance in both ecological and human domains is more likely to be attained if more co-operative approaches to problem solving are followed and if these approaches are supported by the application of systems thinking. An organizational culture which exhorts intra-organizational competition, or enforces a mechanistic structure, is less likely to develop the sense of ownership of problems and the organizational learning which enables sustained compliance and the shift to 'compliance-plus'.[80]

The introduction of an array of voluntary mechanisms for compliance has underpinned a shift in the concept of compliance. It is now seen as a broad agenda going beyond the implementation of clean technology techniques to the redesign of organizational structures and systems that support further initiatives in sustainability.

Moving along the sustainability spectrum to the efficiency phase

Developing compliance systems requires building a baseline level of human and technical competence. Moving towards 'compliance-plus' enables change flexibility as the internal corporate system is modified to address the requirements of external stakeholders. However, voluntary initiatives alone often lack rigorous performance criteria and specific objectives. To ensure rigour, the voluntary phase should be tied firmly to efficiency and strategic objectives. In the shift to the next stage of efficiency, human resource management becomes resource management.[81] Specific targets include how to identify cost inefficiencies and how to develop natural capitalism by increasing resource productivity and operational efficiency.

We have seen that for an organization to move from rejection to compliance requires incremental organizational learning in the form of gradual shifts in culture and structure. However, the organization at the compliance stage remains in a defensive position on sustainability. It is not directly targeting sustainability in order to operate more efficiently or to gear the organization to benefit in a strategic sense from these reforms. To achieve this shift in organizational thinking requires transformative learning. The next chapter explores this process.

Appendix 3.1

Phases in the development of compliance

 ### Phase 1: Rejection

Human sustainability (HS1)

Employees and subcontractors are regarded as a resource to be exploited. Health and safety features are ignored or given 'lip service'. Disadvantages stemming from ethnicity, gender, social class, intellectual ability and language proficiency are systematically exploited to advantage the organization and further disadvantage employees and subcontractors. Force, threats of force and abuse are used to maintain compliance and workforce subjection. Training costs are kept to a minimum necessary to operate the business; expenditure on personal and professional development is avoided. The organization does not take responsibility for the health, welfare and future career prospects of its employees nor for the community in which is a part. Community concerns are rejected outright.

Ecological sustainability (ES1)

The environment is regarded as a 'free good' to be exploited. Owners/managers are hostile to environmental activists and to pressures from government, other corporations, or community groups aimed at achieving ecological sustainability. Pro-environmental action is seen as a threat to the organization. Physical resource extraction and production processes are used which directly destroy future productive capacity and/or damage the ecosystem. Polluting by-products are discharged into the biosphere causing damage and threatening living processes. The organization does not take responsibility for the environmental impact of its ongoing operations nor does it modify its operations to lessen future ecological degradation.

 ### Phase 2: Non-responsiveness

Human sustainability (HS2)

Financial and technological factors dominate business strategies to the exclusion of most aspects of human

Ecological sustainability (ES2)

The ecological environment is not considered to be a relevant factor in strategic or operational decisions.

resource management. 'Industrial relations' (IR) or 'Employee relations' (ER) strategies dominate the human agenda with 'labour' viewed as a cost to be minimized. Apart from cost minimization, IR/ER strategies are directed at developing a compliant workforce responsive to managerial control. The training agenda, if there is one, centres on technical and supervisory training. Broader human resource strategies and policies are ignored, as are issues of wider social responsibility and community concern.

Financial and technological factors dominate business strategies to the exclusion of environmental concerns. Traditional approaches to efficiency dominate the production process and the environment is taken for granted. Environmental resources which are free or subsidized (air, water and so on) are wasted and little regard is given to environmental degradation resulting from the organization's activities. Environmental risks, costs, opportunities and imperatives are seen as irrelevant or not perceived at all.

 ## Phase 3: Compliance

Human sustainability (HS3)

Financial and technological factors still dominate business strategies but senior management views the firm as a 'decent employer'. The emphasis is on compliance with legal requirements in industrial relations, safety, workplace standards and so on. Human resource functions such as training, IR, organization development, TQM are instituted but there is little integration between them. Basically the organization pursues a policy of benevolent paternalism with the expectation of employee loyalty in response. Community concerns are addressed only when the company faces risk of prosecution or where negative publicity may have a damaging impact on the company's financial bottom line. Compliance is undertaken mainly as a risk-reduction exercise.

Ecological sustainability (ES3)

Financial and technological factors still dominate business strategies but senior management seeks to comply with environmental laws and to minimize the firm's potential liabilities from actions that might have an adverse impact on the environment. The most obvious environmental abuses are eliminated, particularly those that could lead to litigation or strong community action directed against the firm. Other environmental issues, which are unlikely to attract litigation or strong community action, are ignored.

Notes

1 Australian Government Corporations and Markets Advisory Committee, *Corporate Social Responsibility Discussion Paper*, Canberra: Commonwealth of Australia, 2005, p. 13.

2 See James Hardie website at www.jameshardie.com/.

3 Peter Prince, Jerome Davidson and Susan Dudley, 'In the Shadow of the Corporate Veil', Research Note No. 12 2004–05, Parliament of Australia Parliamentary Library, Law and Bills Digest Section, 10 August 2004.

4 F. Buffini, 'Reform on the horizon as asbestos pain continues', *Australian Financial Review*, 30 November 2005, 61.

5 Ibid.

6 Australian Government Corporations and Markets Advisory Committee, *Corporate Social Responsibility Discussion Paper*, Canberra: Commonwealth of Australia, 2005, p. 14.

7 Ibid.

8 J. Bakan, *The Corporation*, New York: Free Press, 2004.

9 Australian Government Department of Environment and Heritage, *The State of Sustainability Reporting in Australia*, Canberra: Commonwealth of Australia, 2005.

10 L. Gettler,' Being responsible is suddenly serious', *The Age*, 17 May 2005, at www.theage.com.au/news/Business/Being-responsible-is-suddenly-serious/2005/05/16/1116095905178.html (accessed 20 May 2006).

11 S. Mitchell, 'Social responsibility still missing' *Australian Financial Review*, 19 May 2005, 23.

12 Gettler, 'Being responsible is suddenly serious'.

13 T. Clarke, 'Introduction', *Theories of Corporate Governance*, London: Routledge, 2004.

14 Ibid., p. 11.

15 C. Deutsch, 'Companies and critics try collaboration', *New York Times*, 17 May 2006, at www.nytimes.com/2006/05/17/business/businessspecial2/17partner.html?_r=1&fta=y&oref=slogin (accessed 21 May 2006).

16 P. Martin and M. Verbeek, *Sustainability Strategy*, Sydney: Federation Press, 2006, p. 62.

17 NSW Department of Environment and Conservation, *The Business Environment*, summer edition, 4 December, p. 1.

18 S. Benn and S. Low, interview with A. Sairanen, Environmental Manager, South Pacific, Hewlett-Packard Australasia, 12 May 2006.

19 P. Kelly, 'Business forced to examine its ledger', *Australian*, 6 February 2002.

20 J. Fava, 'A flexible framework to select and implement environmental strategies', *Strategic Environmental Management*, 1998, 1, 21–33.

21 K. Bondy, D. Matten and J. Moon, 'Codes of conduct as a tool for

sustainable governance in MNCs', in S. Benn and D. Dunphy (eds), *Corporate Governance and Sustainability*, London: Routledge, 2007.

22 Clean Clothes Campaign, quoted in Bondy *et al.*, 'Codes of conduct'.

23 G. Avery, *Leadership for Sustainable Futures*, Cheltenham: Edward Elgar, 2005.

24 W. Baue, 'Insurers at the crossroads: intersection between insurance and sustainability is a busy corner', *SRI News from SocialFunds.com* 11 November 2005, at www.csrwire.com/sfarticle.cgi?id=1850 (accessed 28 May 2006).

25 I. Palmer, R. Dunford and G. Akin, *Managing Organizational Change*, New York: McGraw-Hill Akin, 2006.

26 The Natural Step, at www.naturalstep.org/com/ (accessed 28 May 2006).

27 The Home Depot Case Summary, The Natural Step, 2003.

28 McDonald's Corporation Case Summary, The Natural Step, 2003.

29 S. Benn, D. Dunphy and P. Crittenden, 'Carlton & United Beverages' Kent Brewery: A Case Study', unpublished case study, Sydney: University of Technology, 2005.

30 Benn, interview with R. Savage.

31 'Environmental impact assessment', in R. Staub, *Environmental Management and Decision-making for Business*, New York: Palgrave Macmillan, 2005, pp. 256–62.

32 Fava, 'A flexible framework . . .'.

33 CSR Starter Pack, www.business-impact.org (accessed 18 April 2002).

34 Roome, 'Developing environmental management strategies'.

35 S. Suthersen, 'Editorial', *Strategic Environmental Management*, 1998, 1 (1).

36 B. Daily and S. Huang, 'Achieving sustainability through attention to human resource factors in environmental management', *International Journal of Operations and Production Management*, 2001, 21(12), 1539–52.

37 Australian Government Department of Environment and Heritage, *The State of Sustainability Reporting in Australia*, Canberra: Commonwealth of Australia, 2005, p. 33.

38 S. Benn, interview with Professor G. Molenkamp, KPMG, The Hague, the Netherlands, 4 February 2002.

39 R. Staub, 'Environmental auditing', in R. Staub, *Environmental Management and Decision-making for Business*, New York: Palgrave Macmillan, 2006, pp. 263–70.

40 S. Bartholomeusz, 'Time to redefine the audit', *Sydney Morning Herald*, 12 February 2002, 19.

41 Institute of Chartered Accountants in Australia, *Extended Performance Reporting*, report prepared by Wua Fong Chua, 2005, at www.icca.org.au.

42 Hoffman, *From Heresy to Dogma*.

43 J. Elkington, *The Chrysalis Economy*, Oxford: Capstone, 2001.

44 Roome, 'Developing environmental management strategies'.

45 Benn, interview with U. Huiskamp.

46 D. Stace and D. Dunphy, *Beyond the Boundaries*, Roseville NSW: McGraw-Hill, 2001.

47 M. Brinded, 'Perception versus analysis: how to handle risk', speech to the Royal Academy of Engineering, London, 31 May 2000.

48 Friends of the Earth, *The Other Shell Report*, reported in 'Shell accused of contempt of court over continued illegal gas flaring', 16 December 2005, at www.foe.co.uk/resource/press_releases.

49 *Sydney Morning Herald*, 'Shell "ignored pollution warnings"', 14 May 1996, http://global.factiva.com (accessed 31 May 2006).

50 Benn, interview with U. Huiskamp.

51 Stace and Dunphy, *Beyond the Boundaries*.

52 P. Gollan, 'Human resources, capabilities and sustainability', in D. Dunphy, J. Benveniste, A. Griffiths and P. Sutton (eds) *Sustainability: the Corporate Challenge of the Twenty-first Century*, Sydney: Angus & Robertson, 2000.

53 B. Piasecki, *Corporate Environmental Strategy: The Avalanche of Change since Bhopal*, New York: Wiley, 1995.

54 Benn, interview with U. Huiskamp.

55 Elkington, *Cannibal with Forks*.

56 A. Griffiths, D. Dunphy and S. Benn, 'Corporate sustainability: integrating human and ecological sustainability approaches', in M. Starik, S. Sharma with C. Egri and R. Bunch, *New Horizons in Research on Sustainable Organisations*, Sheffield, 2005, Greenleaf Publishing, pp. 166–86.

57 Benn, interview with Hans Nooter, Nuon Energy, Hardewijk, Netherlands, 7 February 2002.

58 A. Griffiths, 'New organizational architectures: creating and retrofitting for sustainability', in Dunphy *et al.* (eds) *Sustainability*.

59 Adler and Tushman, *Competing by Design*.

60 Ibid.

61 Benn, interview with R. Savage.

62 Benn, interview with Hans Nooter.

63 J. Huxley, 'For richer, for poorer: devoted to the boss', *Sydney Morning Herald*, 16 October 2001.

64 Gollan, 'Human resources, capabilities and sustainability'.

65 P. S. Adler, 'Building better bureaucracies', *Academy of Management Executive*, 1999, 3, 36–46.

66 Canadian Chemical Producers' Association, *Codes of Practice*, at www.ccpa.ca/english/who/rc/Codes/statement.html (accessed 18 April 2002).

67 Information from the GRI website, www.globalreporting.org (accessed 18 April 2002).

68 Frank Hubbard, Director, Worthwhile Projects Pty Ltd, Sydney, Environment, Safety and Sustainability Management Consultants, Info@WorthwhileProjects.com

69 Ibid.

70 Ibid.

71 Piasecki, *Corporate Environmental Strategy*.
72 P. Senge, *The Fifth Discipline: The Art and Practice of the Learning Organization*, Sydney: Random House, 1992.
73 A. de Geus, 'The living company', *Harvard Business Review*, 1997, 75, 51–9.
74 C. Laszlo and J. Laugel, *Large-scale Organizational Change*, Boston, MA: Butterworth-Heinemann, 2000.
75 J. Pfeffer and J. Veiga, 'Putting people first for organizational success', *Academy of Management Executive*, 1999, 13, 37–48.
76 I. Palmer and R. Dunford, 'Organizing for hyper-competition: new organizational forms for a new age?' *New Zealand Strategic Management*, summer 1997, 38–45.
77 Pfeffer and Veiga, 'Putting people first . . .'.
78 Winsemius and Guntram, 1992, quoted in N. Gunningham, 'Beyond compliance: management of environmental risk', in B. Boer, R. Fowler and N. Gunningham, *Environmental Outlook*, Annandale, NSW: Federation Press, 1994.
79 Ibid.
80 Roome, 'Developing environmental management strategies'.
81 Gollan, 'Human Resources, capabilities and sustainability'.

Part III
The dominant current reality: understanding and reconstructing second wave corporations

4 Achieving sustainable operational efficiencies

- Beyond low-hanging fruit
- What is efficiency?
- How can the search for efficiency contribute to sustainability?
- Potential benefits of efficiency
- Efficiency choices: high or low paths to competitive advantage?
- Creating eco-efficiencies
- Creating human efficiencies
- The challenge: integrating human and ecological efficiency
- Moving beyond efficiency approaches

Beyond low-hanging fruit

'Picking the low-hanging fruit' is an expression that managers use to describe the easily achieved efficiency gains made within their corporations. However, once all the low-hanging fruit is picked, where are new efficiency gains to be achieved? This chapter takes the search for efficiency beyond the obvious cost reduction exercise. We identify three paths to efficiency:

- Efficiencies via cost reduction.
- Efficiencies through value adding.
- Efficiencies through innovation and flexibility.

These are not mutually exclusive paths to efficiency. Together, they represent a radical shift in the way that corporations approach efficiency – both human and ecological. They form the basis of a strong and compelling business case for managers to engage in sustainability activities.

The Scandic hotel chain provides insights into how organizations can capitalize on these three paths to efficiency. Today Scandic is the dominant operator of full-service three and four-star hotels in Scandinavia and one of the major hotel chains in Europe.[1] However, this was not the case in 1992, when the hotel chain was in crisis. The newly appointed CEO, Roland Nilsson, instigated a major turnaround project that lasted two years. The successes achieved in the turnaround enabled the corporation to shift its focus from crisis management to future strategy. Central to this achievement was a change in values and philosophy. The company adopted 'profound caring' as its value statement. This reflected a commitment to care for all major stakeholders: customers, employees, shareholders, communities and the environment.

Environmental and social responsibility became a central focus of the organization. A corporate-wide programme, the Natural Step, was instigated to instil the new values approach throughout the corporation. Nilsson, the former CEO of Scandic, viewed the Natural Step as a powerful tool for communicating the importance of achieving sustainable outcomes. All managers and employees were exposed to the ideas of the Natural Step through workshops. Scandic managers and employees then sought to translate the principles of the Natural Step into concrete actions that would reduce the 'ecological footprint' of the corporation and simultaneously harness efficiencies to deliver in a practical way on the commitment of 'profound caring'.[2]

The first efficiency impacts at Scandic were felt almost immediately. Employees identified much 'low-hanging fruit', ripe for picking. For instance, the overall amount of soap and shampoo used was reduced by twenty-five tons and refuse by eight and a half tons annually. This was achieved by the introduction of recyclable soap and shampoo and the elimination of waste by the use of refillable containers. The implementation of ideas such as these continues to generate cost efficiencies for Scandic. As a consequence of these initiatives, Scandic now claims that it now uses 200 million fewer items of disposable packaging in seven years – demonstrating that it has continued to build on the cost approach to efficiency.[3]

Second, Scandic moved towards efficiency gains through the adoption of value-adding activities. In order to generate value-adding outputs, the company had first to build the capability of its employees. Anticipated efficiency gains were shared with employees by investing in their skills. Emphasis was placed on developing and training employees (enhancing human capital) to identify value-adding opportunities. Employees developed and used a range of metrics such as environmental barometers (quarterly benchmarking reports) and an environmental index. In addition, a resource hunt was initiated to gain resource efficiencies in energy, water, waste and dematerialization. In its first year, average energy consumption in its Nordic hotels was reduced by 7 per cent, water consumption by 4 per cent and unsorted waste by 15 per cent. This resulted in estimated financial benefits of US$800,000. Scandic has continued to build on these developments by reducing water consumption by 13 per cent and energy by 24 per cent.[4] Through investment in such value-adding activities, Scandic built on its initial cost-cutting approach to deliver more fundamental efficiency improvements in resource utilization. This strategy is now being applied to Scandic's supply chain and procurement practices.

Finally, at Scandic innovation has become another means of gaining further sustainable efficiencies. Renewing and refurnishing are major investment activities in hotels. One major innovation Scandic has developed is the 97 per cent recyclable 'eco-room'. Rooms are designed and built for disassembly and all components that cannot be reused or recycled are sold: 'Approximately 2,000 rooms are being refurbished each year with an estimated decrease per year of plastics by 90 tons, metals by 15 tons and mercury by 50 per cent.'[5] Currently, Scandic has created over 9,500 environmental rooms and seven eco hotels.[6] Innovation – a change in mind set – has led to huge cost savings, reduced ecological impact and enhanced the reputation of the corporation with its customers. Scandic has also sought to add value in other areas of its operations. For instance, the hotel demands that its suppliers share Scandic corporate values and are responsible to both the environment and society. In order to demonstrate transparency, Scandic has made the terms of its suppliers' agreement available on its Web site.

The Scandic case reinforces two important messages contained in this chapter. First, the move to efficiency often starts with an emphasis on using cost measures to capture short-term efficiencies. However, to achieve sustainable longer-term gains, the appropriate human systems and cultural values must be built to support value adding and innovation. For instance, some 9,000 people at Scandic have now undertaken training to 'learn to think sustainably'.[7] Second, in a world where population is still increasing, the stewardship of natural and social resources is critical. An economy made up of efficient organizations may simply devastate the natural and social world more efficiently by, for example, using up natural resources at a greater rate or generating a larger pool of unemployed. Efficiency is a contestable term that can be defined only by reference to values. At Scandic Corporation efficiency gains are shared with employees and a broader set of stakeholders, as well as being used to build internal competences and the reputational capital of the firm. These strategies create a virtuous circle of steadily increasing efficiencies. The three-pronged approach to sustainability exemplified by Scandic provides a compelling business case for sustainability.

In this chapter we detail these three approaches to efficiency: cost reduction, value adding and innovation. While we discuss all three, we emphasize the importance of the latter two in creating positive benefits for the natural and social worlds. We refer to these as the high road to sustainability. Cost reduction alone is not necessarily a positive achievement for the organization, society or the environment. However, it can become a significant first step on the journey towards achieving sustainable competitive advantages and benefiting society and the environment. Some commentators, such as Renato Orsato, have provided a compelling case for understanding under what conditions and strategies corporations should engage with sustainability practices (cost or differentiation) in order that they may be able to generate long-term value and potential competitive advantages.[8] His work further reinforces the business case for sustainability.

What is efficiency?

Efficiency is a concept that means different things to different people. So what is efficiency? How can efficiency contribute to creating a more sustainable world? Who owns the increased efficiency? And how is the pay-off shared?

The search for corporate efficiencies has a long history that provides a useful framework for understanding current approaches. As organizations became larger and more complex in the late nineteenth century a movement emerged focused on controlling the complexities that had arisen in the new factories. Frederick Taylor, the father of scientific management, was one leader who responded to this challenge. He involved himself in studying the new factories and trying to improve their productive efficiency. Taylor aimed to tame organizational complexity through the systematization of work and to increase organizational profitability through incremental improvements to the efficiency with which work was performed. Taylor's scientific management was only one historical source of traditional bureaucratic attempts to improve the efficiency of organizations. A comparable

European source was the work of Henri Fayol. Both Taylor and Fayol had visions of more productive organizations which they and their followers were able to implement in the real world.[9] Their ideas on what constitutes efficiency were, however, limited in scope and unrelated to issues of sustainability.

The principles generated by these approaches were simply an extension of Newtonian science. Success in scientific endeavour had been achieved by breaking the whole into duplicate parts with highly specialized functions and making these parts interchangeable. Scientific management extended these principles to the creation of a logical, linear work flow, the selection of applicants best suited to the job, training workers in the skills needed, measuring output and motivating workers by suitable rewards for performance. One result was the assembly line, which dominated manufacturing through most of the last century.

The systematizing of work that Taylor captured in his *Principles of Scientific Management* still remains an influential concept in much work redesign. Many of the principles embodied in Taylor's work were later taken up by industrial engineers and incorporated in operations management: the application of mathematical and technical solutions to solving managerial problems.

More recently, business process re-engineering (BPR) has built on these earlier incremental approaches to creating corporate efficiencies. It has attempted to do this by designing organizational transformations which 'bust silos', that is, break down the boundaries between functional management areas such as marketing, manufacturing and sales. The aim is to reorganize corporations into discrete lateral process and/or product flows.[10] Re-engineering can result in positive benefits such as a reduction in the number of levels in the organizational hierarchies, a refocusing of activities and resources on the core business, the elimination of non-value added activities, the outsourcing of non-core businesses and simplification of work flows that cross traditional functional boundaries. This in turn requires the devolution of authority and in some cases the introduction of team-based work,[11] with BPR, efficiency moved from being treated as simply an operational issue to being a corporate-wide performance improvement strategy. However, issues of social responsibility, the systematic building of human capability in the work force and environmental regeneration were largely ignored by BPR specialists.

So how do we understand corporate performance? Hilmer identified three factors affecting organizational performance: cost, value and flexibility.[12]

We shall deal with each of these potential components of performance in turn.

If they are working within a conventional business perspective, corporations seeking efficiency are primarily concerned with the first factor – cost. If a firm is to compete against other firms producing similar products or services on price alone, then cost becomes the vital factor in success, and the search for ongoing cost reductions is the way to sustain success. This may include reducing the costs of inputs, redesigning work, product and process flows to generate internal efficiencies, reducing labour inputs and better utilization of company resources (see Figure 4.1). Most firms compete on cost to some extent, but cost is less likely to be the most important factor in success where the firm has developed a unique product, service or production process. In other words, many cost advantages are short-lived. Take for example a beverage company that introduces new water-saving technology as part of an eco-efficiency initiative and in the process doubles its water efficiency in five years. For instance, the Carlton United Brewery at Yatala in Queensland previously used 6l of water per litre of beer brewed; it has since reduced this down to 2l. However, as one manager put it: 'We need to keep extending our efficiencies and looking for new breakthroughs. It won't be long before our competitors follow.'

A second approach to performance improvement comes from improving the quality of the product or service through adding value of some kind. Innovation around adding value is a potential source of performance improvement. Being an innovator is a strategic choice, with very different

Figure 4.1 *Traditional cost efficiencies*

implications from competing primarily on cost, because adding value usually incurs extra costs, such as those associated with research and development and new product design. In the words of Orsato, 'being green costs more, a differentiation strategy is the only way out for the company to pay off ecological investments'.[13]

Environmental performance at S. C. Johnson

S. C. Johnson is a family owned company, established in 1886. Its headquarters are located in the United States but the company operates in over sixty countries. S. C. Johnson is a leading manufacturer of household products for floor, furniture, air care and insect control. The firm has a long history of philanthropy and corporate social responsibility. When faced with increasing consumer awareness and resulting pressure for regulatory compliance, the management of the company initiated an eco-efficiency approach to improve the environmental performance of its manufacturing operations. Rowledge *et al.* point out that, initially, 'it was not a particularly explicit or integrated strategy designed to carefully position itself in customer minds . . . it was clear that there were business benefits to be won from reducing waste, improving efficiency and minimising liabilities'.[14]

S. C. Johnson's strategy at first focused on improving operational efficiencies by finding engineering and technical solutions in the areas of waste management, filtering, recycling and in some cases the use of gas from landfill to produce steam power.[15] However, as the programme of change continued, its success became more reliant on company-wide educational programmes, eco-efficiency workshops, communication strategies and developing the abilities of its people. The experience of this company highlights a central theme of this book: that it is important to make a start somewhere, where at least small wins may be readily made. But where a company ends up may be very different from what management envisaged at the beginning. S. C. Johnson's initial endeavours were devoted solely to the capturing of eco-efficiencies and reducing risk by removing noxious chemicals. But now the emphasis has changed and the company is asking, 'How can we create products without any chemicals at all?' Eco-efficiency often starts with the idea of improving the environmental performance of existing operations. However, its inherent logic carries those involved into a more substantial change process. They have continued to add value to these initial improvements via their Greenlist programme – the Greenlist programme forces the company to invest in research and development in order to look for replacement natural resources that are environmentally best or better than existing products. Furthermore, the company has sought energy and greenhouse gas improvements as part of its overall innovation drive. For instance, it has reduced its greenhouse gas emissions by 29 per cent from its baseline year in 2000 and its Waxdale plant has cut greenhouse gas emissions by 47 per

continued

cent by installing a process to burn waste methane gas from a landfill to produce electricity. S. C. Johnson seeks to build innovation in sustainability by valuing people, place and environment.[16]

Source: Rowledge *et al.* (1999)[17]

A third approach to performance improvement comes from increasing flexibility through innovation, that is, maintaining the ability to monitor, respond to or even anticipate changing market demands. The key to success here is to move in speedily with appropriate products or services to meet emerging demands. Innovation, speed to market and organizational flexibility become key components of success in this approach to creating a high-performance organization.[18] The emphasis is placed on competing by developing unique bundles of competences and organizational capabilities, particularly those involved with reshaping the organization.[19]

The efficiency approach to sustainability is therefore not only a way of reducing costs to ensure competitive advantage but also an approach that can involve investments in value-adding and innovation-based activities which lead on to strategic sustainability initiatives. When managers apply efficiency approaches to ecological issues, for example, they initially recognize that poor environmental practice may result in fines, boycotts or expensive clean-up operations. Product or service redesign may eliminate these risks, which are avoidable costs. On the human sustainability side, efficiency-driven organizations regard employees as a necessary resource required to make returns to the corporation, but a significant source of expenditure. Reducing employee numbers by process redesign can minimize these costs. But this is only one way to achieve that end. In addition, they are a denominator-driven approach. Another way to increase profitability is to make better use of the work force to increase the numerator. Adding value through more effective use of employees is another approach to efficiency. This is clearly the path that has been pursued by organizations such as Scandic and S. C. Johnson.

Efficiency approaches to sustainability are recognition of the scarcity of organizational resources and are about finding efficiency improvements through changing the resource mix or through better utilization of resources. We argue that these latter two approaches to efficiency require significant mind-set changes within organizations.

How can the search for efficiency contribute to sustainability?

Efficiency rests on value judgements – particularly about whose interests will be served by the changes. For instance, there is 'efficiency for the firm on the cheap'. It is relatively easy to increase the efficiency of any sub-unit of an organization or of society by externalizing costs to others. A simple example from managing a household economy is to throw the garbage over the neighbour's fence or on to the common. All that does is transfer the cost to someone else. While efficient in the short term, we do not see it as leading to sustainability. Similarly we may reduce household costs in the short term by chopping up the floorboards for heating and selling off basic facilities like the refrigerator and stove. In that case we have externalized cost to the future. So when we are evaluating efficiencies we cannot evaluate them solely on whether they benefit the organization: we also have to look at their impact on the environment and society.

In many cases the efficiency approach to sustainability is a natural extension of an organization's engagement in compliance activities. Compliance involves reviewing and monitoring organizational performance in order to identify inefficiencies. Efficiency approaches to sustainability have been particularly popular with organizations engaged in activities that significantly impact on the environment such as those operating in the resource extraction industries, in manufacturing and in petrochemicals.[20] Companies in these industries have typically moved over time beyond compliance activities towards the adoption of efficiency approaches to sustainability. In other words, the new lens of sustainability helps management and others see current organizational activities in a fresh light so that new opportunities to make efficiency improvements become apparent.

The message is simple: the efficiency approach represents a natural move towards sustainability because it builds on existing operational and technical capabilities and is a natural extension of installing compliance systems and the application of quality management principles. However, efficiency defined solely as cost reduction and the simplification of product, process and service flows is insufficient to achieve fully sustainable communities and a sustainable world. Some commentators argue that the 'greening of industry' associated with these initiatives is not sufficient to deal with the significant environmental and social shocks that organizations may face under conditions of discontinuous change.[21]

In addition, such efficiencies will provide only limited competitive advantages for the organization, as efficiencies of these kinds are readily copied by competitors. Nevertheless, the cost efficiency paradigm can help organizations lay the foundation for a more comprehensive approach to becoming a strategically sustainable organization.

We argue that a radical rethink of efficiency is required. The Scandic case highlights this in practical terms. The Scandic change programme started with a cost-cutting focus but went on to initiate value-adding and innovation approaches. In *Natural Capitalism* Lovins *et al.* provide many detailed examples of efficiency and resource gains to be made in organizations and societies as they engage seriously with protecting the natural environment.[22] The examples they give demonstrate the need for a mind shift in how managers look at and value natural resources. Similarly, Hardin Tibbs argues that a paradigm shift in thinking on resource use is required:

> At the moment, the industrial system is less a system than a collection of linear flows. Industry draws materials from the earth's crust and the biosphere, processes them with fossil energy to derive transient economic value and dumps the residue back into nature. For every 1 kilogram of finished goods we buy, about 20 kilograms of waste have been created during production, and within six months 0.5 kilograms of our average purchase is already waste.[23]

In other words, if close to 95 per cent of the material used in the production process doesn't make it into the final product, then there must be dramatic opportunities for more efficient use of the waste and for major productivity increases. There is a need to replace the current 'extract and dump' mind set with one that seeks to create virtuous cycles of resource use and utilization.[24] For instance, this can be achieved through developing an industrial ecology where we begin with the principle of maximizing overall benefit to the total system. Efficiency based on value adding places the full cost of disposing of anything dangerous or not used (waste) on the producer. This leads the producer to search for 'beginning of pipe' design solutions to eliminate pollution and waste, to maximize the use of all resources and to recycle material output. This in turn can lead to the creation of new industries which use waste as valuable inputs to further production. Such industries represent new strategic opportunities.

While technologies are important in generating new efficiencies, as in the case of Carlton United Breweries, fundamental shifts in mind set are also required to maximize the value of new technologies so that they contribute towards value-adding and innovation-based approaches to efficiency.

As the Scandic case highlights, human abilities are crucial in creating and capitalizing on these higher-level efficiencies. In a rapidly changing world, marked by unforeseen discontinuities, the capability for flexible response, the ability to change and to reshape the organization to meet new challenges, is vital. Therefore it is false to imagine that anything which reduces this capacity to create higher-level efficiencies is itself an efficiency. It is easy to cut costs in the short term by putting off skilled and experienced staff and cutting back on investing in capabilities and competences. But these human capacities are crucial to generating long-term competitiveness. Roland Nilsson, the former CEO of Scandic, has the last word here when discussing the decision to invest in people and the environment: 'So we can accept a higher investment today, because it will lower the cost in the future. It hasn't cost us anything. No one can claim that this has cost us more money.'[25]

Potential benefits of efficiency

There are potential benefits to the organization, society and the ecosystem from the adoption of efficiency initiatives that build on compliance activities. First, efficiency approaches to ecological sustainability are the front line of action on sustainability for the majority of organizations today. Efficiency initiatives of this kind usually take place within the functional 'silos' of these organizations. These ecological initiatives can be relatively isolated and limited interventions such as the implementation of 'end of pipe' filtering systems and the use of programmes such as Total Quality Environmental Management or Design for the Environment. Alternatively, they can be much more comprehensive interventions such as the development of fully integrated industrial ecosystems or the launch of corporate-wide programmes such as the Natural Step. Central to the successful adoption and utilization of such programmes is the development of a high degree of engineering, operational and technical competence and the use of compliance-based monitoring systems to drive ongoing business performance. The benefits for the organization of the development of such programmes are:

- The building of technical capabilities.
- The development of integrated human resource management systems.

- Cost savings through waste reduction.
- The development of corporate specific knowledge on product design, process and service layouts that can result in future competitive advantages.

There can also be societal benefits from the application of efficiency approaches to sustainability. These include the more efficient use of scarce natural resources and the development of industrial ecosystems that protect and promote healthy communities by recycling and reusing industrial waste. Similarly, there may be some forms of community involvement – such as the funding of public programmes or the establishment of community consultative committees.

Finally, efficiency approaches can have positive benefits for the natural environment. Lovins *et al.* (1999) provide several examples of how organizations, by changing the way that they approach efficiency – looking through the lens of sustainability – have not only garnered cost savings themselves but have also benefited the environment. Consider the case of the Center for Holistic Management in Albuquerque, New Mexico. The members of this community have introduced more efficient ways of range feeding cattle based on the 'natural' methods used by the moving herds of native grazing animals.[26] As Lovins *et al.* point out: 'It turns out that changing industrial processes so that they actually replenish and magnify the stock of natural capital can prove especially profitable because nature does the production; people just need step back and let life flourish.'[27] The full range of potential benefits of efficiency can be realized only when efficiency is maximized simultaneously for the organization, society and the environment.

Efficiency choices: high or low paths to competitive advantage?

Efficiency is the dominant concern of many organizations today; so the key issues here are understanding what efficiency is and making it happen. The drive towards enhanced corporate performance through efficiency gains diverges in two directions: the first path is based primarily on the search for internal efficiencies and cost reductions, and is related to competition on cost alone. The second path leads to the development of specific capabilities and strategies that can add value – a major feature of high-performance organizations. Organizations can often choose the direction they take. If they follow the first path, they run the risk of creating only temporary competitive advantages that are ultimately easy to imitate so that the immediate advantage can be leapfrogged by more strategically focused organizations. If they follow the innovation and flexibility path, new opportunities for business growth and sustainability emerge.[28]

In Australia, for instance, whole industry sectors – such as the resource-based meat industry – have formulated their strategies on low-cost factor endowments. For most of the industry's history they have used the low-cost production of range-fed cattle to compete in export markets. Institutional arrangements, government policies and corporate strategies created an industry environment based on low-quality inputs. This caused significant environmental damage to semi-arid land and made the industry vulnerable to other low-cost competitors. However, some organizations have pursued alternative strategies. For instance North Australia Pastoral Company (NAPCO) with over 120 years of heritage has sought smaller economic returns in the short term in order to create longer-term viability via a commitment to quality; a recognition of the need not to overgraze and over-use natural resources and the need to commit to and build local communities that support their properties. In the NAPCO case, value adding is achieved not via the exploitation of resources but, in the words of one manager, 'by living and learning to live with the land'.[29] The high road to efficiency provides both organizations and societies with greater choices and significant added value.[30]

Sony and the high road to ecological efficiency

Sony provides us with an example of an organization that is attempting to pursue the high road to ecological sustainability. Sony is a leading Japanese multinational company involved in the development, design and provision of consumer and industrial electronic equipment and devices.[31] Sony's first attempts at ecological efficiency in the 1970s focused on the reduction of hazardous waste in the production process and the introduction of health and safety initiatives for its work force. These initial efficiency approaches were 'production'-oriented and focused on process improvements – much in the same vein as quality management. However, these production-oriented approaches became the springboard from which the company launched and extended its efficiency approaches to ecological sustainability. For instance, the company has gone about implementing environmental management systems, furthering its work on process efficiencies, product redesign for the environment and product recycling.[32] In the case

continued

of its second-generation television these programmes have reduced plastics by 52 per cent, increased recyclability to 99 per cent and reduced the cost of the cabinet by 30 per cent.[33] Sony Corporation is now moving beyond the production and cost efficiency basis of earlier initiatives to integrate environmental issues into its corporate strategy.[34]

Creating eco-efficiencies

In the previous chapter the case for compliance was examined. Compliance-based companies focus primarily on the implementation of monitoring and performance-based systems and the early experimentation with programmes that bring the organization into alignment with external stakeholder demands. The major aim is to reduce the organization's exposure to liability and the risk of penalty, fines and loss of reputation. As we pointed out, the failure to do so by many organizations can be costly in terms of the loss of reputational and social capital and the organization's overall ability to develop internal competences. However, we now discuss positive examples of organizations creating eco-efficiencies. We build on the distinction made earlier between low and high approaches to efficiency, concentrating on examples of corporations following the high road.

What is eco-efficiency? The World Business Council for Sustainable Development and the United Nations Environment Programme (UNEP) define eco-efficiency in this way:

> Eco-efficiency is reached by the delivery of competitively priced goods and services that satisfy human needs and bring quality of life while progressively reducing ecological impacts and resource intensity, through the life-cycle, to a level at least equal with the Earth's estimated carrying capacity.[35]

The World Business Council for Sustainable Development and the United Nations Environment Programme have also outlined what they regard as the major principles of eco-efficiency. These include:

● Reducing the material intensity of goods and services.
● Reducing the energy intensity of goods and services.
● Reducing toxic dispersion.
● Enhancing material recyclability.
● Maximizing sustainable use of renewable resources.

- Extending product durability.
- Increasing the service intensity of goods and services.[36]

Pursuing these changes amounts to the more efficient use of environmental resources. The efficiencies, however, provide benefits both to the firm and to the environment. Lovins *et al.* refer to this as Natural Capitalism. In attempting to implement these changes, they recommend that managers seek to address four key areas:

- Increase the productivity of natural resources through changes in the production design, layout and technologies of operations.
- Use biologically inspired production models, that is, 'closed loop' production systems.
- Develop new business models based on value and service.
- Reinvest in natural capital.[37]

Organizations, particularly those based in the manufacturing sector, are increasingly using these principles to design their eco-efficiency programmes. This efficiency approach to ecological sustainability is driven primarily by technocultures associated with engineers and scientists. Eco-efficiency builds incrementally on the compliance approaches and revolves around the establishment of and commitment to environmental programmes and the introduction of technologies to capture these benefits or the design of better facilities. Rockcote is an example of this.

Rockcote Sustainable Design Centre[38]

Eco-efficiency highlights:

- The creation of a sustainable design centre – that generates its own energy needs, recycles and has closed its water loop.
- Waste-free factory and the formation of partnerships with other eco-friendly organizations that exist in the same geographical area.
- Valuing employee input and ownership of the programme to generate home-grown sustainability and eco-efficiency initiatives.
- The creation of a new range of eco-paints and a focus by the R&D section on eco-products.

Eco-efficiency is characterized by a variety of programmes such as: Total Quality Environmental Management; industrial ecology; end-of-pipe solutions; design versus labelling; and environmental management systems. While these systems are primarily technological, they also involve developing the human abilities that enable the effective use of these systems. These abilities include identifying, collecting and understanding information and taking action to implement the programmes.

Furthermore, it appears that several key issues drive corporations towards the pursuit of eco-efficiency. These include the degree of alignment between market opportunities and eco-efficiencies, the internal structure and culture of the company and pressure from external stakeholders demanding action.[39] We have discussed the full range of these pressures for change in Chapter 2.

Consider the case of the Canon Group. Facing increasing regulation over the use of toxins in its manufacturing operations and increasing consumer awareness, Canon instigated technical and cultural changes designed to deliver eco-efficiencies. Emura states that Canon's corporate philosophy is 'Kyoseri' – harmonious coexistence.[40] This has been interpreted as coexistence both within human communities and with the natural environment. As Emura points out: 'the pursuit of Q (quality), C (cost) and D (delivery) are allowable only under conditions that fulfil environmental protection and businesses that cannot protect the environment have no right to manufacture products. Under the EQCD policy, the E (environment) must be given higher priority than management efficiency.'[41]

What are the strategies that Canon has employed to create a high-value road to eco-efficiency? The first initiative was to improve resource productivity, through efforts to reduce energy consumption, reduce waste and thereby save on resources and the removal of hazardous substances from production. In the second initiative, the environmental focus shifted from these product and process improvements to the issue of eco-design. Eco-design has involved the examination of the environmental impact of Canon's products and the introduction of environmental considerations in the initial stages of the product design process (see Table 4.1).

The third initiative in the Canon approach to eco-efficiency has been to reorganize the supply chain through the use of 'green' procurement policies and accreditation systems. Emura states: 'Canon requested 1,200 suppliers in Japan . . . 200 suppliers in South East Asia and China and

Table 4.1 *Characteristics of product eco-efficiency at Canon*

Resource conservation	Ease of recycling	Ease of disposal
Energy consumption	Energy conservation	Environmental preservation
Resources	Ease of assembly	Ease of disposal
Layout	Ease of sorting	
	Ease of reusing	

100 suppliers in North America to supply environment-conscious products.'[42] In the 1960s and 1970s Japanese automotive producers introduced quality improvement and just-in-time (JIT) programmes to create lean production systems. Similarly today Canon is using its influence over the supply chain to set standards for 'green' products and provide suppliers with the capabilities to develop 'green' components.

The final initiative in the eco-efficiency strategy at Canon is inverse manufacturing – or product recycling (remanufacturing). Along with other companies such as Volvo and Fuji-Xerox, Canon realizes that eco-efficiency is a transition phase to strategic sustainability. The pursuit of eco-efficiency enables the firm to develop and build broad environmental management capabilities signified by EMS accreditation and environmental management information systems and environmental accounting systems that leverage this transition.[43] Canon sees that its environmental mission is to move the focus from internal company changes to broader societal changes requiring community co-operation, particularly through 'green' procurement, product recycling and environmental disclosure. The Canon experience aligns with that of other major companies. For instance Bristol-Myers, Squibb, IBM and Xerox encourage their suppliers to develop environmental management systems consistent with ISO 14001. Ford, General Motors and Toyota actually require their suppliers to obtain ISO 14001 certification.[44]

Key issues in creating eco-efficiency

What lessons can we draw from these examples of collective organizational attempts to become eco-efficient? The characteristics of a winning formula for the creation of eco-efficient organizations are:

- Establishment of measurement systems to monitor performance in key areas of energy, waste and quality, for example systems such as Life

Cycle Assessment, Eco Productivity Index or Design for Environment.[45]

- Development of environmental programmes, similar to the quality management initiatives of the 1980s, that provide guidelines, tools and basic knowledge which can be diffused to line managers and employees alike or alternatively, rather than using such tools, development of an internally generated approach closely tailored to the needs of the particular organization.

- Building strong support of these initiatives by middle management (if the initiatives are isolated to functional or business units) and by senior management if these programmes are corporate-wide. For instance, at Interface, Ray Anderson, CEO, has set stretch targets and goals to reduce greenhouse gases and become footprint-neutral. He estimates that they are about a third of the way on that journey. Specifically, they have reduced their carbon intensity by a third, greenhouse gases down by 46 per cent and water use down 78 per cent per yard of carpet and 40 per cent per yard of broadloom.[46]

- Systematically identifying significant inefficiencies, unnecessary steps in the production or service process, poor layout, physical waste, old technologies and wasteful procedures. In the process of addressing inefficiencies, managers at Portland Aluminium in Victoria, Australia, found that they were dumping $1,000m^3$ of solid waste into landfill at a cost of A$1.3 million a year. They have since made a 60 per cent reduction in solid waste through selling much of it, such as carbon dust to cement manufacturers.[47]

- Accessing the tools available to address these issues: TQEM; environmental management systems; new technologies; industrial ecology opportunities and eco-design. Off-the-shelf solutions are generally less useful than combinations of these approaches.

- Using the tools identified above to introduce extensive value-adding activities such as eco-design, recycling of products and conversion of products into services.

- Piloting initiatives in a variety of business units and then progressively integrating them across the organization.

- Measuring and monitoring the costs of the improved systems using both 'hard' measures (financial improvements, waste reduction, production quality) and 'soft' measures (capability development, knowledge transfer, change agent development, consumer awareness and value changes in employees).[48]

- Including external stakeholders in the sustainability/eco-efficiency process through adopting, for example, procurement and supply chain management practices that involve suppliers also adopting eco-efficiency approaches. For example, BHP Billiton has introduced a stewardship programme into its supply chain and is now insisting that partner organizations demonstrate their own sustainability initiatives and use a stringent set of environmental criteria when assessing suppliers. The result has been a significant change in sustainability practices across a range of industries.

- Linking human capabilities and knowledge to generate new value-adding and innovation opportunities. For instance, Electrolux's environmental product line is more profitable than that of its conventional products. The development of this product line has involved investing in people capabilities and creating a culture of innovation. This is a learning process which feeds back into the generation of new products.[49]

We have emphasized here both the technical elements of generating a winning formula for eco-efficiencies and the vital links that must be made to human sustainability to maximize gains for both the organization and society. As Tibbs states:

> Change in either values or in technology alone is not enough: the two must happen in conjunction. One of the reasons for this is that technology – and new technology in particular because it is more powerful – can either help provide solutions or make the situation worse. What makes the crucial difference is human intention.[50]

Creating human efficiencies

We have all heard the mantra 'People are an organization's most valued asset.' In many cases they are its most valued asset only until the organization experiences a crisis and then they are seen as disposable.

Even when the organization does not downsize, the stated value placed on people is often demonstrated by low pay and failure to invest in employee competence development or to use fully employees' knowledge and skills. Many corporations have been trading on rhetoric for decades and in the process they have been losing their intellectual capital and consequently the basis of competition in the knowledge economy:

> If employers do not bridge the current gap between their rhetoric and workplace reality, then the likely outcome will be an exodus of bright and enthusiastic people to organizations that do. For true corporate

sustainability, an organization must recognize value and promote the capability of its people. For human resource sustainability to be achieved, therefore, the HR policies and practices need to be integrated for sustained business performance and positive employee outcomes of equity, development and well being.[51]

Placer Dome and Scandic Hotels

The case of Placer Dome, a gold-mining company, highlights the potential conflict between narrow and broader views of human sustainability. In the 1990s Placer Dome's human resource policies and strategies had a strong focus on employee development, training and safety and on valuing employee contributions to the company's sustainability efforts. A range of human sustainability initiatives were aimed at developing the capabilities of both employees and local communities affected by mining operations. However, a dramatic decline in the gold price caused a setback in the pursuit of sustainability. The decision to downsize led to a substantial reduction in one area of the company's core capabilities: for instance, at the Marcopper mine site a retrenched employee was rehired to undertake negotiations with key stakeholders when executives realized that he was the only one in the company who had developed a strong and trusting relationship with the community stakeholders. This example is an instance of a managerial decision, made in the name of efficiency, which can threaten the corporate capabilities required for future competitive advantages.

The Placer Dome approach is similar to the approach initially adopted by Scandic Hotels during its period of crisis. However, after the implementation of turnaround management strategies which lasted two years, Scandic's CEO realized that the best way to deal with future problems was to develop the human capital and competences of its people that would enable the corporation to adapt. Therefore investments were made in training people to deliver on the hotel chain's stated value of 'profound caring'. In the process Scandic rebuilt its reputational capital and shared the efficiency gains with a range of stakeholders.[52]

Corporations can achieve human efficiency by downsizing and retrenchment. While these policies provide short-term financial benefits and efficiency gains for companies, they provide few, if any, efficiency benefits for the societies in which they operate. Efficiency approaches dominated by such practices as cost cutting through downsizing and poor work environments such as exist in many call centres may create short-term efficiencies for corporations. However, they may also create long-term inefficiencies for the company and significant inefficiencies for society as a whole.

For instance, in the United States, Marriott Hotels was finding it difficult to attract new recruits and to retain good managers. The company had a strong culture of 'face time', that is, managers stayed at their hotel and pretended to work even if they had completed their work! In the Marriott culture, having managers put in long hours at the hotel was regarded as a benefit for the corporation. But there were heavy hidden costs in increased turnover and difficulty in recruiting new managers. When these costs were identified, the senior executive team instigated a programme of 'flexible work' which encouraged managers to adopt a different approach. If they had a busy week and put in more hours at work they were encouraged to work fewer hours in down times. So far the pilot programme has proved successful and Marriott is reaping the rewards of these new efficiencies, as reflected in a reduction of management turnover.[53]

What then is human efficiency? The high road to human efficiency involves organizations making maximum use of their human capabilities; that is, efficiency for the organization is primarily about ensuring that the organization has the requisite number of people, the mix of skills to perform its goals effectively and a strong base for future development. In the drive towards efficiency through added value, the human resource function increasingly develops an integrated approach to the management of a corporation's human capital. This is evidenced through:

● The development of human resource information systems.
● The identification of core competences.
● Focused training and organization development initiatives to enhance managerial and supervisory skills or to create core competences.
● Introduction of displacement technologies; outsourcing of those areas identified as not cost-efficient.

The development of well organized corporate human resource capabilities makes a significant contribution to human efficiency. Furthermore, research has identified a strong link between a company's investment in its work force and its stock market performance.[54] In other words, companies that invest more in their employees, for example in training and development and knowledge creation, show increased profits and productivity improvements.[55] These are characteristics of the value-adding and innovation approaches to efficiency.

Aristocrat and the development of internal human capital

Aristocrat Leisure Industries is the world's second largest designer and manufacturer of gaming equipment. One of its key undertakings during the 1990s was the introduction of efficiency improvements to its production processes to control spiralling costs, reduce waste and promote the desire to manufacture to quality, speed and flexibility. The major change has involved the transformation of the production system from a push to a hybrid pull system reliant on just-in-time approaches. This has in turn required a change in management style from autocratic and controlling to one that is more inclusive and empowering. This led to: the up-skilling of employees; the shift from a culture of fear and mistrust to one of trust; linking people systems (teams) to the new process layouts; a focus on the creation of a group culture through teaming; and the involvement of employees in addressing quality issues. Aristocrat approached the capability-building process of its people through the introduction of quality teams. This quality programme showed immediate improvements, increased production efficiencies and reduced waste across the plant. Over time the quality teams were turned into production-based teams focused on running 'mini-factories'. The social changes at Aristocrat lagged behind the technical changes. However, executives realized that an important prerequisite for increasing performance further was a significant investment in human capital designed to build on the production and process efficiency improvements. Consequently, Aristocrat is now also adopting a high value-added approach to human sustainability.[56]

The Aristocrat case highlights an interesting dilemma in the creation of sustainable corporations. Aristocrat is pursuing an efficiency approach to sustainability. However, many would argue that its products (gaming equipment) can damage the social fabric of communities and most ethical investment groups avoid investment in gaming activities. Gaming corporations respond that they have initiated programmes on responsible gambling and have created community benefit funds. This debate illustrates the usefulness of our framework, which can point to the real contribution of a firm like Aristocrat in one area of human sustainability (employee relations) and raise issues about its impact in another – social responsibility.

The external stakeholder relations of the organization can also contribute significantly to efficiency because they are often strongly affected by the reputation of a company. There is increasing realization of the value of reputational capital. Reputational capital takes years to build, cannot be bought but can be quickly and easily damaged. As Petrick *et al.* note, organizations that systematically build this aspect of intangible assets do so by demonstrating: trustworthiness to employees; credibility with investors (through profitability); reliability to customers and suppliers; and responsibility with communities for the stewardship of community and natural resources.[57] The payback can be significant: 'The reputational capital of Coca-Cola, for example, has been estimated at \$52 billion, of Gillette, \$12 billion, of Eastman Kodak, \$11 billion.'[58] In other words these corporations have added value via their enhanced reputation and public profile.

So how does reputational capital contribute to efficiency? As organizations gain cost efficiencies by picking the low-hanging fruit, that is, by using their resources more effectively, increased emphasis is placed on leveraging those fewer resources that the organization has to increase value. As McIntosh *et al.* state: 'As businesses have become leaner, tighter organizations with fewer staff, key relationships and brand image are the company's greatest assets and their management becomes more important.'[59] That is, organizations need to leverage the resources that they have more effectively, such as reputation, to gain further value-added outcomes.

Steps to the creation of reputational capital

Petrick *et al.* suggest four practical steps that managers can take to build reputational capital in the area of sustainability:

- Provide leadership education to managers and all levels of the organization in the areas of stewardship, behavioural skills so that sustainability competences become commonplace.
- Create senior executive roles for co-ordination of stakeholder relations that impact on reputational capital.
- Conduct an annual audit of global reputation.
- Use competitions for various product, organizational, social and leadership rewards to develop and maintain reputational capital.[60]

For organizations that seek to compete on efficiency there is a clear choice. The challenge is to look beyond a simple-minded cost-cutting approach – the low-cost path. The value-adding route to efficiency offers greater returns to the organization, to society and to the natural world. In this approach, the organization continues to reinvest in technologies, in research and development, and in developing knowledge-based competition. This in turn involves a shift away from an unskilled or semi-skilled work force to a work force with high skill levels and an extensive knowledge base. Organizations taking the added-value path have an efficiency focus in the present, but it is tempered by a future vision of adding value and innovating.

Ray Anderson's approach to eco-efficiency and industrial ecology is based on employee involvement and engagement. As Borial states, 'the participative program QUEST (Quality Utilizing Employee Suggestions and Teamwork) . . . were designed to foster involvement in and environmental awareness covering all the company's activities'.[61]

As a result, companies that have a future vision of value adding do not cut costs in a way that would jeopardize the progressive development of a highly skilled, well paid work force and the customizing of products and services. This choice involves a fundamentally different way of leading and managing organizations: it demands new structural forms and flexible work systems for the organization, a transformed approach to work design and new cultural values that reflect the shift to a knowledge-based economy. Managers who locate their organizations within the paradigm of value-adding/innovation efficiency are in a prime position to move to the next phase of developing a strategic approach to sustainability.

Potential pitfalls in pursuing human efficiencies

Several key issues for organizations emerge in the pursuit of human efficiencies. First, human resource managers often find it difficult to convince senior management and line managers that their efficiency programmes work, because of the intangible nature of the benefits of many HR programmes and also because of the longer time frame involved before the efficiency gains become apparent. The contrast is between short-term cost efficiencies but medium to long-term negative impacts (as in the case of downsizing or re-engineering) versus short-term increased costs (such as in training and development) and medium to long-term benefits. However, evidence has been accumulating over the last thirty years showing that advanced human resource policies, procedures and practices do contribute to the performance and financial competitiveness of organizations. More recently these case-based examples of advanced human resource performance are supported by surveys of large numbers of organizations.[62]

Table 4.2 *Human sustainability orientation*

Compliance	Cost efficiency	Value added/innovation efficiency
Characteristics	*Characteristics*	*Characteristics*
• Industrial relations emphasis on awards, legal agreements, formal negotiations	• Early capability development often subjected to cost cutting in times of crisis • Downsizing for realignment • Core values focus on short to medium-term profitability and return on investment	• Capability enhancement • Integration of sustainability programmes at all levels of the organization • Value adding and flexibility enhancement are linked to long-term financial goals
Aims	*Aims*	*Aims*
• Survival, 'licence to operate'	• Utilize resources to maximize financial returns from resources	• Increasing emphasis on employee rewards • Capability building • Adding value, cost minimization (without damaging capabilities and flexibility)

Second, efficiency alone will not deliver sufficient long-term competitive advantage in turbulent and competitive markets. Skinner has referred to the 'productivity paradox'. He found that organizations that were obsessed with increasing the productivity of labour capital and technology became locked in a vicious cycle of their own making and that this inhibited their ability to develop new ways of competing and enhancing their performance.[63] The relentless search for short-term productivity gains or efficiencies resulted in long-term decline. One danger of adopting a single-minded cost efficiency focus is that, in tough times, it can lead managers to cut programmes designed to up-skill the work force and create positive corporate cultures, thereby reducing the organization's ability to pursue a value-adding path.

Hamel and Prahalad make a similar point in their discussion of the way management fervently embraced re-engineering. They argue that re-engineering focuses too much attention on immediate efficiencies and neglects the vision of future innovative strategies; so there are real limits to an organization's ability to develop a fully sustainable human and ecological approach based on cost efficiency alone. In an extension of these ideas, some commentators argue that the pursuit of efficient and lean organizational designs increases the potential vulnerability of organizations to disruptive change events by reducing slack resources and hence the ability of the organization to adapt to changes in its external environment.[64] Managers need to ensure that cost-cutting today lays the organizational basis for moving towards the next phase of sustainability, the adoption of the strategic paradigm, rather than undermining it.[65]

So how can an organization pursue efficiency goals in a way that lays the basis for adding value? Here are some guidelines:

- Where possible managers need to establish the costs of compliance and present an emerging business case to the organization's senior managers based on piloting efficiency measures, which are then used to offset the costs of compliance-based activities.
- Shift the efficiency orientation of the organization away from cost towards value and innovation. This can be achieved by demonstrating the value of building human capital and by changing management reward systems to ensure that they do not encourage short-term cost-cutting measures that destroy human capabilities for enhanced performance in the medium and long term (see Figure 4.2 on building cost reducing, value adding and innovation cultures).
- Develop and implement systems which reflect increases in human capital, reputational capital and intangible assets at the corporate level. At the operational level, demonstrate the value-added contribution of HR programmes to operations.
- At the corporate level, develop integrated human resource information systems (HRIS) that enable the HR professional to identify the organization's existing core competences so that they can provide informed advice to senior managers about human capital competence areas of the organization.
- Initiate and implement trials of high-performance work environments and practices such as multi-skilled teams, value-adding programmes, culture change programmes.
- Protect innovative units of the organization from cost-cutting initiatives until they have had a reasonable time to demonstrate the value of their innovations to the corporation.
- Diffuse demonstrably successful high-performance practices and experiment with new organizational structures such as virtual teams, networks and communities of practice.

- Give line managers responsibility for the human sustainability agenda; establish support networks which include line and staff innovators and use corporate HR as a centralized resource facility to encourage and inform value-adding initiatives.
- Integrate and or establish links between corporate human resources and sustainability departments to generate complementary programmes – i.e. linking human resource reward systems and training with sustainability initiatives.
- Recognize that not all areas of the organization will be value-adding and develop appropriate policies to maintain cost efficiencies in those areas.
- Seek opportunities to build reputational capital and develop monitoring systems that measure the movement away from physical and financial assets to intangible assets.
- Ensure that the head of the HR function is included in senior management and board decisions regarding corporate strategy.
- Challenge the organization to calculate the costs of eco-services (land, energy, water) to generate broader awareness of emerging business opportunities by valuing innovation.

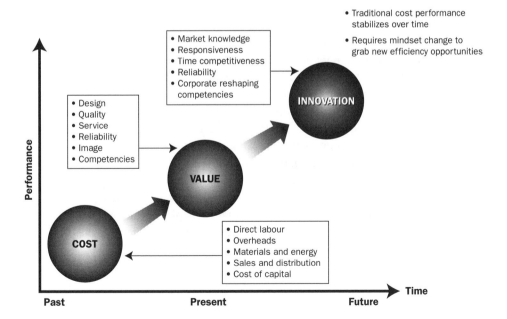

Figure 4.2 *The changing nature of performance*

The challenge: integrating human and ecological efficiency

Integrating the human and ecological approaches to efficiency is a key challenge at this stage of the journey to sustainability. Initially energies are often directed to one approach or the other, or initiatives are undertaken independently. It is only as these initiatives have been implemented that opportunities emerge to develop an integrated approach to efficiency. However, as organizations move further down the efficiency path, particularly in the development of eco-efficiencies, human capabilities become more important to the success of these programmes.[66]

Daily and Huang found that human sustainability factors, such as senior management support, environmental training, empowerment, teamwork and reward systems, were key elements in the implementation of environmental management systems.[67] This evidence has been backed up by research that has found that operational level employees in the Canadian chemical industry contributed significantly in reducing pollution and in undertaking environmental initiatives.[68] The evidence suggests that the pursuit of value-oriented eco-efficiencies is reliant upon the parallel development of human capabilities. However, the development of human capabilities is not reliant upon eco-efficiencies.

Who leads in the pursuit of eco and human efficiencies? The cases presented in this chapter show that senior managers play an important role in championing efficiency programmes. The case evidence also suggests that responsibility for making efficiency measures work belongs with line managers. They must take on the major responsibility for building future capabilities and for identifying future value-added opportunities. Efficiency approaches, by their very nature, are operational in focus and content. Efficiency programmes, whether human or eco-based, focus on such measures as the application of new technologies, the development of integrated and systematic information systems, cost and waste reduction and the effective utilization of a company's human, physical and resource assets. Line managers play an important stewardship function in addressing these issues: they must make the overall approach work.

Moving beyond efficiency approaches

In this chapter we have outlined a case for a radical rethinking of efficiency approaches to sustainability. We have argued that cost-reduction approaches are only one path corporations can use to achieve efficiency gains. For corporations to develop long-term competitive advantages and position themselves to make the leap to strategic sustainability there is a need to invest in capabilities and competences that capitalize on value-adding and innovative paths to efficiency.

The cases we have used demonstrate that once people become committed to developing human and ecological sustainability the momentum builds. In the cases presented here, all organizations started with simple cost reduction measures but went on to adopt a value-added/innovation approach to efficiency performance. In the process they found that this value-added approach unleashed a momentum of its own that led to the development of distinctive competences. These competences can be turned into competitive advantages. Technology initiatives are easily imitated; however, configurations of organizational capabilities – such as those found at Scandic or Canon – are harder to emulate. This is particularly so when these investments lead to and enhance the firm's reputational capital. Efficiency approaches based on adding value and innovation provide organizations with a strong impetus for moving into the next phase of achieving strategic sustainability. This is the subject of the next chapter.

 Phase 4: efficiency

Human sustainability (HS4)

There is a systematic attempt to integrate human resource functions into a coherent HR system to reduce costs and increase efficiency. People are viewed as a significant source of expenditure to be used as productively as possible. Technical and supervisory training is augmented with human relations (interpersonal skills) training. The organization may institute

Ecological sustainability (ES4)

Poor environmental practice is seen as an important source of avoidable cost. Ecological issues that generate costs are systematically reviewed in an attempt to reduce costs and increase efficiencies by eliminating waste and by reviewing the procurement, production and distribution process. There may be active involvement in some systematic approach such as Total Quality programmes of teamwork around significant business functions and generally pursues a value-adding rather than an exclusively cost reduction strategy. There is careful calculation of cost–benefit ratios for human resource expenditure to ensure that efficiencies are achieved. Community projects are undertaken where funds are available and where a cost benefit to the company can be demonstrated.

Environmental Management (ISO 14001). Environmental issues are ignored if they are not seen as generating avoidable costs or increasing efficiencies.

Notes

1 B. Nattrass and M. Altomare, *The Natural Step for Business*, Gabriola Island: New Society Publishers, 1999, p. 75.
2 The sustainability strategy pursued by Nilsson was significantly embedded into the culture and values of Scandic. In 2001 the Hilton Group acquired Scandic but has continued to expand its sustainability initiatives
3 Scandic, 'Environmental Common Sense', corporate publication, 2003, p. 6; Nattrass and Altomare, *Natural Step*, p. 80.
4 Scandic, 'Environmental Common Sense', p. 5; Nattrass and Altomare, *Natural Step*, p. 92.
5 Ibid., p. 97.
6 Scandic, 'Environmental Common Sense', p. 1.
7 www.scandichotels.com (accessed 21 March 2006).
8 R. Orsato, 'Competitive environmental strategies: when does it pay to be green?' *California Management Review*, 2006, 48 (2), 127–43.
9 D. Dunphy and A. Griffiths, *The Sustainable Corporation*, Sydney: Allen & Unwin, 1998.
10 M. Hammer and J. Champy, *Reengineering the Corporation*, London: Nicholas Brealey, 1990.
11 D. Stace and D. Dunphy, *Beyond the Boundaries*, Sydney: McGraw-Hill, 2001, p. 238.
12 F. Hilmer, *Coming to Grips with Competitiveness and Productivity*, Canberra: Economic Planning Advisory Council Paper 91/01, 1991; Stace and Dunphy, *Beyond the Boundaries*, p. 143.
13 Ibid., p. 135.
14 L. Rowledge, R. Barton and K. Brady, *Mapping the Journey: Case Studies in Strategy and Action towards Sustainable Development*, Sheffield: Greenleaf Publishing, 1999, p. 170.
15 Ibid.

16 2005 Environmental Report, CSR Newswire, www.scjohnson (accessed 25 April 2003).

17 Ibid.

18 Stace and Dunphy, *Beyond the Boundaries*.

19 D. Turner and M. Crawford, *Change Power: Capabilities that Drive Corporate Renewal*, Sydney: Business & Professional Publishing, 1998.

20 J. Keegan, 'Corporate Environmentalism and Market Performance: An Analysis of US Corporate Annual Reports, 1988–1999', honours dissertation, School of Management, Brisbane: Queensland University of Technology, 2002.

21 M. Winn and M. Kirchgeorg, 'The siesta is over: a rude awakening from sustainability myopia', in S. Sharma and M. Starik (eds) *Research in Corporate Sustainability: The Evolving Theory and Practice of Organizations in the Natural Environment*, Northampton, MA: Edward Elgar, 2002.

22 E. von Weizsacker, A. Lovins and L. Lovins, *Factor Four: Doubling Wealth – Halving Resource Use*, London: Earthscan Publications, 1998; P. Hawken, A. Lovins and L. Lovins, *Natural Capitalism: Creating the Next Industrial Revolution*, Boston, MA: Little Brown, 1999.

23 H. Tibbs, 'The technology strategy of the sustainable corporation', in D. Dunphy, J. Benveniste, A. Griffiths and P. Sutton (eds) *Sustainability: The Corporate Challenge of the Twenty-first Century*, Sydney: Allen & Unwin, 2000, pp. 191–216, esp. pp. 202–3.

24 Ibid., p. 203.

25 Nattrass and Altomare, *Natural Step for Business*, p. 80.

26 Example cited in A. Lovins, H. Lovins and P. Hawken, 'A road map for natural capitalism', *Harvard Business Review*, 2000, May–June, 145–58, esp. p. 156.

27 Ibid., p. 155.

28 R. Day, 'Beyond eco-efficiency: sustainability as a driver of innovation', *Sustainable Enterprise*, World Resources Institute, at www.wri.org/meb/sei/beyond.html (accessed 15 September 1998).

29 A. Griffiths, 'NAPCO: A Sustainable Company', case study, Brisbane: University of Queensland Business School, 2006.

30 A. Griffiths and R. Zammuto, 'Institutional Governance Systems and Variations in National Competitive Advantage: An Integrative Model', Technology and Innovation Management Centre, Brisbane: University of Queensland, unpublished manuscript, 2002.

31 Rowledge *et al.*, *Mapping the Journey*, pp. 129–50.

32 Sony have also instigated new approaches to the collection, use and recycling of electrical goods. They have taken part in a pilot programme in Minnesota. See: 'US begins to wrestle more earnestly with electronic waste', *CutterEdge Environment*, environment@cutter.com.

33 Rowledge *et al.*, *Mapping the Journey*, p. 131.

34 Ibid., p. 134.
35 World Business Council for Sustainable Development and the United Nations Environment Program (UNEP), *Cleaner Production and Ecoefficiency: Complementary Approaches to Sustainable Development*, 1992, p. 3.
36 D. Buzzelli, 'The challenge of eco-efficiency', in P. Allen (ed.) *Metaphors for Change*, Sheffield: Greenleaf Publishing, 2001.
37 Lovins *et al.*, 'Road map for natural capitalism', 145–58.
38 A. Griffiths, 'Rockcote: A Case in Sustainable Entrepreneurship', case study, Brisbane: University of Queensland Business School, 2006.
39 J. Cramer, 'Environmental management from stretch to fit', *Business, Strategy and the Environment*, 1999, 7, 162–72.
40 Cited in Y. Emura, 'Environmental management of Canon group', in P. Allen (ed.), *Metaphors for Change*, Sheffield: Greenleaf Publishing, 2001, p. 57.
41 Ibid., p. 58.
42 Ibid., p. 60.
43 Ibid., p. 59.
44 Global Environmental Management Initiative, *New Paths to Business Value*, Washington DC: GEMI. 2001, p. 7.
45 H. Pulm, 'Eco-performance evaluation', in J. Köhn, J. Gowdy and J. van der Straaten (eds) *Sustainability in Action*, Cheltenham: Edward Elgar, 2001.
46 R. Anderson, 'Interface celebrates Ten Years of Sustainability in Action', corporate document, Alexandria NSW: Interface, 2004.
47 B. Collis, 'Green bucks', *Qantas: The Australian Way*, 1999, 75, 23.
48 For sustainability indicators at the firm level see D. Tyteca, 'Sustainability indicators at the firm level', *Journal of Industrial Ecology*, 1999, 2 (4), 61–77.
49 G. Hedstrom, S. Poltorzycki and P. Stroh, 'Sustainable development: the next generation of business opportunity', *Prism*, 1998, 4, 15.
50 Tibbs, 'Technology strategy of the sustainable corporation', p. 201.
51 A. Wilkinson, M. Hill and P. Gollan, 'The sustainability debate', *International Journal of Operations and Production Management*, 2001, 21 (12), 1492.
52 J. Benveniste and D. Dunphy, *The Path towards Sustainability: A Case Study of Placer Dome Asia Pacific*, Centre for Corporate Change, Australian Graduate School of Management, Sydney: University of New South Wales, 1999.
53 B. Munck, 'Changing a culture of face time', *Harvard Business Review*, 2001, November, 125–54.
54 L. Bilmes, K. Wetzker and P. Xhonneux 'Value in human resources', *Financial Times*, 21 September 1997, 11.
55 P. Gollan, 'Training and the bottom line', Sydney: Graduate School of Management, Macquarie University, 1998.

56 A. Griffiths, A. Morgan and R. Waldersee, *The Implementation of World Class Manufacturing: The Case of Aristocrat Leisure Industries*, Case Study Series, Australian Centre in Strategic Management, Brisbane: Queensland University of Technology, 1998.

57 J. Petrick, R. Scherer, J. Brodzinski, J. Quinn and M. Fall Ainina, 'Global leadership skills and reputational capital: intangible resources for sustainable competitive advantage', *Academy of Management Executive*, 1999, 13 (1), 60.

58 Ibid.

59 M. McIntosh, D. Leipziger, K. Jones and G. Coleman, *Corporate Citizenship*, London: *Financial Times* Management, 1998, p. 62.

60 Petrick *et al.*, 'Global leadership skills . . .', p. 60.

61 O. Borial, 'The impact of operator involvement in pollution reduction: case studies in Canadian chemical companies', *Business Strategy and Environment*, 2005, 14, 339–60, p. 384.

62 J. Pfeffer, *Competitive Advantage through People*, Boston, MA: Harvard Business School Press, 1994.

63 W. Skinner, 'The productivity paradox', *Harvard Business Review*, 1986, July–August, 55–9.

64 A. Griffiths and M. Winn, 'Slack and Sustainability', Academy of Management conference paper, Hawaii, August 2005.

65 Hamel and Prahalad, *Competing for the Future*.

66 A. Griffiths, J. Petrick and V. Fung, 'Proactive environmental management of ecological information', Technology and Innovation Management Centre, Brisbane: University of Queensland, unpublished manuscript, 2002.

67 B. Daily and S. Huang, 'Achieving sustainability through attention to human resource factors in environmental management', *International Journal of Operations and Production Management*, 2001, 21 (12), 1539–52.

68 Borial, 'The impact of operator involvement in pollution reduction'.

5 Sustainability: the strategic advantage

- Turning sustainability to advantage
- The importance of strategy
- What is strategic sustainability?
- How strategic sustainability contributes to competitive advantage
- Risks of the strategic approach
- Beyond rhetoric and greenwash
- The winning formula
- Moving beyond strategic sustainability

Turning sustainability to advantage

> To avoid making the same mistakes, managers must recognize environmental improvement as an economic and competitive opportunity, not as an annoying cost or an inevitable threat. Instead of clinging to a perspective focused on regulatory compliance, companies need to ask questions such as What are we wasting? And how could we enhance customer value? The early movers – the companies that can see the opportunity in sustainability first and embrace innovation-based solutions – will reap major competitive benefits.[1]

This quotation from the work of Porter and van der Linde, two of the world's leading strategy theorists and free-market proponents, is a manifesto to managers and corporations alike: it is now time to link the firm's competitive advantage with environmental issues. Many firms have already responded to this emerging challenge and are developing corporate strategies that make sustainability a critical component of competitive success. Leading CEOs are now outlining the challenges of sustainability – not only in terms of their own businesses but also in terms of its potential impact on society at large. Their calls to action do not amount to 'greenwash' but rather are a rallying point for further corporate action and strategic change on sustainability and challenges of climate change (see box). This shift is a significant one, but those organizations that succeed in making the new integration will be the strategic leaders in the new economy.

What CEOs are saying

We see climate change as a business issue . . . and we're accelerating our efforts to find solutions.

(Bill Ford, CEO, Ford Motor Company)[2]

We believe climate change is one of the most significant environmental challenges of the twenty-first century and voluntary action alone cannot solve the climate change problem.

(Henry Paulson, chairman, Goldman Sachs)[3]

The vision is not just to change our company and eliminate our environmental footprint, but through the power of our influence on others become restorative.

(Ray Anderson, chairman, Interface)[4]

As business leaders representing a cross-section of the Australian economy, we believe that climate change is a major business risk and we need to act now . . . the longer we delay acting the more expensive it becomes for business and for the wider Australian economy.[5]

(Gerry Hueston, president, BP Australasia; Michael Hawker, CEO, Insurance Australia Group; Grant King, managing director, Origin Energy; Keith Scott, head of Australia and New Zealand Swiss Re; Harry Debney, CEO, Visy Industries; David Morgan, CEO, Westpac)

The Royal Dutch Shell Group was a pioneer of workplace innovations in introducing teams and strategy formation in the 1960s and 1970s. It is now a corporate pioneer in integrating sustainability into its corporate strategy. In 1996, stung by critics over its handling of the decommissioning of the Brent Spar oil rig and alleged human rights abuses in Nigeria, the Shell group undertook a major review of its stakeholders' expectations. The review showed that Shell's reputation had suffered substantially as a result of these incidents. Rather than acting defensively and dismissing the review, senior management used it as a basis for transforming the business principles and strategy of the corporation.[6] As part of its strategic review process, Shell has since committed itself to:

- Measuring and reporting its greenhouse gas emissions and reducing them through continuous improvement.
- Using efficiencies in production processes to achieve these goals.
- Working with governments and international bodies to find solutions to emission problems.
- Promoting product innovations that are energy-efficient and encouraging their use by consumers.
- Developing alternative energy sources, including renewables.

On each of these goals Shell outlined its progress in its 2005 sustainability report. This included:[7]

- A reduction in greenhouse gas emissions, which fell by 7 million tonnes. This reversed a six-year rise.
- Announced major research support for the capturing of carbon dioxide and focusing on alternative energies – biofuels, hydrogen and wind and thin-film solar technologies.
- Furthermore, the report actively outlines Shell's corporate mistakes and established an external review panel to assess the report's validity and Shell's performance.

This external review committee found that:

> We believe that Shell has missed an opportunity to use the Report to express important positions on energy in the public policy debate. These include: more prominent statements of belief and commitment on climate change; more on how to mitigate the 'curse of oil'; greater emphasis on the importance of upholding human rights when operating in poorly governed countries; and more clarity about how the benefits of natural resources could be shared with host communities. But we remain concerned at how the Report covers human rights and social issues, in particular:
>
> - The lesser coverage given to human rights and social concerns in comparison to other sustainable development issues.
> - The narrow selection of issues that focuses on traditional topics like discrimination, health and safety and child labour, while avoiding the complex challenges of wealth distribution in poorly governed countries and operating in zones of conflict.
> - Shell's patchy engagement record with local stakeholders – the pattern demonstrates an insufficient ability to transfer learnings and best practice.[8]

Managers at Shell see that future competitive advantages can be achieved by integrating three key elements: human and social capital, ecological sustainability and financial performance. They are now actively pursuing these strategies, setting targets and ensuring transparency in delivering these outcomes.[9]

BP has adopted a similar strategic approach to sustainability. As one of the world's largest extractive resource-based companies and energy producers, BP has strategically repositioned itself to be seen as moving 'beyond petroleum'. Like Shell, BP has committed to:

- The development of alternative energy products and technologies.
- Reduction in greenhouse gas emissions.
- The implementation of the Kyoto agreement.
- The pursuit of social and community sustainability by enhancing opportunities in local communities.
- The development of its internal human capital by enhancing the quality of life of employees.

BP has incorporated these goals into its corporate strategies in five broad areas of business policy: ethical conduct; employees; relationships; health, safety and environmental performance; and control and finance. BP executives have also decided that they need to develop core competences in these areas if BP is to make further significant contributions to sustainability.[10] In line with stakeholder transparency, they have also outlined the criteria they will use to assess corporate performance. The *Financial Times*, reporting the findings of a survey of media, non-government organizations and leading CEOs, announced that BP was viewed by all these parties as the company that best manages environmental resources.

How did BP win such diverse and unanimous support? One survey respondent framed their selection of BP this way:

> They are huge – a damaging company . . . Their business causes a lot of damage to the environment. However, over the years they have accepted their responsibilities and are constantly making efforts to reduce their impact on environmental resources. Although they have a long way to go, they deserve credit for their effort.[11]

For instance, BP has established an Emissions Markets Group to manage its extensive carbon trading activities.[12] The Global 100 list unveiled in 2005 argued that it was due to BP's leadership in a host of strategic areas – recycling, energy efficiency, climate change and the development of alternative technologies, to name a few, that led to BP's high ranking.[13] Clearly, BP is in the early stages of the sustainability journey but already it is positioning the company as an industry leader.

Previous chapters have demonstrated that managers increasingly face consumer boycotts, public scrutiny, internet blog sites and activism, regulatory monitoring and fines over any failure to meet expectations around sustainability issues. The wish to avoid liability and reduce risk is a major driver for companies to review their strategies to include sustainability objectives. But sustainability can also be seen as presenting opportunities rather than potential problems. There is a better way of doing business that enables corporations to progress beyond pursuing efficiency measures to improve financial outcomes. The key to achieving this is to link corporate strategy with sustainability and progressively build relevant capabilities to support that strategy.[14]

Corporations willing to adopt a strategic approach to sustainability can generate important ecological and community benefits.[15] However, these initiatives can also have other positive outcomes for the organization, such as:

- The generation of brand and reputational capital; for example, BP, Swiss Re, IAG, Toyota, Westpac and Alcoa are consistently singled out as leading corporations in strategically managing social and environmental resources.[16]
- The development of innovative products and services for emerging markets – such as Westpac's development of green renovation home loans.
- Local community support for the organization's activities.
- Difficult-to-imitate human and knowledge capabilities that are the basis of future competitive advantage; for example, Nucor Steel in the United States and Hewlett-Packard and Unilever worldwide.
- Industry leadership and in some cases the creation of a new industry. For instance, the development and release of the hybrid Toyota Prius has created new product and industry divides. Consequently, Toyota and Honda have put other automotive manufacturers on notice. Some of their competitors have found themselves lacking in terms of their research and development capabilities.

Amory Lovins, research director of the Rocky Mountain Institute, emphasizes the business advantages of sustainability in relation to just one issue – climate change:

> I'd like to suggest that actually protecting the climate will be highly profitable rather than costly if we do the cheapest things first; and that pursuing profit motive will put industry in its rightful place as the largest part of the solution . . . The obstacles to achieving this

profitable resolution are not technological or economic. Rather they are cultural and procedural.[17]

In other words, Lovins is arguing that our current corporate strategies, structures, cultures and norms prevent us from seeing solutions that can be both environmentally and economically beneficial. Similarly, Stead and Stead argue that 'achieving sustainability is not just about changing how humans do things; it's about changing how humans view things'.[18] Taken together, the collective view that is emerging from sustainability academics, practitioners, investment funds and managers is that the relationship between corporations and their environment is too complex to represent as either win–win or win–lose.[19] There are costs in incorporating sustainability objectives into corporate strategy but there are also very significant potential gains. This chapter builds the case for corporations to adopt a strategic approach to sustainability.

The importance of strategy

The last fifteen years of the twentieth century were a critical time for traditional organizations. In the preceding period of economic growth and relative stability, strategy was seen as developing and implementing top-down corporate plans and annual monitoring to see whether plan outcomes and objectives had been achieved. Like the five-year plans of the command economies of the former Soviet Union, corporate planning sometimes did not reflect the realities of corporate activity but nevertheless remained an important corporate ritual. Corporate strategic planning and its implementation are a very different process today and, to see why, we shall briefly review how the field developed.

The field of corporate strategy emerged in the 1960s from the work of several managerial thinkers, particularly Philip Selznick, Kenneth Andrews, Alfred Chandler and H. Igor Ansoff. They were actively involved as consultants to some of the leading US companies, including multinationals. These companies were confronting a series of problems emerging out of the growing pace of environmental change and the increasing size and complexity of their organizations. The executives were seeking more effective ways to control the activities of these growing organizations and to develop strategies to seize industry leadership and ensure the success of their international operations.[20]

Strategic management was subsequently popularized and developed further by the leading consulting companies, particularly the Boston

Consulting Group and McKinsey's in the 1960s and 1970s. By the early 1970s most large corporations were attempting to develop or had developed a corporate strategic approach with long-range plans to deal with environmental threats and opportunities. However, they were using what Lynda Gratton refers to as 'the top-down model of strategy'.[21] The top-down model is characterized by senior management formulating strategy and then pushing it down through the organization.

This approach to strategy suffered from several major limitations. First, it assumed that managers were rational decision makers who could make accurate forecasts and that organizations were passive tools to be directed to produce the desired outcomes. In fact, accurate forecasting is increasingly difficult in a turbulent world and organizations are often more political, chaotic and disorganized than a rational decision-making model implies. In addition, the environment was generally taken to mean only the competitive market environment. Other major political and social factors (including the ecological environment) were generally left out of the analysis.[22] Finally, strategic planning often focused on the content of strategy and neglected the process of achieving it.[23] The assumption was that, if the strategy was formulated by the senior executive team, it would be automatically implemented throughout the organization.

The overly rational assumptions of the early strategic planners were widely questioned and led to a major debate in the field about the value of deliberate and emergent strategies.[24] As a result of this debate, researchers are now paying much more attention to three key issues that were formerly ignored:

- The open-ended nature of strategy.
- The impact of political groups in shaping the strategy process.
- The importance of an organization's resources and dynamic capabilities in shaping its ability to respond rapidly to turbulent and competitive environments.[25]

In particular, the debate on strategy has shifted beyond the traditional external elements of strategy such as industry structure, positioning and resources.[26] Current debates now emphasize that sustainable competitive advantages can be achieved by implementing value-adding strategies and by developing organizational innovation and agility. These strategies require the development of particular bundles and sets of capabilities that are not easily imitated and that can be used to transform and adapt the organization to changes over time. In other words, these capabilities are future-oriented and dynamic.[27] This approach to strategy can be characterized as a learning process which brings people together in an active engagement to design the future of the company.[28] In this chapter we outline how strategic thinking will develop further as we move into the twenty-first century.

Hitt *et al.* argue that the following capabilities and competences play an integral role in achieving strategic outcomes. We have linked some sustainability issues to these concepts:[29]

- *Strategic flexibility*. The ability to adapt to fast-paced environmental change. The implication for sustainability is the ability to respond quickly to consumer and community demands and to create business opportunities.
- *Strategic leadership*. The ability to develop a vision and mission and help build the values of the company that will achieve the stated intent of the mission. The challenge here is to incorporate sustainability objectives into the mission, which can be acted upon.
- *Dynamic core competences*. The development and evolution of core skills and training and competence development. This requires investment in resources and people. Sustainability strategies require the development of core competences to create value-adding opportunities.
- *Developing human capital*. Focus on the development of organization learning, capturing and developing employee knowledge and identifying when to develop or rely on contingent workers. This amounts to a capability of higher-order learning – found in organizations such as Hewlett-Packard.[30] The focus is on long-term competence development.
- *Effective use of new technology*. Extension of information systems into systems of procurement and supply management for value adding; design of environmentally responsive technologies and products/ services. For instance, Interface has pursued a strategy based on the pursuit of long-life leasing deals for its products.
- *Engaging in valuable strategies*. Taking advantage of global opportunities and developing strategic alliances and co-operative strategies. An extension of this to the ecological approach focuses on the development of partnerships with key stakeholders and local communities to review and monitor performance, to redesign products or services or to build local community capacity.
- *Developing new organizational structures and cultures*. Valuing human capital and contributing to the sustainability outcomes and strategic goals of the organization. Such structures are designed to enhance and

reward continuous innovation – this may be product or process oriented. The implication for sustainability is that the development of human and ecological competences is reliant upon changes in structure and culture. Creating the conditions whereby these competences become the basis upon which future competitive advantages are generated.

We think that Hitt *et al.*'s points are perceptive but we would add one further key characteristic of successful strategy: strategy is more than a set of business goals, financial objectives and means of pursuing competitive advantage in the market place. This is the traditional province of business strategy but it means nothing if the strategy is not known to all the members of the organization, strongly committed to by them and actionable in their terms. To be effective, strategy must be clearly articulated and embodied in specific action plans for every unit and individual in the organization.

We have explained how the current view of strategy differs from the traditional strategy model. But the current model of business strategy is only now beginning to take into account the importance of the ecological environment and human factors in achieving success. This is the issue we take up now. How can the strategy field incorporate the new demands of sustainability?

What is strategic sustainability?

What is meant by the term 'strategic sustainability'? There is no clear-cut definition and several parallel interpretations exist. The first interpretation is the use of the word 'sustainability' to mean corporate longevity and survival. If we were interested in how to achieve this kind of strategic sustainability then we would examine characteristics of those corporations that are long-lived and strong performers.[31] For instance, de Geus has identified four characteristics of long-living companies. They show fiscal responsibility – these companies are not high-risk takers in the financial arena. They are aware of and in tune with their environment; they scan it constantly and respond quickly to emerging consumer demands. They have developed ways to experiment and to examine peripheral ideas and turn these into core activities or important side businesses. Finally, these companies have a sense of identity and community, and they work at maintaining good communal relationships.[32] De Geus's research highlights the fact that long-living companies, such as

Shell, value human capital and seek to integrate the development of human capabilities into their long-term strategic approach.

There are limitations to adopting longevity as the measure of sustainability. Longevity is a poor indicator of whether an organization is pursuing goals that sustain the natural environment or society. However, the characteristics of long-living organizations do provide insights into how organizations adapt to changing environments. They are therefore useful in creating sustaining organizations.

North Australian Pastoral Company (NAPCO): long-living and sustainable

NAPCO is a privately owned Australian pastoral company that was founded in 1877. The company owns sixteen properties spread over 6.5 million ha (larger than some European countries) and runs 190,000 head of cattle. NAPCO is an interesting example of a long-living organization that has survived and prospered as a business while operating under some of the harshest environmental conditions. How do we explain its longevity and its success? As an organization NAPCO learnt that it survival under these conditions relied on building 'sustainability driven slack'. Core to this has been the organization's willingness to 'listen' to the environment. This approach of listening to the needs of the managers of its pastoral stations has meant that NAPCO has successfully avoided issues to do with overgrazing and environmental degradation. The organization also has a philosophy of engaging and embedding itself in its local communities. The organization has stumbled upon the realization that it needs to support local communities so that they can provide the services and support which are required to run large-scale cattle properties. Furthermore, local communities become an important source of local knowledge and understanding of environmental issues and an important source of social capital. A stewardship approach to the land and willingness to sacrifice short-term economic gains for long-term viability make NAPCO an example of a long-living sustainability-driven organization.[33]

The second use of the term 'sustainability' focuses on an organization's engagement with its ecological environment. This is the approach adopted by Andrew Hoffman, Stuart Hart, John Elkington, Nigel Roome and others.[34] According to this approach, organizations which are seeking to realize strategic opportunities from the natural environment will develop a range of capabilities for understanding, processing and acting on ecological threats and opportunities.[35] This includes the generation of 'green' products and services, the refinement of supply-chain procurement practices and the implementation of environmental management programmes, practices and techniques. Hoffman uses Volvo as an example of a company that was able to shift from environmental management to environmental strategy because it was able to adopt environmental values rapidly. In Volvo's case the new environmental values were congruent with its existing values of safety and corporate responsibility. This enabled it to enlarge its existing values base to take in these other aspects of sustainability. Nevertheless, Hoffman claims that the adoption of a strategic sustainability perspective requires a cultural and behavioural shift within firms.[36] Such shifts do not occur easily or overnight but the resulting capabilities are hard to imitate and are a key source of competitive advantage.[37]

Interface

In 1994 Ray Anderson, Interface CEO and founder, instigated QUEST: a corporate programme designed to address the environmental consequences of manufacturing commercial carpets made primarily from petrochemicals. Anderson confronted the issue of huge quantities of Interface carpets ending up in landfill around the world.[38]

QUEST was aimed at waste minimization through a variety of processes, including the recycling of carpet. However, for QUEST to succeed as a programme, the organizational members needed to be strongly motivated to address the negative environmental impacts of key elements of the Interface 'value-adding' chain. This required a dramatic shift in the mind sets and motivation of everyone in the organization, from Ray Anderson to shopfloor workers.

While QUEST was a company-wide programme, decisions on how it was to be undertaken were delegated to each of the individual production facilities. Plants in individual countries were given the autonomy to pursue the QUEST programme according to local needs. Under these conditions, the Australian plant, for example, went from being No. 27 – or worst in the organization – to No. 1 by 1997.[39] In facilities across the world, small teams were established to address internal issues, such as waste reduction and minimization, and external issues, such as customer and supplier requirements. Company processes were then altered so that they aligned with the new focus on quality, waste reduction and recycling. For example, individuals and groups of employees were rewarded for attaining these goals. At Interface the distinction between human and ecological issues has been increasingly integrated; new structures and processes have been established that reward progress in both areas and encourage the pursuit of excellence in each. Some of the impressive achievements from 1996 to 2006 have been:

- Carbon intensity down by one-third.
- Greenhouse gases down by 56 per cent.
- Cumulative avoided costs from waste elimination are US$299 million since 1995.
- Total energy used in carpet manufacturing down 41 per cent since 1995.
- Renewable energy use increased to 13 per cent.
- The introduction of Terratex, the industry's first post-consumer recycled polyester commercial fabric.
- The use of third-party certification to ensure that the company is not greenwashing on its claims of environment success and environmental product development.

Source: Interface (2004, 2006); Dunphy *et al.* (2000)[40]

The third use of sustainability focuses on strategic sustainability as a suite of human resource practices and clusters of human capabilities that lead to high performance and enduring competitive advantages.[41] Such HR practices include the redesign of jobs to develop autonomy in decision making, the use of skills training to increase the organization's flexibility and the adoption of team-based organizational architectures to enhance work and increase innovation. High-performance workplaces require organizational systems which integrate HR practices such as particular approaches to recruitment and selection, the remuneration and the distribution of resources to value-adding activities, and knowledge management systems. Consequently, within this tradition, the focus of strategic development has been on creating value-based corporate cultures made up of committed individuals and supportive organizational systems. Hewlett-Packard and Westpac for example have built their strategic sustainability success on the commitment, pride and trust of their employees – their competitive advantage has been based on the development and utilization of their human capital to design new products, processes, services and community engagement.[42] According to Gratton, the development of human capital is a complex task that requires years of management commitment, action and skill. But the result is sustainable high performance.[43]

Human capital at Hewlett-Packard

A key factor in Hewlett-Packard's success has been the effective development of a workplace culture which attracts and retains skilled people committed to working in an

continued

entrepreneurial team-based environment that supports innovation. Hewlett-Packard has achieved a global reputation for building and utilizing human capital in the creation of innovative products and processes. For instance, Hewlett Packard was ranked as No. 2 in the *Business Ethics Magazine* 100 Best Corporate Citizens for 2006. This is the seventh year that HP has been in the top ten. On top of its impressive corporate capability and development approach, HP has instigated programmes such as its 'Digital Village' programme designed to deliver information technology to Africa, Asia and Latin America. In the process, it has been able to create community centres and increase the skill base of local populations.[44] It is now utilizing this same human capital in its shift towards the development of sustainable strategies and eco-design. At the core of the Hewlett-Packard approach to developing its human capital lie the following strategies:

- Emphasis on creating careers, not jobs.
- Promoting from within.
- Developing and encouraging a culture of continuous learning and the expression of innovative ideas and practices.
- Programmes designed to encourage diversity, profit sharing and the creation of a better work–life balance.
- Programmes designed to build human capability in local communities.
- Delivering its global citizenship programmes at local level, with state and local governments in Australia signing sustainability compacts to deliver recycling and sustainability improvements across HP's operations.

These strategies rely on the development of enabling organizational structures such as the use of smaller division and cross-functional teams that enable employees to communicate freely, diffuse ideas and exchange knowledge. In turn, this has created an environment in which Hewlett-Packard is able to respond quickly and in an innovative fashion to customer and consumer expectations.[45]

For the purposes of this book we identify strategic sustainability as being an organizational commitment to achieving competitive advantage through the strategic adoption and development of ecologically and socially supportive production processes, products and services and innovative human and knowledge resource management practices. What distinguishes our approach from the earlier strategic approaches we identified is the integration of the human and ecological sustainability traditions as a means of generating long-term competitive advantages. We have combined elements from all three traditions of strategic sustainability to define strategies to sustain the organization, society and the environment.

How strategic sustainability contributes to competitive advantage

What is the evidence that the strategic approach to sustainability can provide corporations with a basis for enduring competitive advantages? Research from the United States shows a positive relationship between a firm's performance on environmental indicators and its economic growth. When it comes to developing capabilities around sustainability, it pays to be green.[46] But the model of strategy we are advocating here goes beyond environmentalism: throughout this book we have viewed sustainability as including both human and ecological factors. Effective strategy in the future will draw competitive advantage from both areas. In this section we outline how this can be achieved and provide examples.

There is, however, an important point to make before we do this. Strategic sustainability represents more than the rhetorical commitment to human and ecological sustainability principles found in the glossy reports published by some corporations. These reports can be public relations exercises designed to conceal the corporation's lack of care for the community and the environment rather than an exercise in transparency. Strategic sustainability, by contrast, is a demonstrated commitment by the executive team and the board actively to pursue and develop corporate capabilities, products and processes that align sustainability initiatives with the corporation's overall strategic orientation. For instance, Westpac, Visy and Origin Energy, along with other members of the Australian Business Roundtable on Climate Change, have taken a proactive role in advancing the debate and arguing in particular for the strategic advantages for corporations and governments to be engaged in corporate sustainability activities.

Strategic sustainability is also about the development and utilization of corporate competences in both the human and the ecological areas. The two are loosely linked because developing ecological competences within the organization necessarily relies on the development of proactive advanced-level human capabilities. Take the example of the Xerox Corporation, where proactive designers and managers working in teams generated new products that were recyclable and reusable. This approach adopted by Xerox defied current trends that build in product redundancy and therefore waste. The team's zero-waste vision resulted in the establishment of a manufacturing plant that created virtually no waste.[47]

This approach pursued by Xerox and HP – focused on product stewardship – contrasts in almost every respect with the 'old strategy' of limited product lifetimes pursued by firms in the new consumable markets of plasma and LCD television technologies. Opportunities exist for companies to take strategic leadership in redefining these dated strategies. Similarly, there are advantages to be gained by extending these strategies to include reorganizing supply chains so that all stages of the chain contribute to the sustainability strategy.

Strategic sustainability involves the organization in developing processes that institutionalize and systematize these capabilities so that they no longer depend on key individuals but are embodied in systems that act as an organizational memory. Based on a statistical analysis of change in over 100 organizations, Turner and Crawford argue that high-performing organizations require both operational and transformational capabilities.[48] Operational capabilities contribute to the efficiency and effectiveness of day-to-day activities while transformational capabilities support change and strategic repositioning. This also holds true for organizations pursuing strategic sustainability.

Gratton argues that human capital contributes to the competitive advantage of organizations in three ways: first, when it is rare, that is, something other competitors lack; second, when it is valuable, that is, it has an impact on bottom-line performance; finally, when it is difficult to imitate. Gratton goes on to argue that only human capacity can create these competitive advantages for corporations. She builds a strong case for managers to develop and integrate human capital into the core strategic directions of corporations in order to build long-term, sustainable competitive advantages.[49]

Volvo

At Volvo a strategic approach to sustainability has meant concentrating on developing both ecological and human capabilities. Volvo has a long history of engagement with human-centred design and sociotechnical systems as a means of developing people capabilities. This has led to the creation of internal cross-sectional project teams formed around the task of addressing key issues such as: changing structures and systems to capture the benefits of product recycling; restructuring organization systems for acquiring and diffusing environmental information; changing production processes for environmental efficiencies, and finally, meeting and extending European standards.[50] Despite being part of the Ford stable, one of Volvo's interesting research and development initiatives has been the creation of an automotive prototype that can run on five different fuels.[51] As Rowledge et al. state:

Volvo's vision of environmental positioning has clearly moved beyond a compliance orientation in response to environmental regulation towards integrating consideration for sustainability into core business plans, products and operations. The most important thing about this evolution is that it is soundly based on prudent strategies and business planning. Rather than approaching environmental issues with an end-of-pipe mentality, Volvo instead addresses environmental considerations upstream in product and process design.[52]

The Volvo process of strategic sustainability is built on four key steps:

1 Planning for sustainable development:

- Leadership priority and organization alignment.
- Diagnosis and analysis.
- A culture of openness and transparency.
- Measurable environmental goals.

2 Organizing:

- Comprehensive education and communication.
- Establishment of infrastructure support for all operations.

3 Implementation:

- Investment of resources in R&D, technology, product and people competence.
- Formation of partnerships and alliances.
- Practical change management strategies.

4 Review and monitoring.

This process is now being extended to the Volvo supply chain with the inclusion of the environment as a factor in the auditing of suppliers.

Sources: Maxwell *et al.* (1997); Rowledge *et al.* (1999)[53]

Up to this point we have argued that strategic sustainability generates competitive advantages when ecological and human sustainability elements have been effectively integrated. Now we show that this integration can be achieved in different ways which result in significantly different sustainability strategies. Each of these strategies provides a different form of competitive advantage. To develop this approach, we combine two influential theoretical frameworks; the first, by Hart and Milstein, outlines different strategies for the creation of sustainable shareholder value and applies these strategies to the sustainability imperative. The second framework, developed by Orsato, outlines a contingent set of circumstances for when it pays to be green.[54]

Hart and Milstein start from a simple assumption (see Figure 5.1)
– that shareholder value is a multidimensional construct. On the vertical
dimension (today versus tomorrow) managers can make decisions
favouring short-term outcomes such as investing in pollution-saving
technologies now or they can make decisions for the longer-term future
such as investing profits in new products and markets. On the horizontal
dimension (internal versus external) managers can choose to build their
current internal capabilities, by for example purchasing new equipment,
or they can choose to gather new information, ideas and innovations
from external sources. The choices that managers make about these issues
determine their dominant strategy and how the firm goes about creating
value.

Hart and Milstein argue that this framework can be used to understand
a firm's sustainability strategy. For instance, firms can choose between a
pollution prevention strategy – that is, a short-term cost-reduction
efficiency strategy (short-term, internal) – or shift their orientation to
a future-oriented clean technology strategy (future, internal). Both
strategies create shareholder value – however, they have different
implications for capability development and represent different strategic
orientations. Defining your firm's strategy in this way provides strategic
focus and helps clarify the kinds of sustainability strategies the firm
needs to develop and implement.

The Hart and Milstein framework elaborates how companies can create
sustainability value. Similarly, Orsato's work outlines a specific set of
environmental strategies that firms can pursue in order to generate
competitive value (see Figure 5.2). For instance, Orsato argues that firms
can either pursue a differentiation or a low-cost strategy (competitive
advantage) and then can decide whether they improve products/service
or organizational processes (competitive focus). For instance, some firms
can generate competitive advantages via the pursuit of eco-efficiency
strategies – such as firms in the beverage industry that need to reduce
water consumption. Carlton United Breweries' Kent Brewery in Sydney,
for example, achieved substantial efficiency savings in this and other
resource areas.[55] Other firms can pursue ISO certification as a means
of branding and differentiating their product from that of their
competitors. This would fit within the clean technology and processes
quadrant of the Hart and Milstein model. For instance NAPCO, the cattle-
producing company, has sought and gained ISO accreditation as a means
of differentiating its product in the highly competitive export markets
of Japan. A clear example of a long-term sustainability vision is the

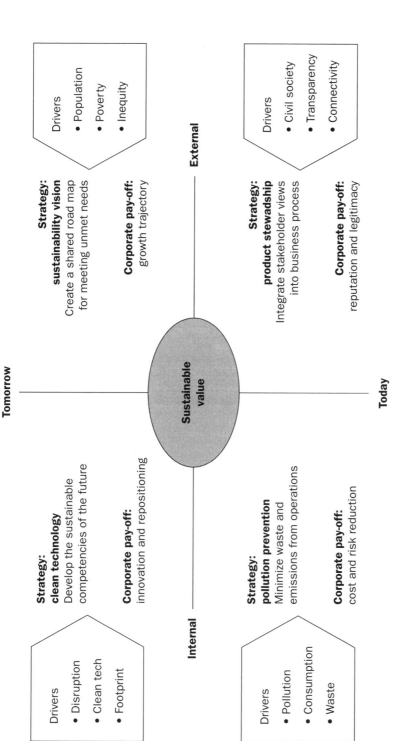

Figure 5.1 Sustainable value framework

Source: S. Hart and M. Milstein, 'Creating sustainable value', *Academy of Management Executive*, 2003, 17 (2), 56–67, p. 60. Reproduced with permission of the Academy of Management (NY).

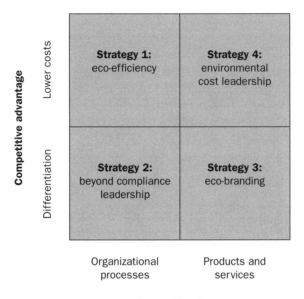

Competitive focus

Figure 5.2 *Generic competitive environmental strategies*
Source: R. Orsato, 'Competitive environmental strategies: when does it pay to be green?'. © 2006, The Regents of the University of California. Reprinted from the *California Management Review*, vol 48 (2), p. 131. By permission of The Regents.

introduction by Toyota and Honda of hybrid cars – the Toyota Prius and the Honda Insight. Both these initiatives have already paid their way but, more important, they have positioned these companies 'to lead the next generation of the automobile industry'.[56]

The two frameworks appear to be converging on a new approach to differentiating sustainability strategies:

Hart and Milstein

- Pollution prevention.
- Clean technology.
- Product stewardship.
- Sustainability vision.

Orsato

- Eco-efficiency.
- Beyond compliance leadership.
- Environmental cost leadership.
- Eco-branding.

We now outline some of the strategic human capabilities required for these four strategy types – our preferred term for each of these strategies is shown in italics below:

- Pollution prevention/*eco-efficiency*. The human capabilities that are required to further this strategy involve the development of engineering and technical understandings and skills for addressing environmental issues. These capabilities focus on reducing resources waste, particularly for water, energy and materials. Many of these types of technical capabilities can be located at the operator level but need to be fully integrated in an overall strategic plan.

- Clean technology/*beyond compliance*. The human capabilities involved here focus on both the development of innovative R&D approaches and the ability to use metrics to further sustainability goals. For instance, to measure and then reduce greenhouse gas emissions demands either the development of new technologies or the application of new technologies to existing production and service systems. This requires high levels of innovation, increased investment in research and development and external environmental scanning for potential new solutions.

- Product stewardship/*environmental cost leadership*. The focus of capabilities in this area will be around the creation of new range of low-cost products for emerging and existing markets or streamlining supply chains and current operations.

- *Environmental vision*/eco-branding. The focus of human capabilities in this area is on developing the relationship skills needed to integrate external stakeholders into the organization, to develop innovative future-oriented strategies and product offerings, and the leadership capabilities needed to influence others in the organization's supply chain to follow this visionary leadership.

Risks of the strategic approach

While the previous section outlined positive examples of corporations that were seeking to gain competitive advantages through the pursuit of strategic sustainability, this approach has some inherent risks. A focus on sustainability alone is clearly not enough to deliver competitive advantages. If the strategy is not viable in business terms, then a focus on sustainability will not save the organization. Consider the rapid rise and fall of many dot.com organizations. As Porter noted, many corporations and dot.coms assumed that the internet changed all the rules of competition. He argues that this led some organizations to make poor business decisions which undermined their own competitive advantage. For instance, many internet companies not only attempted to compete on speed, quality and innovation but also on being the lowest-cost provider of products and services. This led to many firms becoming unprofitable.

As he states, 'The Internet *per se* will rarely be a competitive advantage. Many of the companies that succeed will be ones that use the Internet as a complement to traditional ways of competing, not those that set their Internet initiatives apart from established operations.'[57] In other words, many companies were swept up in the notions of the 'new economy', forgetting that conventional strategic rules about competing on value and cost still applied.

Similarly managers of organizations engaging in strategic sustainability need to understand that, as corporations, they must be profitable, add value and provide quality products and services. These are the conventional elements of any viable corporate strategy. For instance, the Body Shop is held up as a successful example of a company pursuing strategic sustainability. However, it has experienced problems in maintaining the financial viability of the business. Elkington reports that the Body Shop lost ground to competitors because its product line was ageing and in need of revamping. He argues that this demonstrates the need for managers to maintain their focus on financial and strategic issues as well as social and ecological ones.[58] As a by-line on these issues, Anita and Gordon Roddick resigned from the board of the Body Shop.[59]

An analogy can be made between current efforts to institutionalize green strategies and earlier corporate experiences with the implementation of flexible manufacturing systems. At the height of competition between US and Japanese manufacturing firms, Jaikumar showed that Japanese firms outperformed US firms using the same or similar technologies. Why? It appears that US firms used traditional organizational structures, systems and processes and did not modify their strategy to take account of the flexibility benefits associated with the new technologies. The Japanese, on the other hand, not only introduced the new technology, they also changed their structures and strategies to maximize the competitive advantages associated with its introduction. The story serves as a powerful reminder of the importance of linking the pursuit of sustainability with organization systems and strategic outcomes. It should also act as a warning: in the haste to develop corporate sustainability strategies, we should not overlook the need to make these strategies deliver competitive advantages.

Another potential risk is that the organization outstrips the understanding of the key external stakeholders on whom the organization's future depends. This is particularly the case with shareholders and financial analysts, whose viewpoints on sustainability are often highly conservative. As Kent *et al.* point out, the investor interface is vital and:

> There is . . . a growing body of evidence to suggest that the attitudes of some institutional investors are beginning to change, with many starting to price in the costs and liabilities associated with social, ethical and environmental issues. In the main, however, their approaches have tended to be defensive, with reduced ratings for poor performers rather than high ratings for achievers.[60]

Consequently, the organization pursuing strategic sustainability initiatives needs to devote time and energy to keeping shareholders informed of the value being added to their investment by the pursuit of these strategies, to communicating the benefits. The authors make concrete suggestions as to how this can be done.[61] They also note that institutional investors are increasingly emphasizing lead indicators rather than historical measures in assessing business performance. As this trend strengthens, the relevance of sustainability strategies will become more obvious.

Beyond rhetoric and greenwash

What can we learn from our discussion of the risks of the strategic approach and from the successes of corporations such as Interface, Hewlett-Packard and Toyota, which continually re-emerge as leaders in areas of strategic sustainability? One conclusion we could draw is that strategic sustainability can be fragile and difficult to maintain.

For instance, in the 1990s Monsanto was hailed as a company that had achieved a remarkable turnaround. It adopted a strategy of moving from being a major polluter to pushing the boundaries of biotechnology and the new agriculturally based industries. In generating this transformation, the issues of strategic sustainability were key drivers. Monsanto's internal sustainability initiatives were promoted as being forerunners to creating the sustainable corporation.[62] They included the establishment of teams, a focus on waste and pollution reduction, and executive leaders who appeared to support key principles of strategic sustainability. Monsanto executives were keen to turn around the company's negative reputation concerning ecological and human resources. They set out to build a new image of an organization that valued community concerns, emphasized building human capabilities and was determined to move away from polluting industrial processes.[63] However, by the late 1990s and into 2000 Monsanto was once again attracting the ire of green and civil liberties groups and its commitment to sustainability was being questioned. See Figure 5.3. What had gone wrong?

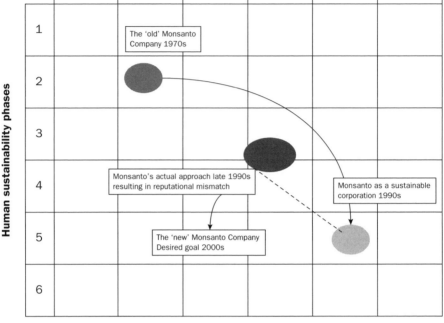

Figure 5.3 *Monsanto's approach to sustainability*

Monsanto had moved strategically to develop a range of genetically modified products. This was a product line which many outside Monsanto found ethically unacceptable. Environmentalists almost universally condemn Monsanto's ethics and its development and promotion of these products. In the case of Monsanto, first-mover advantages were quickly lost owing to external stakeholder criticism, which was very public and evoked broad consumer cynicism. Strategic proactivity in the new areas of biotechnology and genetic engineering requires the application of the precautionary principle. Monsanto provides an illustration of how easily a company can overlook this fundamental requirement of strategic sustainability. Had Monsanto maintained active and open links between strategic decision makers and third-party monitoring groups it would have received early warning that its developments in this area were unacceptable. These consumer concerns about genetic modification have now spread to food manufacturers, with many food manufacturers, particularly in the European Union, discarding genetically modified foods in order to avoid having to display GM food labels. As Robert Hadler, corporate affairs director of Goodman Fielder, stated: 'The customer is always right and the customer is concerned about the effects of GM ingredients. The major retailers don't want products with GM in them.'[64]

Despite the strong commitment of its CEO and the introduction of sustainability teams, Monsanto found that strategic sustainability can be fraught with potential problems and hazards. In a thought-provoking article Stuart Hart and Sanjay Sharma argue that companies such as Shell, Nike and Monsanto had experienced legitimacy problems generated by remote but increasingly connected 'fringe stakeholders'. They ask, how is it that a company that had broken no laws in the pursuit of its strategy and engaged all key stakeholders managed to get it so wrong?[65] As Figure 5.3 illustrates, Monsanto started out as a low-margin polluting chemical company. From 1993 to 1998 it made around US$8 billion in acquisitions as it implemented a strategy of being a life sciences company – a significant commitment of which was to become a sustainable corporation. However, questions were increasingly asked over genetic modification of crops and food: farmers from Canada to India were concerned about Monsanto protecting its patent ownership.[66] As fringe stakeholders found collective and connected voices, a mismatch appeared between Monsanto's stated goals and where the company was seen to be. By the year 2000 Monsanto's US$8 billion vision of being a global life science company had disappeared – the company was taken over by competitors.[67]

There are some lessons to be learned from the Monsanto case. To achieve sustainability, companies need to remain nimble and continually reinvest in ecological and human sustainability capabilities. They need to maintain active and open links between strategic decision makers and third-party monitoring groups. In particular, strategic proactivity in the new areas of biotechnology and genetic engineering requires the application of the precautionary principle and transparency in operations.

The building of the human and ecological capabilities of an organization also contributes to its reputational capital. In their efforts to turn around poor or bad reputations, companies sometimes turn to 'spin doctors' and advertising, but this can expose the gap between what the organization says and what it does. Reputation must be realistic, monitored and constantly assessed, particularly in the global economy.[68] As Charles Handy puts it, 'Reputations matter and brands are fragile things.'[69]

Furthermore, he argues, corporations have to redefine social responsibility – it is not enough to think of it as giving a little of your profits to the poor; it is about how you run your business and balance this with the demands of different stakeholders: 'Increasingly we want to know how they are making their money as well as how much they make.

They cannot turn over as much money as whole countries and not expect to be held accountable for the way they do it.'[70]

Table 5.1 outlines false postures that organizations sometimes adopt in dealing with sustainability issues. If your organization is adopting one of these postures, attempting to pass it off as strategic sustainability, the deception will almost certainly be uncovered.

The winning formula

What is the winning formula to achieve strategic sustainability? What can we learn from our discussions of company cases and emerging research about how to integrate sustainability into strategy? First, corporations moving towards the attainment of strategic sustainability focus on building key capabilities for value adding and innovation. Second, they develop and utilize the corporate competences needed to develop and enact these business strategies in the human and ecological spheres.[71] Third, the corporation develops processes that institutionalize and systematize these capabilities so that the organization is no longer reliant upon key individuals for best-practice operations. The capabilities are embodied in the organization's systems and culture and are simply seen as 'the way we do business around here'. Finally, corporations must be embedded into local communities so that they are sensitive to community needs. The strategically sustainable organization will therefore give priority to cutting-edge human resource practices and look towards the creation of values-based cultures for sustainable outcomes. They will aim to become high-performance organizations (see Figure 5.4).

Achieving successful strategic sustainability also involves the following:

- *The move from efficiency to strategy.* Building capabilities around achieving strategic goals involves moving beyond the compliance and efficiency phases to a strategic approach to sustainability. Strategic

Table 5.1 *Strategic sustainability: false postures*

What strategic sustainability is not	Risk to the organization
Greenwash	
The use of corporate reports and misinformation to promote the public image of being sustainable	Damage to reputational capital as a cynical public votes with their dollars and shifts loyalties. For instance, Exxon lost US$3 billion in shareholder value after the *Exxon Valdez* incident. Similarly, protests and consumer boycotts over its factories in developing countries hurt Nike's bottom line
Green marketing	
Green product labels and the use of animals such as dolphins to create the image of green branding while obscuring the actual environmental impact of a company's processes, products and services	Consumer backlash against the organization and heightened cynicism about corporate and institutional pledges of self-regulation
EMS/TQEM	
These tools are useful in addressing complex sustainability issues but will not in themselves deliver strategic sustainability	A technological fixation: organizations can slip into the assumption that the implementation of such tools necessarily generates sustainability outcomes. A focus on tools alone can lead to missing strategic advantages, which are eventually developed by competitors
Fad surfing in the area of human resources	
Rhetoric about teams, virtual organizations, empowerment, culture change. Most employees have heard it all before. If translated into strategically relevant actions these concepts may help build sustainable capabilities and employee capital but, if rhetoric only, they create cynicism and resistance	Alienation/cynicism and the flight of human capital as employees leave to find better employment prospects and to pursue their own values in a more honest corporate environment

proactivity is much more externally focused and involves calculated risk taking. This is a significant value shift because the compliance phase reinforces risk avoidance and the efficiency phase reinforces cost minimization. By contrast, the development of new strategic options demands thoughtful risk taking and investment in research and development. Consequently, many organizations have to run an 'analyser' strategy, that is, they pursue a low-cost, low-risk strategy in traditional operational areas while accepting higher costs and significantly greater risks in areas involving new strategic developments.[72] To be successful this requires a more flexible managerial approach.

- *Introducing new tools and techniques.* Various tools and techniques can be used to guide the development of strategic sustainability initiatives and in third-party monitoring and audits. One well known example is the use of the triple bottom line. John Elkington defines TBL as: 'sustainable development [that] involves the simultaneous pursuit of economic prosperity, environmental quality and social equity. Companies aiming for sustainability need to perform not against a single, financial bottom line but against the triple bottom line.[73] Other companies, such as Hewlett-Packard and Du Pont, have experimented with the Balanced Environmental Scorecard, which links environmental performance with four key indicator areas: financial, customer, business processes and organizational learning.[74]

- *Linking operational processes to sustainable strategy.* This involves the systematic and rapid translation of successful experimental ventures into standard operating procedures company-wide. For instance, Texas Industries operates a steel mill reliant on recycled scrap. A separate division, in the same town, then turns the slag from the mill into the raw material for its cement works. This has created synergies in product, resource use and a reduction in energy waste while increasing profits.[75]

- *Creating new product and service process improvement opportunities.* A strategic approach to sustainability enables an organization to look for new opportunities to create new markets, reinvent existing products or add value to services. The Toyota Prius illustrates how Toyota has made significant strategic R&D investments in hybrid technologies and then integrated those into Toyota's lean production systems of production to create new products and consumer demand.

- *Creating enabling structures and design.* The development of sustainable business models and new organizational architectures can enhance an organization's responsiveness to environmental and social issues. Many traditional organizations have structures and designs that actually impede the development of sustainable business models. Networks and alliances in particular are appropriate to supply chain reorganization, recycling and stakeholder involvement. Queensland

Rail, a national freight transport company, installed a series of flexible and dispersed sustainability hubs across the organization with a mandate to initiate sustainability projects and deliver on the organization's strategic goals.[76]

- *Building employee knowledge and commitment.* Firms adopting innovative and value-adding approaches to sustainability have emphasized the development of employee capital and corresponding competences and have acknowledged their importance for long-term competitive advantages. They have set about creating commitment rather than control-based cultures and structures. For instance, NAPCO relies on its station managers to make the call on the stocking of their pastoral properties with respect to local climatic conditions. The organization's commitment to its employees is to rely on the decisions that they make in these strategic business units.

- *Executive leadership and stewardship.* Innovative firms and corporations committed to the attainment of strategic sustainability have executive teams which support the development of sustainable products, services and processes for existing, emerging and future markets. Building an informed executive team takes time and may involve some change of membership. For instance, consider the comments by Bill Ford, chairman of the board at Ford Motor Company. He states: 'We see no conflict between business goals and social and environmental needs. I believe the distinction between a good company and a great one is this: A good company delivers excellent products and services; a great one delivers excellent products and services and strives to make the world a better place.'[77] The vision being outlined for Ford involves the shift from a traditional manufacturing company to a company that values its stakeholders: 'Our shared vision and my sincere hope is that Ford can become a company whose decisions and choices restore the environment and contribute to the creation of social and economic equity in communities around the world.'[78]

- *Developing differentiated stakeholder strategies.* This involves designing and implementing various strategies that reflect the needs and interests of different stakeholders.[79] To achieve this, stakeholder representatives need to be actively involved. As examined earlier in this chapter, Shell has opened itself up to third-party scrutiny and has also publicly admitted failings and issues that they have experienced on particular projects. Similarly, Interface has given a commitment to have its 'green' products independently tested and verified by external parties. BHP Billiton's Carrington silver, lead and zinc mine in Queensland has used third-party auditing by the North Queensland

Conservation Council as a means of independently monitoring and reporting on the company's sustainable operation of the site. While the council found that BHP performed better than their own targets and legislative requirements, they recommended that the mining operations look further into developing a product life cycle analysis and seek greater community involvement in risk assessment and revision of mining operations. Third-party scrutiny can be used to push organizations further towards the attainment of strategic sustainability and this can also prove to be of strategic advantage to the firm.[80]

We shall now expand on each of these points in the remainder of the chapter.

Figure 5.4 *The strategic target*

The move from efficiency to strategy

What does a review of the existing literature and case examples tell us about what the shift from the efficiency phase to the strategic phase involves? First, it is important to note that much of the literature in this area concentrates on environmental management rather than human sustainability. We shall deal with this literature first. Andrew Hoffman argues that the move from environmental management to environmental strategy requires organizations to shift their cultures, structures, reward systems and job responsibilities. In his view, the shift to strategic sustainability requires a radical overhaul of how corporations value their assets and how they define what is an asset.[81] The current strategic approaches are only starting to recognize the importance of culture and human capital in the attainment of strategic outcomes.

Furthermore, Hoffman argues that engagement with sustainability issues requires a holistic change. Piecemeal solutions such as retro-fitting, firefighting, end-of-pipe solutions and other technical programmes such as total quality environmental management (TQEM) and environmental management systems (EMS) are not enough. To be effective these programmes must be accompanied by a series of broader supporting organizational changes. Hoffman acknowledges that technical solutions can provide efficiency gains. However, he argues that they are easily imitated and will not provide long-term competitive advantages.[82] Increasingly companies will also require their suppliers to adopt a strategic approach to sustainability. For instance, the movement from efficiency to strategy has implications for a range of small and middle-sized companies. In their pursuit of new markets for green products and services, larger corporations will increasingly require their suppliers to obtain environmental accreditation and reach quality standards. The implication for those companies that supply the larger corporations is clear. They must act now to avoid the risk of having such systems imposed or, worse still, losing market share to others who have already implemented such systems. This has happened in some cases. Ikea, for example, now requires its furniture manufacturers, subcontractors, transport and logistics companies to implement and adhere to Ikea's high environmental standards. Customers are demanding high environmental standards and Ikea insists that those who participate in their supply chain deliver on Ikea's commitment to meet them.[83]

Key steps to strategic sustainability

This section outlines the five key steps required to shift an organization from an efficiency focus to strategic sustainability.

Step 1: top team elaboration of corporate goals relating to sustainability. For corporations to shift to strategic sustainability, corporate goals need to measure and be redefined to include sustainability. This involves a thorough assessment of the strategic advantages that sustainability can provide. The executive team then needs to work with line managers to turn the revised goals into actionable strategies for individual business units. This is an iterative process as each individual business unit searches for new business opportunities in line with the corporation's overall sustainability agenda. Individual managers can also build on initiatives already undertaken through TQEM/EMS programmes or on skills development programmes, job redesign and pilot teaming initiatives.

In the process, widespread involvement of staff at all levels leads to upward feedback about the goals and strategies which may result in some modification of them. For instance, at Ikea this required all senior managers to undertake training in the Natural Step and their mission and strategies to incorporate an environmental focus. Once this occurred, environmental training was diffused throughout the organization.[84] It is important at this stage that the projects developed have clear strategic relevance and are not simply the *ad hoc* projects of individual enthusiasts.

Ikea's environmental goals

Ikea has adopted a systematic approach to environmental issues since the mid-1990s. It has followed a step-by-step approach to improving the environmental performance of the organization. This has typically involved the development of three-year plans – with clear objectives against which performance can be managed. In the three-year plan 2000–03 Ikea targeted the following areas for improvement:

- *Products and materials*. Reduce the use of resources and increase the use of recyclables and reusable materials.
- *Forestry*. Obtain forestry products from certified forests.
- *Suppliers*. Ensure that all suppliers adhere to the four-point supplier environmental accreditation scheme developed by Ikea.
- *Transport*. Measure and monitor the impact that the transporting of Ikea products has on the environment.
- *Environment – retail*. Concentrate on reducing waste and implementing energy efficiencies in retail outlets.[85]

Step 2: development and systematic alignment of measurement systems with corporate goals. This step involves the design and use of measurement systems to monitor ecological and human performance. Such systems are aligned with corporate objectives and linked with broader performance systems such as the triple bottom line. The aim is to use the resulting information to further drive the development of capabilities in product and process design to increase sustainability. At Ikea, for instance, cross-functional project teams were initially set up to identify environmental issues and to help integrate policies and practices across the organization.[86]

Step 3: diagnosis of opportunities. Opportunities for 'quick wins' are identified and resources channelled into those areas. In other areas of business activity constant scanning is taking place of internal opportunities to achieve strategic sustainability. Resources are shifted into R&D and future opportunity areas. Competitors and potential allies are identified. Resources are also shifted to the individual business unit level to support new developments there. Culture change programmes are designed, aimed at modifying corporate culture to support the drive to achieve sustainability goals. For example, the diffusion of the Natural Step programme at Ikea followed a cascading model. Managers undertook the programme, followed by employees, so that everyone in the organization had a shared understanding of the emerging strategies. Opportunities had been identified for improvements in key areas. The focus of attention shifted to product design, then to purchasing, then to wholesale activities and, finally, to retail.

Step 4: implementation and diffusion of successful practices both internally and externally. Successful product and service practices, measurement systems and human resource approaches are then diffused internally. Slow-moving business units are linked with 'star' or good performers to improve the performance of these areas. At the senior management level, more time is devoted to engaging suppliers and other external parties to take part in the initiatives. At the grass-roots level, business unit performance is supported by the provision of new resources, training and development initiatives and the development of key performance indicators (KPI) for all relevant staff.

Step 5: review, monitoring and alignment. Results of initiatives on both the ecological and human sustainability fronts are made available internally and externally. Third-party auditors are invited to review the strategic directions, challenge strongly held corporate assumptions and generate ideas for future opportunities for competitive advantage.

Employees and managers alike are rewarded for strong performance on TBL measures. Feedback mechanisms are used to further develop and enhance human and ecological capabilities and develop the next range of sustainable products, processes and services.

Introducing new tools and techniques

The movement towards strategic sustainability has raised new issues over the tools, techniques and methods that corporations use to monitor their performance (for example, the triple bottom line) and inspire corporate transformation (such as the Natural Step). Earlier chapters referred to programmes and systems such as total quality environmental management (TQEM) and environmental management systems (EMS). In this section we outline the benefits of such programmes – particularly the measurement systems that enable organizations to collect information on their performance and that enable them to set targets and goals. This monitoring of human and ecological performance, established in the compliance phase, is an essential element in the attainment of strategic sustainability. We shall examine first the operational benefits of such systems, then move on to explore how they can be used to inform the strategic directions of corporations and, finally, outline some risks involved with the use of measurement systems.

As we saw in Chapters 3 and 4, moving through the compliance and efficiency phases requires organizations to develop systems for collecting and evaluating information on performance. Generally, in these early stages, monitoring and data collection systems focus on operational activities. For example, environmental reporting systems may focus on monitoring pollution or waste levels, with the goal being to use TQEM programmes to move towards zero waste or zero emissions at particular business unit locations. In pursuing human sustainability in the compliance and efficiency modes, organizations will often monitor their performance in terms of operational factors, such as health and safety incidents and absenteeism. Such monitoring systems allow individual managers and business units to comply with legislative requirements and track costs. These systems form the base from which broader strategic sustainability initiatives can be launched.

As corporations develop strategic sustainability initiatives, they systematize and expand such information systems. The Fuji Xerox eco-manufacturing plant in Sydney, Australia, exemplifies this approach.

When they began to retrieve components of their damaged office equipment, instead of allowing them to be thrown into landfill, they found that they could analyse where faults had occurred and why. This product information was then used to redesign components to extend their life. For instance, the redesign of a small roller spring, worth only five cents, saved millions of dollars by significantly extending the working life of each roller. Or, in the case of their new team-based organization, teams become responsible for collecting information on their own performance in terms of product, processes and customers. They use this information to leverage further performance improvements, identify gaps in their skills and knowledge base and develop proactive programmes to address these limitations.

Corporations that have moved into the strategic phase increasingly align their internal tools and systems with other reporting initiatives of environmental and social performance. For instance, such ambitious initiatives are being undertaken by Shell, BP, ABB, Daimler-Benz, BT and Toyota.

Clarke notes the following trends in the movement towards broader measurement systems:[87]

- Increased willingness to use such systems to engage with a broader range of stakeholders interested in different elements of the company's performance.
- A shift towards complementing the measurement of tangibles with that of intangibles – that is, the social capital of the firm.
- The broadening of social and environmental reporting both within the organization and in public forums and the development of more systematic ways of reporting.
- The creation of a sense of legitimacy in the process by increasing involvement of external parties in the auditing and verification process.

Finally, however, as with any reporting system, there exist some inherent challenges. We know of one corporation in the process of implementing TBL reporting systems that has faced difficulties in several areas. These include: the problem of aligning current internal systems with the more macro variables associated with TBL reporting, uncertainty over what to measure – particularly when it comes to external factors such as community engagement and satisfaction – and working out how to integrate different measures to create broad indices of performance, particularly on environmental and social reporting. New forms of auditing such as triple bottom line are important mechanisms for leveraging the corporation to achieve strategic sustainability. However, they need adapting and customizing to the needs of specific organizations and by themselves do not deliver a strategic commitment to sustainability.

Linking operational processes to sustainable strategy

We mentioned earlier in this chapter that, in the efficiency phase, the prime focus of sustainability initiatives was on creating effective operational systems. As the organization moves into the strategic phase, these systems have to be linked to the emerging sustainability strategies so that they can support them.

However, to be effective, the linking of operational systems to sustainability strategy requires a shift in values and culture. Several writers have identified the need to change traditional values, the way managers typically view organizations and technical problems.[88] Value shifts by employees, engineers and other key stakeholders are important prerequisites in identifying innovative solutions to existing problems and potential new opportunities.

For instance, Amory Lovins provides examples of how strategic knowledge can be linked with operational processes and emphasizes the importance of changing values to identify such opportunities: for instance, realizing that 'changes in the size of pipes' could modify the flow of processes in a plant and result in efficiencies for business units. This case provides a clear example of the linking of operational knowledge, embedded in the minds of scientists, engineers and employees of the organization, with the strategic approach of gaining long-term sustainability outcomes, embedded in the minds of executives.

In other words, organizations need to create cultures which provide opportunities for employees to undertake 'out of the box' thinking and play 'maverick roles' in identifying strategic sustainability opportunities. The human sustainability tradition already has developed processes which can be utilized to solve problems – such as TQM practices. However, TQM systems are tightly controlled and managed problem-solving approaches and must be modified to provide for creative thinking if organizations are to integrate operational and strategic practices. Operational thinking cannot be allowed to dominate: managers also need creative thinking for strategic initiatives. Contradictions need to be managed so that the two mind sets can coexist.

At a more macro level, the new field of industrial ecology also provides insight into the benefits of linking operational and strategic processes. The operational processes revolve around finding industrial synergies in the industrial ecosystem in order to create closed-loop industrial systems. This involves the creation and management of strategic alliances between different firms within the industrial ecosystem. It requires the development of competences in the management of strategic alliances, in the exploration of industrial interconnections and in the management of trust. Cohen-Rosenthal believes that central to the success of effective industrial ecology applications are skills in human decision making, imagination and learning.[89] He reports a comment made by Tachi Kiuchi, managing director of Mitsubishi Electric and chairman of Future 500, a high-level group exploring industrial ecology:

> When I visited the rainforest, I realized that it was a model of a perfect learning organization. A place that excels by learning to adapt to what it doesn't have. A rainforest has almost no resources. The soil is thin. There are few nutrients. It consumes almost nothing. Wastes are food. Design is capital. Yet rainforests are incredibly productive. They are home to millions of types of plants and animal, more than two-thirds of all biodiversity, so perfectly mixed that the system is more efficient, and more creative, than any business in the world. Imagine how creative, how productive, how ecologically benign we could be if we could run our companies like rainforests.[90]

Creating enabling structures and designs

Organizations will fail to address ecological and social issues unless systems, designs and structures are changed to support sustainability initiatives. Organizations can impede the attainment of sustainability in three ways. First, rigid corporate structures can insulate organization systems and processes from a broad range of relevant information: systems that rely on inspired leaders rather than establishing structural or systemic solutions are particularly vulnerable. Second, the established routines and systems of many corporations promote and protect the *status quo*: sustainability initiatives, particularly in the strategic sustainability phase, can be a threat to command and control style management systems; managers who have risen to power in the command and control systems frequently resist the transition to alternative enabling organizational structures. Finally, many current organization designs limit or deny access to a range of stakeholders whose participation is vital for the pursuit of sustainable initiatives. Traditional organizations tend to be focused on a limited set of stakeholders, in particular boards of directors and shareholders. Other stakeholders, such as unions, green groups and community groups, are often seen as hostile forces that may harm organizational performance. Redefining these groups as resource and information opportunities rather than problems demands a significant shift of perspective.

However, organizational design can play an important contributing role in the development of human and ecological capabilities. Hierarchies are killers of creativity and initiative and impede the use of employee knowledge. Companies such as Xerox and Monsanto found that team-based structures were more conducive to the generation of employee knowledge and empower employees to use such knowledge. Team-based structures enable employees to have input, discretion over decision making and provision of information. Team-based organization architectures, which include project teams and virtual teams based on new information technologies, provide the basis for capturing and utilizing employee knowledge and competence in real-time situations.

Building employee knowledge and commitment

Strategic sustainability requires employee input and commitment. The successful implementation of various operational programmes such as total quality environmental management is reliant on human capital and workforce skill. The experience of firms such as Interface and Placer Dome demonstrates the need to develop and utilize employee capital and knowledge to achieve innovation, agility and high performance.

Organizations that have shifted to the strategic approach value human resource practices around new workplace cultures, enhanced adaptability, team-based work and project work and are keen to experiment with new ventures, such as virtual teams, that characterize 'silo busting' approaches to sustainability. The focus in these organizations is on developing and promoting talent, increasing autonomy and being responsive and flexible. Similarly, these firms typically create reward structures that allow managers to foster these conditions and that encourage employees to look beyond their organization by rewarding their efforts in community assistance and community building.

In a recent empirical study it was found that within organizations there exist at least four distinct categories of understanding of corporate sustainability. These included: a corporation working towards sustainable long-term economic performance; a corporation working towards positive outcomes for the natural environment; a corporation that supports people and social outcomes; and a corporation with a holistic approach. One implication from this study is that the change agents guiding strategic sustainability programmes can motivate people by designing change management programmes to appeal to people holding these different views, to deliver sustainability products and services.[91] We would add a third implication – that it is important to define very carefully the outcomes to be achieved by any sustainability strategy rather than to leave the strategy couched in ambiguous abstractions like 'sustainability' and 'corporate social responsibility'.

The innovative performance of Nucor Steel, a US-based firm, is reliant in part upon the development and utilization of its human capital. At the heart of this strategy lies a social ecology that enables Nucor to: create knowledge internally through the encouragement of experimentation; acquire external knowledge as a consequence of good reward structures and a reputation for being an 'ideal employer'; and finally, retain and use the knowledge it has developed. By social ecology we mean the culture, structure, information systems, processes, people and leadership that enable the company to pursue its knowledge management approach. The concrete actions that Nucor have taken include: the use of group incentive schemes; the encouragement of experimentation and 'play'; risk taking; rewards for knowledge sharing; and transfers within the company to diffuse knowledge. These have helped create Nucor's innovative approach to knowledge management and human capital development.[92]

Building executive leadership and stewardship

Strategic proactivity is a demonstrated commitment by the senior executive team and the board to actively pursue and develop corporate capabilities, products, processes and designs that align sustainability with the corporation's overall strategic orientations. Strategic proactivity encourages the use of distributed leadership approaches – rewarding innovation and initiatives that drive the company further towards its sustainability goals. Strategic proactivity opens the corporation to third-party scrutiny, as a way of improving or embedding sustainability practices within the organization. In particular, one of the key drivers of sustainability performance for an organization is the commitment by the executives to the large-scale changes and reforms required for sustainability to take place. They outline and live a compelling vision for the organization.

While executive leadership is crucial for sustainability, such leadership needs to be reinforced by the corporate values, the funding of corporate change programmes and willingness to transform organizations towards these ends. CEOs such as Ray Anderson of Interface, David Morgan of Westpac and Bob Cameron of Rockcote highlight the importance of social strategies in building and developing the human capital of the organization. These executives believe that it is important for CEOs and other senior managers to address people's needs and expectations and to reward their efforts by taking time to communicate openly and honestly. They not only believe in these values but enact them in their day-to-day activities. Because they model these values with integrity, others follow their example and the values then become 'human capital assets' within the organization.

The success of senior managers in this area is also determined by the skill with which they draw together different sustainability initiatives within the overall strategy of the organization and its ongoing programmes and operations. The senior executive role is not only about formulating commitment but about integrating the transformation into the business strategies of the organization.[93] Reinhardt argues that 'Managers need to go beyond the question: "Does it pay to be green?" and ask instead: "Under what conditions do particular lines of environmental investment deliver benefits to shareholders?"'[94]

Developing differentiated stakeholder strategies

Business alone cannot achieve sustainability. To achieve sustainability, corporations also require inputs from both governments and communities. Some organizations have already built capabilities associated with forming internal communities of practice that are fluid structures formed around areas of interest and expertise in organizations. An example of a community of practice may be a community of professionals who gather and share information around particular technical problems or solutions. Such communities generate the diffusion and acceptance of tacit knowledge that can be transferred into innovative solutions and actions within organizations. Their contribution to the attainment of sustainability outcomes for organizations lies in their ability to collect, process and diffuse knowledge of a technical and specialized nature to find rapid and innovative solutions. This is a vital component of strategic success.

One method to use in developing a stakeholder strategy is values-based environmental management. It is an approach that aims to develop a strong relationship between corporate strategy and how stakeholders view the organization. The questions posed by values-based environmental management include: 'Do stakeholders value your performance?' 'Do products and services contribute to solving environmental issues?' 'Does the stakeholder see you as a problem or part of the solution?'[95] Attracta Lagan, foundation director of the St James Ethics Centre, states,

'We're finding that values-based companies are outperforming others on the stock exchange when performance is measured over the long term.'[96]

One of the authors (Dunphy) is a member of Westpac Bank's Community Consultative Council, which consists of about twenty leaders mostly from community-based not-for-profit organizations. Once a year the CEO, David Morgan, meets with this council for about three hours and asks them what issues are at the centre of their attention when they think five to ten years ahead. Morgan then sits and listens as each community leader addresses this question, occasionally asking for clarification. The points raised are summarized and fed into Westpac's strategic planning process. Members of the council may be involved at various points as the issues they have raised are integrated into the bank's business strategies and actioned. The following year Morgan reports on the issues that have been addressed and the results that have been achieved. More detail is also reported in the annual environmental report against specific targets that have been set. Westpac's business performance speaks to the value of this simple process of environmental scanning. Westpac is rated among the top ten ASX listed companies, has global assets of A$260 billion and in 2005 made a net after tax profit of A$2,818 million.

Analysing stakeholders

It is vital to engage key stakeholders and to ensure that they understand and support the new strategic thrust of the organization. Thames Water, for instance, states that 'We listen to clients, customers, local communities, workers and neighbours. Before we make recommendations, we keep our eyes, ears – and minds – open.'[97]

Polonsky suggests a four-step process to analyse stakeholder approaches and identify strategic actions:

1 *Identify the stakeholders.* That is, identify those who have a vested interest in the outcomes of environmentalism.
2 *Determine the stakes.* What is each group's stake in the issue? Is it large or small? What specific issues do they revolve around?
3 *Determine how expectations are met.* Use this to assess the gap between expectations and performance.
4 *Adjust the strategy.* Strategy is adjusted to minimize/deal constructively with the stakeholder expectations and the gap in performance.[98]

Grayson and Hodges provide a detailed approach to engaging stakeholders that is consistent with Polansky's steps above.[99]

Moving beyond strategic sustainability

Hart and Milstein state:

> To capture sustainable opportunities managers must fundamentally rethink their prevailing views about strategy, technology and markets. Managers who treat sustainable development as an opportunity will drive the creative destruction process and build the foundation to compete in the twenty-first century.[100]

We agree with Hart and Milstein. To attain strategic sustainability managers must develop ecological and human capabilities within the organization. These capabilities enable the organization not only to keep abreast of sustainability issues but to obtain sustainable competitive advantages.

This chapter has outlined some organizational pathways to strategic sustainability. The challenge now, for those who aspire to move beyond strategic sustainability, is to generate the new business models of corporations that move beyond the pursuit of competitive business advantage in order to contribute to a fully sustainable society. This emerging model of business we take up in the next chapter.

 ## Phase 5: strategic proactivity

Human sustainability (HS5)

Ecological sustainability (ES5)

The workforce skills mix and diversity are seen as integral and vitally important aspects of corporate and business strategies. Intellectual and social capital are used to develop strategic advantage through innovation in products/services. Programmes are instituted to recruit the best talent to the organization and to develop high levels of competence in individuals and groups. In addition,

Proactive environmental strategies supporting ecological sustainability are seen as a source of strategic business opportunities to provide competitive advantage. Product redesign is used to reduce material throughput and to use materials that can be recycled. New products and processes are developed that substitute for or displace existing environmentally damaging products and skills are systematized to form the basis of corporate competences so that the organization is less vulnerable to the loss of key individuals. Emphasis is placed on product and service innovation and speed of response to emerging market demands. Flexible workplace practices are strong features of workplace culture and contribute to the work force leading more balanced lives. Communities affected by the organization's operations are taken into account and initiatives to address adverse impacts on communities are integrated into corporate strategy. Furthermore, the corporation views itself as a member of the community and as a result contributes to community betterment by offering sponsorship or employee time to participate in projects aimed at promoting community cohesion and well-being.

processes or satisfy emerging community needs around sustainable issues (reforestation; treatment of toxic waste). The organization seeks competitive leadership through spearheading environmentally friendly products and processes.

Notes

1. M. Porter and C. van der Linde, 'Green and competitive: ending the stalemate', *Harvard Business Review*, 1995, September–October, 130.
2. D. Cogan, *Corporate Governance and Climate Change: Making the Connection*, Boston, MA: CERES Investor Responsibility Research Centre, 2006, p. 14.
3. Ibid.
4. R. Anderson, 'Interfaces celebrates Ten Years of Sustainability in Action', corporate report, 2004.
5. Australian Business Roundtable on Climate Change, *The Business Case for Early Action*, 2006, p. 2.
6. Anon., 'Action agenda for the private sector', *Business Week*, 3 May 1999.
7. Csrwire.com, 09 May 2006, 'Shell: sustainability at the heart of our business'; The Shell Report, 2005.
8. Royal Dutch Shell, 'The Shell Sustainability Report, 2005', The Hague: External Review Committee, 3 April 2006 (accessed 9 May 2006).
9. Consequently Shell and BP rank second and first in the energy sector,

according to some investor reports, owing to their strategic efforts at addressing corporate governance and climate change. See Cogan, *Corporate Governance and Climate Change*.

10 BP, *Environmental and Social Review*, 2000, at www.BPamoco.com/alive (accessed 4 December 2001).

11 Michael Skapinker, 'Best environmental companies', *Financial Times*, 1 February 2002.

12 Carbon Disclosure Project, Cleveland, OH: Innovest, 2005, p. 53.

13 www.global100.org (accessed 2 March 2005).

14 For a detailed insight into the creation of strategic sustainability outcomes see Bob Willard, *The Sustainable Advantage*, and Edward Stead and Jean Garner Stead, *Sustainable Strategic Management*, London: Sharpe, 2004.

15 N. Roome, 'Developing environmental management strategies', *Business, Strategy and Environment*, 1992, 1 (1), 11–23.

16 Visy aims to be a leading provider of packaging and recycling services in the paper and paper products industry.

17 A. Hoffman, *Competitive Environmental Strategy*, Washington DC: Island Press, 2000, p. 162.

18 Stead and Stead, *Sustainable Strategic Management*, p. 28.

19 P. Hawken, A. Lovins and L. Lovins, *Natural Capitalism*, Boston, MA: Little Brown, 1999.

20 D. Dunphy and A. Griffiths, 'Corporate strategic change', in M. Warner (ed.) *International Encyclopaedia of Business and Management*, London: Thomson Learning, 2002.

21 L. Gratton, *Living Strategy: Putting People at the Heart of Corporate Purpose*, London: *Financial Times*/Prentice-Hall, 2000.

22 A. Schaefer and B. Harvey, 'Stage models of corporate greening: a critical evaluation', *Business Strategy and the Environment*, 1998, 7, 109–23.

23 A. Pettigrew, *The Awakening Giant*, Oxford: Blackwell, 1985.

24 H. Mintzberg and J. Waters, 'Of strategies deliberate and emergent', *Strategic Management Journal*, 1985, 6, 257–72; H. Mintzberg, *The Rise and Fall of Strategic Planning*, New York: Free Press, 1995; Gratton, *Living Strategy*.

25 Dunphy and Griffiths, 'Corporate strategic change'.

26 M. Porter, *The Competitive Advantage of Nations*, New York: Free Press, 1990.

27 K. Eisenhardt and J. Martin, 'Dynamic capabilities: what are they?' *Strategic Management Journal*, 2000, 21, 1105–21; C. Prahalad and G. Hamel, 'The core competence of the corporation', *Harvard Business Review*, 1990, 68 (3), 79–91.

28 Gratton, *Living Strategy*.

29 The basic competences outlined are based on: M. Hitt, B. Keats and S. de Marie, 'Navigating in the new competitive landscape: building strategic flexibility and competitive advantage in the twenty-first century',

Academy of Management Executive, November 1998, 22–47; M. Hastings, 'Oil companies in sensitive environments', *Business Strategy and Environment*, 1999, 8, 267–80; S. Sharma and H. Vredenburg, 'Proactive environmental strategy and the development of competitively valuable organizational capabilities', *Strategic Management Journal*, 1998, 19, 729–53.

30   Gratton, *Living Strategy*.

31   A. de Geus, *The Living Company*, Boston MA: Harvard Business School Press, 1997; J. Collins and J. Porras, *Built to Last*, London: Century, 1994.

32   De Geus, *Living Company*.

33   A. Griffiths, 'NAPCO: Long Living and Sustainable', case study, Brisbane: University of Queensland Business School.

34   J. Aragon-Correa, 'Strategic proactivity and firm approach to the natural environment', *Academy of Management Journal*, 1998, 14 (5), 556–67; M. Starik, *Management and the Natural Environment*, Fort Worth TX: Dryden Press, 1997.

35   B. Piasecki, K. Fletcher and F. Mendelson, *Environmental Management and Business Strategy*, New York: Wiley, 1999.

36   Hoffman, *Competitive Environmental Strategy*, pp. 160, 181.

37   S. Hart, 'A natural resource based view of the firm', *Academy of Management Review*, 1995, 20 (4), 986–1014.

38   Anderson credits part of his conversion to reading Hawkins's *Ecology of Commerce*, which he described as 'a spear in the chest': 'Interface celebrates Ten Years'.

39   A. Griffiths, 'New organisational architectures: creating and retrofitting for sustainability', in D. Dunphy, J. Benveniste, A. Griffiths and P. Sutton (eds) *Sustainability: The Corporate Challenge of the Twenty-first Century*, Sydney: Allen & Unwin, 2001, pp. 219–35; R. Orsato, 'Competitive environmental strategies: when does it pay to be green', *California Management Review*, 2006, 48 (2), pp. 127–43.

40   For further information on the Interface case see L. Rowledge, R. Barton and K. Brady, *Mapping the Journey: Case Studies in Strategy and Action towards Sustainable Development*, Sheffield: Greenleaf Publishing, 1999; Interface, 'Interface celebrates ten Years of Sustainability in Action', corporate communication, 31 August 2004; www.interfacesustainability.com (accessed 6 March 2006).

41   J. Pfeffer, *Competitive Advantage through People*, Boston MA: Harvard Business School Press, 1994; D. Dunphy and A. Griffiths, *The Sustainable Corporation*, Sydney: Allen & Unwin, 1998.

42   D. Raths, '100 best corporate citizens', *Business Ethics* magazine, 2006, 20 (1), 1–9.

43   Gratton, *Living Strategy*.

44   Raths, '100 best corporate citizens'.

45   P. Crittenden and D. Dunphy, *Hewlett-Packard: A Corporate*

Sustainability Case Study, Faculty of Business Working Paper No. 19, Sydney: University of Technology, 2000.

46 M. Russo and P. Fouts, 'A resource based perspective on corporate environmental performance and profitability', *Academy of Management Journal*, 1997, 40 (3), 534–59.

47 P. Senge and S. Carstedt, 'Innovating our way to the next industrial revolution', *MIT Sloan Management Review*, 2001, winter, 24–38.

48 D. Turner and M. Crawford, *Change Power: Capabilities that Drive Corporate Renewal*, Sydney: Business and Professional Publishing, 1998.

49 Gratton, *Living Strategy*, p. 11.

50 J. Maxwell, S. Rothenberg, F. Briscoe and I. Marcus, 'Green schemes: corporate environmental strategies and their implementation', *California Management Review*, 1997, 39 (3), 118–34.

51 Justin Thomas, 'A car that can run on five fuels from Volvo', www.treehugger.com/files/2006/06/a_car_that_can.php (12 June 2006).

52 Rowledge *et al.*, *Mapping the Journey*, p. 49.

53 J. Elkington, *Cannibals with Forks*, Gabriola Island: New Society Publishers, 1998, p. 119.

54 S. Hart and M. Milstein, 'Creating sustainable value', *Academy of Management Executive*, 2003, 17 (3),56–67; R. Orsato, 'Competitive environmental strategies: when does it pay to be green?' *California Management Review*, 2006, 48 (2), 127–43.

55 A. Griffiths, S. Benn and D. Dunphy, 'Organisational structures and roles', in R. Staib (ed.) *Environmental Management and Decision-making for Business*, New York: Palgrave Macmillan, 2005, pp. 169–91.

56 M. A. Schilling, J. Johng, Y-J. Kang, J. Sul and M. Takanashi, 'Honda Insight: development and launch of a hybrid electric vehicle', in M. Starik and S. Sharma, *New Horizons in Research on Sustainable Organizations*, Sheffield: Greenleaf, 2005, pp. 123–43, p. 143.

57 M. Porter, 'Strategy and the internet', *Harvard Business Review*, March 2001, 63–78.

58 J. Elkington, *Cannibals with Forks*, p. 333.

59 Anon., 'Anita Roddick off Body Shop board', *Sydney Morning Herald*, 15 February 2002, 7.

60 V. Kemp, A. Stark and J. Tantram, 'To Whose Profit? Evolution – Building Sustainable Corporate Strategy', London: Worldwide Fund for Nature, 2004, p. x.

61 Ibid., pp. 51–62.

62 S. Hart, 'Beyond greening', *Harvard Business Review*, 1997, January–February, 66–76; J. Magretta, 'Growth through global sustainability', *Harvard Business Review*, 1997, January–February, 79–88.

63 J. Elkington, *The Chrysalis Economy*, Oxford: Capstone, 2001, p. 96, L. Pregelj, 2005 Monsato Case Study, unpublished, figure 5.3.

64 M. Metherell, 'Gene labels scare off food makers', *Sydney Morning Herald*, 15 November 2001, 1.

65 S. Hart and S. Sharma, 'Engaging fringe stakeholders for competitive imagination', *Academy of Management Executive*, 2004, 18 (1), p. 7–18.

66 Ibid., p. 7.

67 Ibid., p. 7.

68 L. Gettler, 'Reputation: it's priceless', *Management Today*, 2002, January–February, 5.

69 C. Handy, *The Elephant and the Flea: Looking back to the Future*, London: Hutchinson, 2001, p. 82.

70 Ibid., p. 83.

71 R. Orsatto, 'The Ecological Competence of the Organization: Competing for Sustainability', paper presented to the XVI EGOS Colloquium, Helsinki, Finland, July 2000.

72 R. Miles and C. Snow, *Fit, Failure and the Hall of Fame*, New York: Free Press, 1994.

73 Elkington, *Cannibals with Forks*, p. 3.

74 G. Wilson and D. Sasseville, *Sustaining Environmental Management Success*, New York: Wiley, 1999, p. 208.

75 Anon., 'Case studies: visionary leadership', *Business Week*, 3 May 1999.

76 A. Griffiths, 'Queensland Rail and Sustainability Hubs for Small Wins', case study, Brisbane: University of Queensland Business School, 2006.

77 Ford Motor Company, *Connecting with Society*, Detroit: Ford Motor Company, 2000, p. 3; www.fordmotorco.com (accessed 4 December 2001).

78 Ibid., p. 6.

79 B. Hirsh and P. Sheldrake, *Inclusive Leadership*, Melbourne: Information Australia, 2000, p. 20.

80 Business Council of Australia, *Towards Sustainable Development: How Leading Australian and Global Corporations are Contributing to Sustainable Development*, Melbourne: Business Council of Australia, 2001.

81 Hoffman, *Competitive Environmental Strategy*. Stead and Stead, *Sustainable Strategic Management*.

82 Ibid.

83 B. Nattrass and M. Altomare, *The Natural Step for Business*, Gabriola Island: New Society Publishers, 1999, pp. 47–74.

84 Ibid.

85 www.ikea-usa.com.

86 Nattrass and Altomare, *Natural Step for Business*.

87 T. Clarke, 'Balancing the triple bottom line: financial, social and environmental performance', *Journal of General Management*, 2001, 26 (4), 1–11.

88 Hoffman, *Competitive Environmental Strategy*.

89   E. Cohen-Rosenthal, 'A walk on the human side of industrial ecology', *American Behavioral Scientist*, 2000, 44 (2), 245–64; J. M. Benyus, *Innovation inspired by Nature*, New York: Morrow, 1997.

90   Cited in ibid., p. 259.

91   S. Russell, N. Haigh and A. Griffiths, 'Understandings of Corporate Sustainability', Academy of Management conference, Atlanta GA, 2006.

92   A. Gupta and V. Govindarajan, 'Knowledge management's social dimension: lessons from Nucor Steel', *Sloan Management Review*, 2000, 42 (1), 71–80.

93   S. Banerjee, 'Managerial perceptions of corporate environmentalism: interpretations from industry and strategic implications for organizations', *Journal of Management Studies*, 2001, 38 (4), 479–513.

94   F. Reinhardt, 'Bringing the environment down to earth', *Harvard Business Review*, 1999, July–August, 149–56, esp. p. 150.

95   J. Blumber, A. Korsuold and G. Blum, 'Value based environmental management and sustainability', in G. Wilson and D. Sasseville (eds) *Sustaining Environmental Management Success*, New York: Wiley, 1999, p. 220.

96   A. Lagan, 'Lively conversations with the future', *Future News*, 1998, 3 (5), 2.

97   RWE Thames Water, 'Water Partner to the World' (2002), quoted in D. Grayson and A. Hodges, *Seven Steps to make Corporate Social Responsibility work for your Business*, Sheffield: Greenleaf, 2004, p. 211.

98   M. Polonsky, 'Incorporating the natural environment in corporate strategy: a stakeholder approach', *Journal of Business Strategy*, 1995, 12 (2), 152–5.

99   RWE Thames Water, 'Water Partner', pp. 204–43, 'Step 6: engaging stakeholders'.

100   S. Hart and M. Milstein, 'Global sustainability and the creative destruction of industries', *Sloan Management Review*, 1999, 41 (1), 22.

6 The sustaining corporation

- Generating a future reality
- The third wave
- Putting the jigsaw together
- Conclusion
- Sustaining corporation

Generating a future reality

In this chapter we aim to present a vivid image of the 'sustaining corporation', that is, the corporation which fully incorporates the tenets of human and ecological sustainability into its own operations and which also works actively to support the application of sustainability principles throughout the rest of the society.

We freely admit that there are few if any organizations today that fully embody this socio- and ecocentric ideal. To date the ones most cited, such as Patagonia and Interface, have not been public companies but are relatively small and privately owned. Some of these innovative small companies have not always been able to maintain the advances they have made, particularly through the transitions of take-over or CEO succession. This indicates a CEO's leadership plays a crucial role in shaping a company's corporate sustainability strategy. The challenge is to learn from these early adventures in sustainability and extend that learning to larger public corporations. There is, however, another source of learning. Many larger companies have experimented successfully with aspects of sustainability and we illustrate the ideal with case examples of what some of these organizations have achieved. Green Mountain Coffee Roasters, for instance, a publicly listed company since 1993, have developed an extensive form of community engagement and consultation in supporting both communities and the environment from locations where they source coffee beans.[1] Others, such as S. C. Johnson, have moved into the development of environmentally safe products and the reduction of greenhouse gas emissions, while some state-owned enterprises, such as BC Hydro, are striving to become 'footprint-neutral'.

None of these organizations yet meets the ideal, but collectively they help us create an image of how a fully committed organization would operate. The future is emerging around us, if we have eyes to see it, as innovative companies explore sustainability practices in a range of operations. The analogy is to constructing a jigsaw puzzle – we assemble one piece from one organization, another piece from another organization, until we have an overall image of the organization of the future which is modelling sustainability in its own operations and supporting the wider sustainability movement. The sustaining organization is not only sustainable itself but is also promoting and supporting the further development of sustainability principles throughout society and for future generations.

This image may seem a dream. It is. Managerial leadership is increasingly about having ambitious dreams and then ensuring that these dreams are realized. Ian Lowe writes, 'in fact, practically all desirable features of modern life were once utopian visions made real by visionaries who worked systematically to achieve their dreams of a better world'.[2] Dreams are only reality waiting to happen.

> At Honda, we turn the dreams of tomorrow into realities.
>
> (Honda website)[3]

The internet was once a dream – until it was put in place and revolutionized the economy and society. Our argument here is that transformational social change is now happening at incredible speed and that the onset of the 'third wave' will make achieving corporate sustainability a political, economic and social priority. For instance a KPMG survey in 2005 found that for the Global 250 companies Corporate Responsibility reporting had increased from 45 per cent in 2002 to 52 per cent in 2005 and, if integrated annual reports were included, the figure was 64 per cent.[4] The challenge is to turn dreams into corporate visions and visions into concrete, practical actions:

> It is simply ridiculous that we allow businesses to continue to destroy our planet. The bottom line is now simple – people are dying because of environmental degradation, people are forced into working for subsistence wages because companies need to increase their

profitability, those who resist the progress of capitalism are subjected to torture and even murdered by the state because they have campaigned for human rights. Yet business still operates in concert with the institutions and governments which cause such suffering and people still buy their products. Doing business in countries which abuse human rights and torture citizens means that you accept that practice. Not protesting when your opponents are hanged is tantamount to killing them yourself. To buy the products of such a company is to agree with its actions.[5]

These are strong statements, but we are moving to a society where more people will support these views and act on them. More ethical investment funds are being created around the world and the capital invested in these funds is growing every day. At first glance, it seems strange that radical green activists and conservative financial institutions are now working together to ensure that corporations act responsibly, but this is a regular occurrence now. Organizations such as the Australian Conservation Foundation work closely with large corporations such as Westpac and Swiss Re and have formed the Australian Business Roundtable for Climate Change. Similarly, WWF has joined forces with large corporations such as IBM, Johnson & Johnson and TetraPak as part of its Climate Savers Programme that is aimed to reduce energy consumption and greenhouse gas emissions. We have examined the way that powerful drivers of change are converging to change the ground rules for corporate activity. The result is that old-style companies face increasing pressure from social and environmental activists and can no longer assume that they will be supported even by financial institutions. The future lies with those organizations that anticipate changes such as this and take the lead as the changes unfold.

The third wave

So we go on to outline the nature of the third wave. The third wave sees society moving into a new paradigm where complexity and interconnectedness are central, where transformational change is more widespread and occurs over shorter time periods, where direction and momentum are achieved through alliances, shared commitment to common goals, high levels of innovation and loose coupling. In this world there will be an increase in the number of temporary organizations formed for specific purposes. Whether long-lasting or temporary, these organizations of the future will be strongly value-driven. They will be responding to an emerging shift in global values that is already becoming evident in a number of ways:

- Growing scientific consensus and concern about the looming environmental crisis.
- International co-operation between governments, corporations and environmental groups to protect the environment.
- Increasing questioning of the value of the dominant neo-liberal economic model accompanied by the rise of ecological economics as an alternative.
- Increasing use of the precautionary principle as a policy tool.
- Increasing support for green political parties, already a significant political force in countries such as Germany, Italy, Australia and New Zealand, to date regularly achieving between 5 per cent and 8 per cent of the popular vote in elections in these countries.
- Development of international regulatory agreements to promote social justice and protect the environment.
- The rise of postmodern philosophy questioning the association between positivist science and materialistic views of progress, and rejecting social and environmental exploitation in favour of care for all humans, other species and the natural world.[6]

This last point represents a re-emphasis on spirituality and the emergence of a new way of conducting science so that it is embedded in values that affirm biodiversity and social justice.[7] Happily, this is taking place as professional scientists set up ethics committees and sign public statements about critical issues of sustainability such as environmental warming.

The most successful of these sustaining organizations will act both locally and globally, will put a premium on speedily repositioning themselves strategically to take advantage of new market opportunities and will add value through providing new levels of customized service. In this regard, they are acting strategically. For these organizations, sustainability is central to their corporate strategies and a vital ingredient in how they assess their effectiveness. They see success as dependent on developing active stakeholder relationships with a variety of community groups – they build 'stakeholder capital'. They regard their success as dependent also on the 'intellectual and skill capital' of their work force. Therefore they systematically develop the skills of those in the core work force and contribute to skill development in the work forces of suppliers and alliance partners. They are consciously committed to actions that increase the human capability base of society and that maintain and restore the biosphere. For those who contribute to the leadership of these organizations the corporation is a vital link in the ecology itself and in the intergenerational continuity of society. They are 'sustaining organizations'.

We contrast this world with the world of the first wave, where organizations were discrete and enduring entities with clear boundaries, were primarily cost-driven, emphasized hierarchy and control and maintained traditional ways of doing things, resisting change unless the traditional ways were clearly failing. We also contrast the third wave world with the second wave, where organizations sought to establish radically new levels of efficiency and to develop more forward-looking business strategies to ensure their futures – we discussed this further in Chapters 4 and 5.

First wave organizations largely took the ecological and social environment for granted. At worst, some actively opposed (and still do) moves to protect the biosphere from destructive exploitation or pressure for their active involvement in community development. Typically they argued that business exists simply to make a profit. Or they ignored sustainability issues, concentrating on a narrowly defined business concept, and treating the natural and social environment as 'free' goods or a regrettable source of cost. At best, they emphasized compliance with legal restraints (health and safety regulations, waste treatment) and pursued positive sustainability policies only when such measures reduced costs or provided a clear competitive advantage. Both first wave and early second wave organizations tended to ignore the wider issues of ecological and social responsibility, generally failing to recognize and measure the negative impacts of their activities on communities and on the ecological carrying capacity of the environment (unless public reaction compelled them to do so). Issues of social and environmental responsibility were, at best, regarded as marginal to the core business of the company and to its business strategies. They emphasized the goods and services they provided and conveniently ignored the 'bads' and 'disservices' they contributed. This, however, undergoes a significant change as organizations move into Phase 5: strategic proactivity.

> The basic development patterns of the industrial era are not sustainable.
> (P. Senge, in *Sloan Management Review*)[8]

If we are to turn around the serious social and environmental degradation we have created, there must be a radical departure from past practices. We argue for a reinterpretation of the role of the corporation in society and for a reintegration of the economy into the ecology and the global community. Economics cannot be separate from issues of species survival, social justice and spirituality. Similarly, science and technology cannot operate without regard to the risks they create for survival, health and human happiness. And businesses cannot ignore the costs, to future generations, of operations that outrun the rate of resource replacement. Hoffman, in an article on climate change, argues that more and more businesses are seeing opportunities and rapidly moving to make the most of them.[9] However, most corporations use accounting practices that ignore the social and environmental costs of their business practices. We are all part of a living system that is dependent on a delicate balance of gases in the atmosphere and a thin residue of soil created over millennia. Our activities must preserve and enrich this precious life support system, not degrade it.

Similarly, we all come into this world as helpless infants and depend for our subsequent development as mature human beings on a society that provides caring relationships, socialization and education. Traditional economics tends to ignore these functions, for example of parents caring for their children in the home. The proper function of the economy is to support a healthy biosphere and quality of social life for the earth's human population. Consequently, the sustaining organization will create a social and ethical balance sheet and be accountable for it. An important part of this approach is the increasing interest in the study of collaborative relationships rather than the past obsession with competition, 'winners' and 'winning'.

The Rabobank group, a large Dutch co-operative bank, is one organization that has demonstrated, for many years, a collaborative commitment to human and ecological sustainability. The bank was founded as a co-operative in 1888 and has expanded to rank thirty-second of banks globally. Rabobank's stated aim is to pursue the goals of 'profit, people and the planet'. Rabobank regards sustainability as central to its business activities.[10] It is strongly involved in several national and international business forums that exchange information and best practice and which engage in public advocacy of sustainability. In 1999 it launched the RG Sustainable Equity Fund, which invests in companies chosen for their ethical approach to social and environmental issues. In the first eleven months 'the fund achieved a return of 59 percent compared to 45 percent for its benchmark, the Morgan Stanley Capital Index'.[11]

Putting the jigsaw together

What then are the characteristics of the sustaining corporation?

A new social contract

We begin with the corporation's connection with its key stakeholders and the notion of a social and ecological contract negotiated by management with these stakeholders or their representatives. This social contract provides the rationale for the corporation's continued existence, for it defines the mutually valuable exchanges that will sustain the firm's ongoing network of relationships. It also defines the organization's mission and legitimizes the organization's right to operate, to produce valued goods and services and its responsibility not to produce 'bads' (pollution, waste and so on) and 'disservices' (socially or ecologically destructive processes). Concomitant with this is the development of a stakeholder accountability process that emphasizes transparency and openness in reporting on delivery to stakeholder expectations. For example, over 52 per cent of the Global 250 corporations now produce comprehensive annual corporate responsibility reports that deal with their impacts on society. These companies have well known names such as BP, Amoco, Nike, Shell, Renault and Hewlett-Packard.

But all this begs the question: who are the stakeholders? There is now a substantial body of work delineating stakeholder theory.[12] There are differences of opinion expressed in this literature about whether to confine the definition of stakeholder to those individuals and groups who are vital to the survival of the firm or to expand it to a wider set of groups whose interests are affected by the firm's actions. These views correspond to the two major uses of the word 'sustainability', which cause considerable confusion in the field: (1) the firm's ability to sustain itself versus (2) its impact on the sustainability of its social and ecological environment.

Both definitions are useful and Factor suggests that we distinguish between 'primary' and 'secondary' stakeholders.[13] Primary stakeholders are those engaged in some transactions with the firm and without whom the firm would cease to exist. Secondary stakeholders are those who are not essential to the firm's survival but who can influence the firm or who are influenced by the firm (or both). The distinction makes it clear that, to pursue its own immediate self-interest, the firm must concern itself with the expectations of primary stakeholders; however, it also has ethical responsibilities to secondary stakeholders. In a similar vein Hart and Sharma differentiate between core stakeholders and peripheral stakeholders. Much of the strategy literature has been obsessed by the core stakeholders of an organization. This focus on a limited number of key stakeholders has had disastrous consequence for some organizations – such as Monsanto (covered in Chapter 5). For others, such as HP and Unilever, the recognition of the importance of peripheral stakeholders has created new product and business opportunities and the formation of new social contracts with communities.[14]

The potential list of stakeholders includes shareholders and owners, suppliers, customers, government, the community, future generations and the rest of nature: that is, all 20 million or so species on earth. Each organization must decide which are primary and which are secondary. Given the insights provided by Hart and Sharma, we argue for a broad definition of the potential range of stakeholders – one that includes future generations, the good of society as a whole and the natural world. As Carl Anderson has noted:

> Over the last fifteen years, many managers have defined the market force doctrine in the narrowest way, as self-interest exploited through *laissez-faire* economics. In the most extreme cases, using ethical principles in decision-making is seen as a sure path to ruin in the Darwinian fight for survival. Competing within an open system is stressed, but preserving the competitive system itself is not. Businessmen and businesswomen have a stake in analyzing systems as a whole, thinking about the overall good of the society in which we are to live. Stakeholder analysis, reasonableness, and enlightened self-interest force decision-makers to consider the situation of the worst off in society as well as of the owners who are obvious targets of attention.[15]

The social contract that emerges out of a company's interaction with its stakeholders has its visible form in clear, written policies and principles that relate to human resource development, community relations and the ecological environment. It is evident also in the firm's core business strategies and in the way they are interpreted in the process of day-to-day decision making. It is clear that the commitment to sustainability matters because it shows up in decisions about what the corporation both does and does not do. It does not exploit its work force or pollute the planet with its products or emissions. It does work collaboratively with a variety of community bodies to solve social and environmental problems and to identify and take up opportunities that build community. It does actively help workforce members develop their personal and professional abilities; it works actively to foster a healthy biosphere. For instance, BHP Billiton has invested significantly in its Mozal aluminium smelter, located in Mozambique. It has made significant investments in the education and health care of the region and has also invested in the development and training of the local work force. Furthermore, the company has attempted to help create the framework via which small and medium enterprises can develop around the smelter. The project demonstrates the potential benefit that corporations can bring to communities through the development of new social contracts.[16]

Already many companies worldwide have significantly modified their traditional approach of measuring the effectiveness of their operations through financial measures alone. Some firms, for example, have adopted the 'Balanced Scorecard' concept. This approach was developed in the 1990s by the Boston-based Nolan Norton Institute, a research arm of KPMG Peat Marwick. Its most comprehensive exposition is by Kaplan and Norton.[17] The Balanced Scorecard uses a wider set of indicators to represent future economic value. Some of the world's leading companies, including Du Pont, General Electric, Hewlett-Packard, EDS, Cigna and American Standard, have adopted this approach.[18]

In Westpac's case, for example, fully 70 per cent of the value assigned to Westpac by the market is not captured in the traditional financial measures. Employee commitment, occupational health and safety, workplace diversity, governance and leadership, customer satisfaction, product and service quality, brand strength, environmental impacts, the quality of relationships with stakeholders, and so on, are all critical to our longevity. But they currently have no place in a traditional P&L and balance sheet.

(David Morgan, CEO, Westpac)[19]

Ensuring that performance measures include these concerns, and engaging in dialogue around them, keeps the firm in touch with the interests of those groups that can affect its future. It assists the firm to co-evolve with its life companions in the way that birds have co-evolved with trees or beetles with flowers.[20]

A focus on human sustainability

We move on now to the issue of how the corporation handles human sustainability. In this area, the organization accepts responsibility for the process of contributing to and upgrading human knowledge and skill formation within the organization itself. It acts this way because it makes good business sense to develop the intellectual and social capital of the work force, particularly in areas relevant to the organization's mission.[21] This upgrading is also valuable for its own sake and reflects the organization's commitment to treating people as having value in their own right. It also contributes to a society where human capabilities are enhanced rather than degraded and this process of continuous upskilling improves the quality of life in society as a whole.

> Everything in this firm works because of social capital.
> (Hobson Brown, Jnr, President and CEO, Russell Reynolds)[22]

Capability enhancement includes developing the organization's capacity for reshaping itself, that is, its ability to identify future strategic opportunities and to initiate action which effectively repositions particular products or services, repositions the organization as a whole to take advantage of changing markets or proactively redefines the industry or a significant segment of it. There is an intimate connection between creating the capacity for organizational and for individual change. Flexible organizations need and develop proactive, flexible individuals who take responsibility for their own personal, professional and spiritual growth. In turn, they are able to raise the level of organizational innovation. Today we find more examples of organizations progressing human sustainability in 'hi-tech' companies in IT, software development, the arts and the service sector.

Consistent with this emphasis on innovation is strong support for a policy of workplace diversity, participation in decision making, gender equity and work–life balance. In addition, the organizational architecture reflects the emphasis on adaptability, flexibility, innovation and speed of response. It is a non-hierarchical, continuously evolving net of interrelated groups and individuals. For example, the Danish maker of hearing aids, Oticon, abandoned all formal structures, supervisory positions, job descriptions, budgets and policies in its head office, established a true paperless office, encouraged any and all of its head office employees, including its R&D

staff, to form themselves on their own initiative into working groups around innovative projects, and made all information on its IT system (except trade secrets) available to all employees. Its multi-storey office building was reorganized to encourage people to communicate informally. After an initial period of disorientation, the result was a significant improvement in the company's market position. This resulted from doubling the rate at which new products were developed, halving new product lead time and growing sales at 20 per cent per annum when global markets were shrinking.[23] These results were achieved under the leadership of Lars Kolnid, CEO from 1988 to 1998. His successor, Niels Jacobson, received the prestigious Employee Empowerment Pioneer award in New York in 1998 on behalf of Oticon, and stated: 'Our goal is to do business in a manner that positively contributes to society in every country where we do business. We support the principle that industry has a responsibility to society and that we have a collective responsibility to the environment.'[24]

One critical challenge for the company of the future will be to attract and retain highly talented people, as either 'permanent employees' or contract workers. There are some managers who imagine that, because there is significant unemployment in most societies, building and retaining a skilled work force is not problematical. But there is intense global and national competition for highly talented professionals and a firm's success is increasingly dependent on attracting, developing and retaining such people. Many executives are responding to this perceived need by trying to define their company as 'the employer of choice'. The fact is that talented professionals are highly mobile, in many cases define the world as their sphere of activity, and take for granted that they will be well paid. The deciding factor in choosing an employer is the opportunity that an organization provides for meaningful work, autonomy and professional development. Consequently human resource management strategies become critical for building a high-performance culture that provides challenge, work satisfaction and effective career development. The success of companies such as Hewlett-Packard and Ericsson comes in part from their development of comprehensive human resource policies that recognize this.

Human sustainability has an external as well as an internal focus. It involves adopting a strong and clearly defined corporate ethical position based on multiple stakeholder perspectives. It identifies key stakeholders with interests in human sustainability, builds positive relationships with them or their representatives, listens to their concerns, identifies their needs, and communicates the organization's mission and strategies to them. This ethical commitment also makes good business sense in that it provides, for example, an up-to-date customer knowledge base which signals previously unidentified customer needs or emerging interests – these represent potential future business opportunities. It also builds customer loyalty. Customers and other key stakeholders ask: 'Why would we go elsewhere when our needs are being identified and met so effectively here?'

> Research drawing from the resource-based view argues that a capability of integrating knowledge from stakeholders such as suppliers and customers will help firms design products for the environment; empirically it has been shown that a stakeholder integration capability helps a firm generate knowledge from collaborative and adversarial stakeholders for continuous learning and innovation around sustainability and for generating competitive imagination and ensuring corporate survival.
>
> (S. Sharma and M. Starik)[25]

> **Cultural diversity**
>
> We recognize and value our multicultural background as a company. We draw on the wealth of diversity as a unique strength to preserve, promote and protect the rich cult character of countries, communities and local regions. We value the variety of our diversity content, which represents our heritage and the world's cultural diversity and we strive to deliver competitively superior services to our local markets.
>
> (Vivendi Universal website)[26]

The sustaining organization seeks to exert influence on stakeholders, other industry participants and society in general to pursue human welfare, equitable and just social practices and to create the social circumstances that contribute to the fulfilment of human potential in all citizens. The concern here is global and multigenerational: 'citizens' includes citizens of other countries as well as our own and future generations. Sustaining organizations are aiming to use their influence to create a generative society. This is not considered an 'add-on' to the organization's activities, as a charitable exercise, but as a demonstration of the organization's integrity as a responsible corporate citizen. We like the story of the organization that always keeps an empty chair at the table when the board meets to consider the organization's strategies. The chair represents unborn generations; it stands as a constant reminder to consider seriously the long-term impact of decisions on the future.

Patagonia is one company that has consistently acted on this principle. Patagonia manufactures sports clothing and gear and has built a strong reputation for quality and innovation. The company's environmental commitment is evidenced, for example, by its use of recycled materials and its decision to convert its entire sportswear line to 100 per cent organically grown cotton fibre even though this incurs higher costs. Despite the sportswear being more expensive, sales have grown, showing that there is public support for environmentally responsible action of this kind.[27]

Furthermore, Patagonia announced its Common Threads recycling programme, as a further extension of its desire to create closed-loop systems. In conjunction with research partners in Japan, Patagonia is able to accept back polyester clothing for recycling into new products. Driving these innovations has been the founder's passion for ecological and social sustainability and also the willingness to invest in technical and non-technical solutions to social and environmental challenges.[28]

The acceptance of these principles has an observable impact on the way the corporation operates. It is strongly and proactively committed to traditional occupational health and safety measures, ensuring that the workplace is safe and healthy. It is also strongly committed to equal opportunity and proactive in recruiting from minority groups and ensuring career progression for women and minorities. It adopts family-friendly policies. But it goes beyond these concerns to place importance on the design of work for job satisfaction, personal and professional development and on creating a learning environment. It also actively encourages all members of the organization to be involved in community activities in which they contribute in their own right and as members of the organization.

Purposive, value-based action

Sustaining corporations are value-based and attract members who are strongly committed to the same values – people who want to make a difference. In such organizations people feel that their work is meaningful and the process of innovation and strategy implementation flows more readily because of the basic alignment between the values of the organization and the majority of those working there. They want to see innovations with positive environmental impact and they are keen to make the developing environmental strategy work.

The sustaining corporation has a codified set of company values – a corporate value statement or credo – that is used as a reference point in decision making at all levels of the organization. This is actively workshopped and discussed throughout the organization and, where appropriate, modified so that it attracts widespread commitment. The company specifies guidelines for how the company will treat its members, the community and the environment. An external body is chosen to collaborate in conducting an independent ethical audit of the company's internal and external relations and their report forms an integral part of the company's annual report published on the company website. All this demands much more disclosure, transparency and accountability than has been the practice in the traditional firm.

One firm that has based its existence on sustainability values is the US chain of quality food supermarkets Whole Foods Market. This is a chain of food stores that actively markets delicious and nutritious foods that are mostly organic. Its core values are:

- Selling the highest-quality natural and organic products available.
- Satisfying and delighting our customers.
- Team member happiness and excellence.
- Creating wealth through profits and growth.
- Caring about our communities and environment.

The net operating profit from 1991 to 2002 showed an annual average growth of 45 per cent.[29]

The range of activities emphasized in sustaining organizations means that different capabilities and skills are developed within the organization – the organization generally needs a broader range of skills than a traditional organization and the emphasis is on process skills. In particular, members develop higher-order skills of personal resilience, self-confidence, adaptation and learning, empathy, communication and influence, coaching, negotiation and conflict resolution. Chapter 9 discusses how leadership becomes increasingly diffused throughout the organization and how leaders develop these qualities.

Some sustaining organizations are not-for-profit and we are confident that, as third wave thinking spreads, we shall see more organizations of this kind emerging, committed to social ideals other than profitability.

As more third wave organizations develop they will begin to bring pressure to bear on politicians to support the development of third wave economies, that is, economies which value people and use resources to develop their capabilities, invest in environmental renewal and redefine progress in ways that are more meaningful than GNP. They will lobby governments to withdraw subsidies from unsustainable industries, to invest in social capital, to encourage innovation and the innovative industries of the future. They will also form alliances with like-minded companies whose activities are complementary to their own. In some cases, the organizations in these alliances will co-locate their production facilities to form what are known as 'industrial clusters' or 'industrial ecosystems'. In these clusters, materials flow in closed loops. As Tibbs points out, this has the potential to create a massive increase in the efficiency of materials use because 'about 95 percent of all the materials we use end up as waste before the finished product is even purchased'.[30] Imagine the productivity increase possible if this material were fully utilized and recycled! The evidence is that focused industrial clusters like this can be highly productive in business terms and support a healthy environment and society. This brings us to the issue of ecological sustainability.

Focus on ecological sustainability

In the area of ecological sustainability, the sustaining organization seeks to define itself as an integral part of the ecology: like an earthworm, it takes up resources from the environment, processes them and, in returning them to the earth, ensures its own growth and enriches the environment. The sustaining organization ensures that resources are economically recycled or returned to the environment in a form which is not destructive of environmental value or actually helps restore and enrich the environment where it has been damaged. This is in contrast to most current industrial processes whose major output is waste, often poisonous waste.

> At Hewlett-Packard, our goal is to provide our customers with products and
> services that are environmentally sound throughout their life cycles and to
> conduct our business worldwide in a responsible manner.
>
> (Hewlett-Packard,
> *Commitment to the Environment*)[31]

In the sustaining organization, environmental best practice is espoused
and enacted because it is the responsible thing to do. The organization
becomes an active promoter of ecological sustainability values and seeks
to influence key participants in the industry and society in general. It is
prepared to use its influence to promote positive sustainability policies on
the part of governments, the restructuring of markets and the development
of community values to facilitate the emergence of a sustainable society.
For instance Green Mountain Coffee Roasters has been a pioneer in the
fair trade movement and is now sourcing 20 per cent of its coffee as 'fair
trade certified' and purchasing 45 per cent of its coffee directly from
farmers. The company sees these as early initiatives in its efforts to create
sustainable coffee growing communities. In third wave firms the
environment is treated as integral to a viable global economy that is
sustainable into the future for the benefit of generations to come as well
as those alive today.

This has some important consequences for how firms with a material
production process can operate in the future. They will be far more
concerned about the initial design of products than with their ultimate
disposal. Much of the problem of pollution and waste can be eliminated
at the design stage by the choice of environmentally friendly,
non-polluting materials and designing out waste. In natural systems
there is no waste and material production processes can increasingly
emulate natural processes.

In 1992 Hewlett-Packard initiated a product stewardship programme:

> Under this program, Hewlett-Packard strives to prevent or minimize
> any negative impacts to human health or safety, or to the ecosystem,
> that may occur at any point in the life of an HP product – from when it
> is designed until it is no longer used.[32]

The programme guidelines outline five key principles in the attempt to
design environmentally friendly products:

- Minimize the energy consumption of our products, fewer raw materials, and increase our use of recyclable materials.
- Reduce waste and emissions from our manufacturing processes.
- Use less material overall and more recyclable material in our packaging.
- Form local covenants for the collection, disposal and recycling of computer equipment – taking responsibility for products from cradle to grave.
- Develop products that are easier to reuse or recycle.[33]

Hewlett-Packard regularly reports progress against these guidelines.

Sustaining organizations conduct a life-cycle assessment for all products. They are concerned with the full production flow, from the extraction of raw materials to their disposal, even where their own operation may control only one link in the total chain. Where this is the case they will actively negotiate collaborative solutions to social and environmental problems with other firms in the chain. In this way they build voluntary partnerships committed to working to raise their awareness of key interdependences and to eliminate the, often unintended, negative impacts of the production process on the community or the ecology. Collectively they view themselves as stewards of the resources they use: they either continue to recycle them or return them to the earth in a form that feeds the earth.

Such alliances can expand even further. In 1997 a Zero Waste New Zealand Trust was established with a vision for New Zealand to become the first country in the world to adopt a national zero-waste strategy and a target of zero waste to landfill. Twenty-five local councils participate in the project, committing themselves to a target of zero waste to landfill by 2015, and the number participating continues to expand steadily. The trust helps them research, develop and implement waste reduction strategies and connects them with best practice around the world. It also provides financial support.

This approach may also mean a reversal of the trend to create short-term, disposable products in favour of creating products that are used for lengthy periods and have lasting value. Sustaining organizations ensure that, all the way along the production chain, manufacturing processes are sustainable, the technology is the best possible from an environmental viewpoint and material and energy use is minimized. Where there is a choice of suppliers, they prefer to buy from those whose production processes are environmentally friendly.

> In 1998 Xerox introduced its first fully digitized copier, the Document Centre 265, more than 90 per cent remanufacturable and 97 per cent recyclable. The product had only about 200 parts, an order of magnitude less than its predecessor. Its sales have exceeded forecasts. According to *Fortune*, remanufacturing and waste reduction saved Xerox US$250 million in 1998.
>
> (P. Senge, in *Sloan Management Review*)[34]

An integral part of the life-cycle assessment is the reduction of packaging, the use of recyclable materials where packaging is necessary and the reuse of packaging and pallets where feasible. Staff at all levels are actively involved in finding innovative ways to improve the sustainability of throughput and innovations are widely diffused, communicated and recognized.

They also carefully consider the location of any new operations in terms of potential environmental impact; and they design the site to respect the natural values of the area, preferring to retain natural features and native vegetation where possible. New buildings maximize the use of natural rather than artificial lighting, use energy-efficient designs that make use of the sun's heat for warmth and natural materials such as rock and earth for cooling. 'Waste' water is purified to an appropriate level and recycled through the plant or used for maintaining the green environment.

A striking example of a major building project of this kind is the Olympic Village constructed for the Sydney Olympics 2000 by the partnership of Mirvac and Lend Lease: the Mirvac Lend Lease Village Consortium. This village, now a new Sydney suburb, consists of around 2,000 homes. The village was constructed on degraded land 15 km from the central business district (CBD). The village exemplifies a set of clearly formulated environmental principles aimed at renewing the local environment and increasing biodiversity in the area. Life-cycle assessments were also made of all materials before the major building material types were selected. All power for the village is created by photovoltaic technology, with excess power delivered to the local grid. The redesign of the site was carried out with participation of key interest groups, including environmentalists, and all site workers received environmental skills and diligence awareness training.[35]

Increasingly there are other examples of sustainable communities emerging – communities like Currumbin Eco Village in Australia that

The sustaining corporation • 213

are designed on sustainable principles – that share, collect and recycle water; that generate their electricity needs and that focus on building community partnerships and facilities.

The sustaining organization seeks partnerships with relevant 'green' groups, actively supports their involvement in assessing the firm's environmental performance and works collaboratively with them to develop improved environmental practices. It goes beyond compliance to develop and update a knowledge base relevant to its core production processes (for example, a register of chemical pollutants), to build general awareness of environmental issues within its work force and a commitment to progressive elimination of pollutants, product redesign for improved environmental impact and support for the 'dematerialization' of physical processes. It collaborates with an external 'green' group to conduct an externally verified environmental audit of its operations and publishes this as an integral part of its annual report and on its web page. This is an increasingly common practice in a number of the companies, as we have discussed in previous chapters (e.g. Shell, Interface, IAG, Westpac).

Frankel argues that there are four principles which companies must adopt to make genuine progress towards ecological sustainability.[36]

- *Towards zero waste*. Rather than reducing waste, every company must eliminate it entirely. One plant that has succeeded in doing this is the Nagoya plant of the Kirin Brewing Group in Japan, which reached zero emissions in 1997.[37] Examples of other major corporations committed to achieving zero emissions are Ogihara and Chichibu Cement in Japan and DuPont in the United States.
- *Whole system thinking*, which fosters the reinvention rather than redesign of industrial processes.
- *Look outward*, which means that companies have to go beyond cleaning up their own operations by helping smaller companies with fewer resources to put their houses in order. It also means working in concert with other companies to create symbiotic cycles of industrial ecology, that is, capitalizing on the notion that one company's waste is another's resource. And in addition it means creating alliances to capitalize on large-scale business opportunities in the greening process.
- *Remember sustainable development*. Businesses need to think more broadly than the ecological environment. As we have pointed out above, sustainable development involves social issues as well as

ecological ones. Because these issues are integral to the core strategies of the organization, they are not considered to be the sole responsibility of an environmental manager or a human resource manager. There may be an environmental manager and a human resource manager but they are regarded as technical experts who are there to provide the specialized input other senior executives need to implement sustainability strategies.

At any one time there will be a range of environmental initiatives being run on a project basis; all these will also have human resource implications. As a consequence, lateral co-ordination is at least as important as vertical.

What are the advantages for the firm of pursuing ecologically sustaining policies with such ardent commitment? We argue that, as the ecological crisis deepens and the third wave moves the values of society towards this ideal, it will be the bold but foolish organization that persists in environmentally destructive practices. As the conditions of the 'risk society'[38] intensify there will be increasing pressure on firms to be 'squeaky clean' environmentally if they are to continue to have a 'license to operate'.[39] But proactive policies in particular can prove a comparative advantage in the market place as consumers, investors and governments increasingly discriminate in favour of firms that are ethical in their approach to their people, their community and the natural world.

Nuon Energy is the second largest energy supplier in the Netherlands. Nuon employs 6,500 staff in its traditional divisions of water, gas and energy and 3,500 staff in its newer divisions responsible for green energy (wind and sun) and relations with other companies. Nuon's mission is to become a leading company in Europe, including a leading company in sustainable energy supply. Only 5–6 per cent of the energy it generates comes from wind and sun but the proportion is growing. Nuon's strategic long-term vision is based on the fact that eventually all energy must be supplied from renewable resources. Nuon is also working in partnership with NGOs in other parts of the less developed world such as Mali, the Sudan and Albania to develop their use of renewable energy sources.[40]

As in the social arena, we are also witnessing a trend to the development of more not-for-profit organizations devoted to environmental protection and renewal. One well known organization of this kind is Greenpeace, which operates globally and has had a powerful influence on international, national and enterprise-level environmental policies. Another that is having a significant impact on the corporate world and in raising community campaigns is the World Wide Fund for Nature. But there is a plethora of such organizations and we are confident that we shall see many more. In addition, a range of new jobs, such as 'environmental manager', 'sustainability manager' and 'corporate sustainability manager' are being established in organizations. Tricia Casswell, formerly executive director of RMIT University's Global Sustainability unit in Melbourne, Australia, has identified ninety-eight different kinds of environmental jobs in the private and public sectors – her own job is one example.[41]

The sustaining corporation is currently a visionary ideal – but it is one that we illustrate with partial case examples to show that there are firms moving towards the ideal. Its visionary nature raises the issue of how the transition can be managed for those corporations that wish to move in this direction. We refer the reader to Chapters 7, 8 and 9, where we deal with the process of managing change, particularly to our discussion in Chapters 7 and 8 of the need for both incremental and transformative change processes. The transition to the third wave represents a significant value shift. Therefore the core of the transformative process that will bring about third wave organizations has to be culture change. We deal here with some of the characteristics of culture change but refer the reader forward to Chapters 7 and 8, where culture change is dealt with in more detail.

Building strategy into the culture

Many standard texts on strategic management describe it as a process that is logical, rational and non-problematical. Empirical studies of strategic management show that in reality strategic management differs substantially from this model. Strategy is created in a political environment where stakeholders have differing and sometimes conflicting interests. Within the organization itself, executives are seldom in full agreement about an appropriate strategy and sometimes in active conflict. This is not surprising, because they face differing environments (for example, customers versus suppliers) and have differing career interests. There is, in fact, no single shared environment for the firm: there are a multitude of environments changing at different rates; there are too many factors to consider and there are legitimate differences of opinion about which are important signals of future trends. When we expand this confusing reality to the organization as a whole, we can conceive of the organization as a constellation of groups all perceiving differing environments, having differing interests and having close relationships with some groups but seldom or never relating to others.

In addition strategic planning is not only a rational process. Any attempt to define a future rouses strong emotions. People care about the future, as Mark Twain remarked, because it is where they will spend the rest of their lives. Strategic planning is an attempt to envisage a desirable future and to take action to bring that future into being. Even where the senior executive team reaches consensus on a strategic plan, there is no assurance that the plan will be implemented as conceived. It relies for its implementation on the actions of other members of the organization, all of whom have interests at stake. Large-scale strategic shifts necessarily involve transforming the established culture (or cultures) of the organization and integrating strategic reorientation and sustainability into the corporate culture itself.

> A shift from environmental management to environmental strategy requires a concurrent and supporting shift in organizational culture, structure, reward systems, and job responsibilities.
> (A. Hoffman, *Competitive Environmental Strategy*)[42]

But what exactly is corporate culture and why is it so important? Organizational culture is usually defined as 'the way we do business around here'. Organizational culture consists of the basic assumptions, values and norms, symbols, myths and 'wisdom' that define the collective approach to day-to-day decision making and action. Culture centres on the creation and continuity of meaning for organizational members. Much of it may be unreflective and unarticulated – it is the 'world taken for granted' – often more visible to visitors than to inmates. One of the most powerful ways to create organizational change is to confront, develop or remould the core cultural values of an organization so that people experience a profound change in their understanding and purpose and, as a result, act differently. Leaders play a major role in this because they can embody a new cultural profile in their speech and action and become catalysts for cultural change.

In their book *Blown to Bits* Evans and Wurster discuss the forces that are massively reorganizing global and local markets and challenging our understanding of what corporations are and how they should do business.[43] They emphasize that the leader's first task is to create a culture and the second task is to develop a strategy. They then search for a way to define the core identity of the corporation of the future. They conclude:

> Theorists have variously seen the corporation as a set of physical assets, a set of property rights, or a body of core competencies. Those can all be deconstructed. What *resists* deconstruction is the idea of the corporation as defined by its culture and its strategy. The corporation as *purposeful community*. And if all else fades, perhaps purposeful community becomes the essence of identity, of management, of leadership. In a world of impersonal, technical change, that is a refreshingly human thought.[44]

To move to the sustaining organization involves members of the organization at all levels internalizing the values of sustainability so that these values become a core theme in their work as a purposeful community. This does not mean that there will necessarily be unanimity about the solutions to be sought to emergent sustainability issues. However, it does mean the development over time of a strong and pervasive shared ideology. The members of the organization derive meaning from their ability to create useful goods and/or services that contribute to the community's quality of life and sustain the natural environment. In reality this is reflected in the fact that all members of the organization, as well as its subcontractors and suppliers, make day-to-day decisions on the basis of a deeply held, internalized commitment to sustainability values. This ideology does not negate the value of work in providing financially for the needs of the work force or running a profitable enterprise. But it does define financial returns to organizational members and shareholders as the appropriate exchange for providing something of real value to society and the environment.

Culture is the glue which holds the pieces of the jigsaw puzzle firmly together so it cannot fall apart. A positive culture blends human and ecological sustainability seamlessly.

Proactive leadership

Critical to this culture-building process is proactive leadership consciously developed and practised at all levels of the organization. Ideally this starts with a fully committed executive team which has reached agreement that sustainability is central to the firm's ongoing strategy or strategic reorientation. The executive team emphasizes creating a strong corporate identity around sustainability values and creates shared experiences and reward systems that reinforce the emerging values. Culture is not created by fiat; rather it grows organically from the experience of working together successfully on meaningful tasks. Leaders are the shapers of the corporate culture and they must embody the core cultural values of sustainability in their actions.

Culture change involves creating an ongoing drama in which the members of the organization are both actors and audience. It is a drama in which heroes and heroic groups emerge who forge new meaning for themselves and others and whose success is embodied in powerful stories and myths. Leaders become attractors and role models, inspiring others to move in the same direction, so multiplying the momentum of change. This surge of human energy and meaning making is the matrix from which the new culture arises, is invigorated and becomes a powerful shaper of the work-related behaviour of all organizational members. The process of continuing cultural innovation is an organizational endeavour to support and renew, rather than exploit and degrade, the world, the community and the planet. It is a process which restores a fuller meaning to human work than the accumulation of capital and material goods.

> I fully expect that we'll no longer be talking about economic,
> environmental and societal values as being distinctly different, but see them
> as integral and interlocking aspects of every business process and activity.
> (Paul Tebo, Vice-president for Safety,
> Health and the Environment, E. I. du Pont de Nemours)[45]

Conclusion

Corporations are the fundamental cells of the modern economy. If we are to transform our economy to make it sustainable and sustaining we must make significant changes in the way corporations operate. Corporations also control most of the resources of our global society; if we are to have effective leadership of the sustainability movement, then much of that leadership must come from the corporate sector. Building sustainable organizations requires a fundamental shift of mind set from traditional mainstream business thought and practice. In the future the corporation will remain profitable by becoming an active partner in the ongoing renewal of global society and of the earth's biosphere.

However, the path to creating the sustaining organization is not travelled quickly and easily. Having sketched the ultimate goal in this chapter, in the remaining three chapters we outline the incremental (Chapter 7) and transformational change strategies (Chapter 8) required to create sustaining corporations. Finally, in Chapter 9 we outline the change agent roles and leadership actions required in creating fully sustainable organizations.

Sustaining corporation

 Phase 6: the sustaining corporation

Human sustainability (HS6)

The organization accepts responsibility for contributing to the process of renewing and upgrading human knowledge and skills formation in the community and society generally and is a strong promoter of equal opportunity, workplace diversity and work–life balance as workplace principles. It adopts a strong and clearly defined corporate ethical position based on multiple stakeholder perspectives and seeks to exert influence on the key participants in the industry and in society in general to pursue human welfare, equitable and just social practices and fulfilment of human potential of all. People are seen as valuable in their own right.

Ecological sustainability (ES6)

The organization becomes an active promoter of ecological sustainability values and seeks to influence key participants in the industry and society in general. Environmental best practice is espoused and enacted because it is the responsible thing to do. The organization tries to assist society to be ecologically sustainable and uses its entire range of products and services to this end. The organization is prepared to use its influence to promote positive sustainability policies on the part of governments, the restructuring of markets and the development of community values to facilitate the emergence of a sustainable society. Nature is valued for its own sake.

Notes

1 D. Raths '100 best corporate citizens for 2006', *Business Ethics* magazine, spring 2006, 20 (1).

2 I. Lowe, *A Big Fix: Radical Solutions for Australia's Environmental Crisis*, Melbourne: Black/Schwartz Publishing, 2005, p. 109.

3 www.hondacorporate.com (accessed 6 February 2002).

4 KPMG, International Survey of Corporate Responsibility Reporting, KPMG Global Sustainability Services, 2005, p. 4.

5 R. Welford, *Hijacking Environmentalism: Corporate Responses to Sustainable Development*, London: Earthscan Publications, 1997, p. xi.

6 W. Fox, cited in J. Dryzek, *The Politics of the Earth: Environmental Discourses*, Oxford: Oxford University Press, 1997, p. 156; M. Fox, *The Reinvention of Work: A New Vision of Livelihood for our Time*, San Francisco: Harper, 1994.

7 R. Welford, 'Rediscovering the spiritual dimension of environmentalism', in R. Welford, *Hijacking Environmentalism: Corporate Responses to Sustainable Development*, London: Earthscan Publications, 1997, pp. 211–27; K. Wilber, *The Marriage of Sense and Soul: Integrating Science and Religion*, Melbourne: Hill of Content Publishing, 1998.

8 P. Senge, 'Innovating our way to the next industrial revolution', *Sloan Management Review*, 2001, winter, 2.

9 A. Hoffman, 'Climate change strategy: the business logic behind voluntary greenhouse gas reductions', *California Management Review*, 2005, 47 (3), 21.

10 G. J. I. Schrama, 'Sustainability banking at the Rabobank', in K. Green, P. Groenewegen and P. S. Hofman (eds) *Ahead of the Curve: Cases of Innovation in Environmental Management*, Dordrecht, Netherlands: Kluwer, 2001, pp. 77–91, p. 85.

11 Ibid.

12 R. E. Freeman, *Strategic Management: A Stakeholder Approach*, Boston, MA: Pitman, *c.* 1984; R. Mitchell, B. R. Agle and D. Wood, 'Toward a theory of stakeholder identification and salience: defining the principle of who and what really counts', *Academy of Management Review*, 1997, 22 (4), 853–86; M. Clarkson, 'A Risk-based Model of Stakeholder Theory', paper presented for the second Toronto Conference on Stakeholder Theory, Toronto: Centre for Corporate Social Performance and Ethics, University of Toronto, 1994; L. K. Trevino and G. R. Weaver, 'The stakeholder research tradition: converging theorists, not convergent theory', *Academy of Management Review*, 1999, 24 (2), 222–7; A. Factor, 'Barriers and Catalysts associated with Environmental Initiatives within Small and Medium-sized Enterprises', unpublished doctoral thesis proposal, Department of Organization and Management, Aarhus School of Business, Aarhus, Denmark, May 2000; D. Goldblatt (ed.) *The Stakeholding Society: Writings on Politics and Economics*, Oxford: Polity Press, 1999.

13 Factor, 'Barriers and catalysts', p. 7.

14 S. Hart and S. Sharma, 'Engaging fringe stakeholders for competitive imagination', *Academy of Management Executive*, 2004, 18 (1), 7–18.

15 C. Anderson, 'Values-based management', *Academy of Management Executive*, 1997, 11 (4), 25.
16 BHP Billiton, Sustainability Report, Socio-economic Case Study: Mozal, A model for integrating Sustainability into Resource Projects, 2005.
17 R. S. Kaplan and D. P. Norton, *The Balanced Scorecard: Translating Strategy into Action*, Boston, MA: Harvard Business School Press, 1996.
18 W. G. Wilson and D. R. Sasseville, *Sustaining Environmental Management Success: Best Business Practices from Industry Leaders*, New York: Wiley, 1999, pp. 208–13.
19 David Morgan, CEO, Westpac, 'Sustainable Prosperity: Confronting the Inconvenient Truths', address to Trans-Tasman Business Circle, 28 June 2006, p. 6.
20 C. Kaesuk Yoon, 'A taste for flowers helped beetles conquer the world', *New York Times*, Science Times section, 28 July 1998, C1.
21 For a comprehensive review of the concept of social capital and its implications for managers see P. S. Alder and S. W. Kwon, 'Social capital: prospects for a new concept', *Academy of Management Review*, 2002, 27 (1), 17–40.
22 Hobson Brown, Jr, President and CEO, Russell Reynolds, quoted in L. Prusack and D. Cohen, 'How to invest in social capital', *Harvard Business Review*, 2001, June, 93.
23 Personal observation and on-site interviews, D. Dunphy, 1995; B. Burnes, Case Study 1 'Oticon – the disorganized organization', in B. Burnes, *Managing Change: A Strategic Approach to Organizational Dynamics*, 3rd edn, London: *Financial Times*/Prentice-Hall, 2000, pp. 319–28.
24 Ibid., p. 327.
25 S. Sharma and M. Starik 'Stakeholders, the environment and society: multiple perspectives, emerging consensus', in S. Sharma and M. Starik, *Stakeholders, the Environment and Society*, Cheltenham: Edward Elgar, 2004, pp. 1–22, p. 7.
26 Extract from 'Our values' statement, Vivendi Universal website, www.vivendiuniversal.com/vu2/en/who-we-are.cfm (accessed 6 February 2002).
27 Corporate essay, 'Global alliance for the Twenty-first century', special advertising section, 'The next bottom line', *Business Week*, Asian edition, 3 May 1999, 45–96.
28 D. Wright, Patagonia: Leading Sustainability', case study, Brisbane: University of Queensland Business School, 2005.
29 L. Langeland, 'Cultivating the sustainable corporation', in M. Starik and S. Sharma (eds) *New Horizons in Research on Sustainable Organizations*, Sheffield: Greenleaf, 2005, pp. 146–165.
30 H. Tibbs, 'The technology strategy of the sustainable corporation', in D. Dunphy, J. Benveniste, A. Griffiths and P. Sutton (eds) *Sustainability:*

The Corporate Challenge of the Twenty-first Century, Sydney: Allen & Unwin, 2000, pp. 191–216.

31 From Hewlett-Packard, 'Commitment to the environment', Mount View CA: Hewlett-Packard, 1998, p. 1.

32 Ibid.

33 Ibid.

34 P. Senge, 'Innovating our way to the next industrial revolution', *Sloan Management Review*, 2001, winter, 2.

35 Case example 9, 'Lend Lease – the Olympic Village', in B. Hirsch and P. Sheldrake, *Inclusive Leadership: Rethinking the World of Business to generate the Dynamics of Lasting Success*, Melbourne: Information Australia, 2001, pp. 121–40. Note, however, that some environmentalists remain critical of remediation measures for the site: see S. Bader, *Global Spin*, Carlton North, Victoria, Australia: Scribe Publications, 2000.

36 C. Frankel, 'Into the fourth era', in *In Earth's Company: Business, Environment and the Challenge of Sustainability*, Canada: New Society Publishers, 1998, pp. 81–94.

37 M. Ota, 'Cutting edge: the zero emissions challenge', *Aichi Voice*, 1998, 9; www.pref.aichi.jp/voice/9_cutting-edge.html.

38 U. Beck, *The Risk Society: Towards a New Modernity*, London: Sage Publications, 1992.

39 J. Elkington, *Cannibals with Forks: The Triple Bottom Line of Twenty-first Century Business*, Oxford: Capstone, 1997.

40 From an interview by S. Benn with Hans Nooter, Human Resource Management, Nuon Energy, at Hardewijk, Netherlands, 7 February 2002.

41 'The greening of life', *Sydney Morning Herald*, weekend edition, 12–13 May 2001, section 8, 1, 'My career'.

42 A. Hoffman, *Competitive Environmental Strategy*, Washington DC: Island Press, 2000, p. 163.

43 P. Evans and T. S. Wurster, *Blown to Bits: How the New Economies of Information Transforms Strategy*, Boston, MA: Harvard Business School Press, 2000.

44 Ibid., p. 229.

45 A. Spencer-Cooke, 'Hero of zero', Environmental Leadership Award 2000, *Tomorrow*, November/December 2000, 10–16, p. 10.

Part IV
Pathways to sustainability: towards third wave corporations

7 The incremental path

Setting the scene

For a significant part of the twentieth century most managers used incremental change programmes to modify their organizations. Transformative change programmes were employed only in times of crisis, which were the exception rather than the rule. So the history of the development of systematic approaches to incremental change extends throughout the twentieth century into the twenty-first. As a result, we now have a comprehensive set of tools available to make incremental change and we know some of the key ingredients for successful change programmes of this kind.[1]

Early in the twentieth century, scientific management theories led to an emphasis on technically and operationally focused change. Later human relations theories dominated and the focus switched to an emphasis on changing the social systems of the organization through interventions such as supervisory training and motivational programmes. All these approaches advocated making relatively slow-paced change. They also tended to ignore technological issues. However, in the 1970s, incremental change theories began to address both social needs and technical efficiencies in a more balanced way. The dominant approaches became organization development (OD) and socio-technical systems (STS) theory. The STS approach developed in the United Kingdom and Scandinavia under the intellectual leadership of Trist and Emery, while they were working from the Tavistock Institute of Human Relations in London. The approach was widely adopted after the Second World War, particularly in Scandinavia and Australia, where it became strongly linked with the industrial democracy movement.[2]

The STS approach derived from general systems theory in the natural sciences and used open organic systems as its metaphor for organizations. The diagnostic model was socio-technical systems analysis, which is a detailed approach to analysing both the technical and social systems. The ideal organization was a representative democratic community composed of work teams, learning through participative action research. STS theory strongly influenced the empowerment movement in the United States, particularly through the work of Davis, Cherns, James Taylor and others at the University of California, Los Angeles, and of Lawler and others at the University of Southern California. It also continues to influence action research in a range of countries, particularly in the Netherlands. STS theory consistently advocated incremental change as a necessary condition of workforce involvement.[3]

While STS and OD theories of change were developing in Europe, North America and Australia, in Japan quality management techniques were adopted with enthusiasm. The Japanese combined the TQM emphasis on statistical controls, stemming from the work of Deming and others, with the participatory shopfloor practices of the earlier human relations movement. The human relations movement advocated employee participation in decision making and strongly emphasized social factors. By including employees in the quality improvement process Japanese managers harnessed employee knowledge and competencies to overcome variances from ideal quality standards. The human relations/OD, STS and TQM approaches to change have all strongly supported incremental rather than transformative changes. Incremental change appeared ideally suited to the operating environments of many organizations in the late 1960s, 1970s and into the early 1980s, particularly when it achieved a balanced emphasis on both technical and human factors.

This emerging movement for incremental change was led by self-proclaimed management heretics (like Emery and Trist) who saw their mission as overturning the prevailing management orthodoxies of the time. The paradigm espoused by the Organizational Renewal Movement heretics contrasted significantly with the dominant managerial ethos of the 1960s and 1970s. Their criticisms were directed at inefficiencies in bureaucratic organizations, but even more at the dehumanizing and exploitative effects of bureaucratic managerialism on the morale and satisfaction of the work force.[4] They advocated incremental change to shift organizations to be more effective in terms of the core business and more responsive to employee needs.

However, in the period from 1985 to 1999, under pressure from economic reforms, increasing globalization and international competition, many companies found that they were significantly out of alignment with their operating environment. For example, they found that their core technology was suddenly obsolete or that their major customer segment had shifted its preference to another type of product or service. In these circumstances, incremental changes were often insufficient to strategically reposition organizations. So in the late 1980s and the 1990s many organizations abandoned incremental change for radical, transformational change. Change of this kind is covered in detail in Chapter 8. Many organizations have moved into a period of mid-range change: that is, many managers are recognizing that their organizations need the flexibility to move between the two approaches in order to stay in alignment with market conditions. Some commentators have suggested that contemporary organizations need to be 'ambidextrous', that is, with the ability to manage both incremental and revolutionary approaches to change.[5]

Incremental versus transformational change

In this chapter we discuss those incremental change approaches that are characterized by participative management and collaborative forms of work that require basic operational change and work redesign. However, our overall approach is not that we should go back to these past approaches, but rather that they represent a part of our armory of change that needs to be utilized under the appropriate conditions. For instance, when some of these change techniques are combined with value-oriented programmes such as the Natural Step and Total Quality Environmental Management, powerful forces for sustainability change are unleashed in organizations.[6] In other words, the approach to change that we advocate is not about pursuing the 'one best way' but rather of identifying the appropriate strategy for the appropriate situation. However, when it comes to the study of the environment and organizations, Orsatto points out:

> The majority of literature on corporate environmental management assumes reformism as the guiding principle for organizational change.

> Incrementalism is the basic principle of the standards of
> environmental management systems such as the ISO 14000 series
> . . . These programs assume that through incremental improvements
> organizations would achieve eco-efficiency and, eventually, ecological
> sustainability.[7]

However, some advocates of sustainability question whether it can
be achieved by changing corporations incrementally. In their view,
incremental change is not enough: transformational changes are required
to achieve sustainability.[8] Hart and Milstein, in their prophetically
titled article 'Global sustainability and the creative destruction of
industries', argue that: 'the emerging challenge of global sustainability
is a catalyst for a new round of creative destruction that offers
unprecedented opportunities. Today's corporations can seize the
opportunity for sustainable development, but they must look beyond
continuous, incremental improvements.'[9] Building on the work of
Joseph Schumpeter, these authors view incremental change as simply
maintaining the *status quo*. Furthermore, they argue that at some point
in the future those organizations that have only changed incrementally
will fail because they did not 'change the fundamental manner, in which
they provide products, processes and services'.[10] In their view, the
operations of current businesses are so inimical to sustainability that
only radical change will create a sustainable world.

Other recent studies examine the relationship between forms of
organizational 'slack' and an organization's ability to respond to
sustainability challenges. These studies too question the drive to
efficiency characteristic of incremental change approaches and, in
particular, the emphasis on removal of forms of organizational slack.
These authors argue that research evidence points to the positive effects
of organizational slack for the development of innovative capabilities and
beneficial responsiveness. However, the more broadly held contrary view
leans toward reducing slack on the grounds that efficiency and leanness
are useful and functional for organizations. This may be the case for firms
situated in economic systems that, as a whole, are relatively stable. In
such circumstances the relative system stability allows incremental
change toward efficiencies derived from an increasingly lean resource
base. However, under conditions of system instability, the benefits of
efficiency may disappear and sustainability suffer, suggesting the need to
qualify past findings in light of broader system conditions.[11]

In other words, lean and efficient organizations have received much
attention and praise in recent years, but they may have a dark side that

has so far been overlooked. They may lack the capabilities needed to respond to large-scale, disruptive and unpredictable events, particularly those connected with sustainability issues, and incremental change programmes may only compound this problem. So what really works best, incremental or transformational change?

We want to make it clear that making change of any kind is difficult. As Beer and Nohria state:

> Despite some individual success, change remains difficult to pull off, and few companies manage the process as well as they like. Most of their initiatives – installing new technology, downsizing, restructuring or trying to change corporate cultures – have had low success rates. The brutal fact is that about 70 per cent of all change initiatives fail.[12]

However, there are circumstances where incremental change can effectively create new values, structures and processes that support the building of sustainable corporations. Our collective experience of consulting and research in organizations indicates that incremental change is often a viable means to achieve sustainability outcomes – this is clear from organizations we have already discussed in this book, organizations as diverse as Scandic (hotels), Interface (carpets), Rockcote (paints and coatings) and NAPCO (pastoral). In these organizations and in many others incremental change programmes have produced impressive results. The approach that we take in this and the next chapter is situational. We argue that managers should adopt the kind of change programme that suits the organization's specific situation. Significant gaps between corporate strategy and performance, or between a culture of Rejection and one of Strategic Proactivity, for instance, do require larger, more robust transformational changes. Smaller gaps, new strategic opportunities, more minor culture shifts, capability development or changes in the workforce skills mix, however, may be achieved through incremental or continuous change initiatives. As Abrahamson states:

> To change successfully, companies should stop changing all the time. Instead they should intersperse major change initiatives among carefully paced periods of smaller, organic change using processes I call tinkering and kludging. By doing so companies can manage overall change with an approach called dynamic stability.[13]

So arguments for transformational change are compelling in some circumstances, but unconvincing in identifying it as the sole means to achieving sustainability outcomes. We agree with O'Reilly and Tushman, who argue that organizations need to become ambidextrous.[14] For instance, if increasing evidence on climate change and other ecological systems changes are consistently ignored by organizations and governments, and action towards sustainability is not taken now, then the luxury of choice of type of change may disappear for many organizations[15] – full-on transformational change may be the only option for organizational survival. Most organizations today, however, as they face up to sustainability issues, will need to be ambidextrous; that is, be able to manage incremental and transformational simultaneously and/or sequentially.[16]

The change strategy employed to make an organization sustainable must be situational and connected with and driven by an organization's strategy. Without this, it becomes 'change for change's sake'.[17] Incremental changes are best suited to organizations that require minimal strategic realignment. Where organizations are already meeting many of the demands of key stakeholders for sustainable practices, incremental strategies are effective in keeping the organization aligned with incremental changes in stakeholder expectations. So this chapter focuses on incremental change showing the important role it can play in the development of the corporate capabilities, cultures and practices that lead to the creation of sustainable organizations.

What is incremental change?

Sometimes it helps to explain a concept by first defining what it is not. For our purposes, incremental change is not large-scale transformational or revolutionary change of the kind often associated with business process re-engineering, downsizing, corporate spin-offs, mergers/ acquisitions or strategic unbundling. Incremental change does not include radical changes in strategy, structure, capability or organizational realignment. Rather incremental change is planned and emergent, continuous and ongoing and for the most part impacts on the organization's day-to-day operational processes.[18] Incremental change includes changes in the way people work (job redesign; teamwork); changes to an organization's business unit processes (quality management; STS redesign); and changes in reward systems, information systems and technologies. As Stace and Dunphy note: 'corporate wide total quality management, service quality and team building programs are often a feature of this type of organization change. Leadership is primarily consultative in style.'[19] Furthermore incremental change can be used to generate new capabilities, for example, through multi-skilling or forming project teams or creating new values and modifying corporate culture (customer service, empowerment and leadership development programmes).

Westpac Bank is a highly successful Australia-based bank that offers general, commercial and industrial banking services as well as insurance and financial services. It has consistently been rated the No. 1 performing bank on the Dow Jones Sustainability Index since 2003.[20] Westpac has used incremental change strategies over the last decade to build its capabilities and reputation in corporate sustainability and responsibility. This approach was initially seen as an effective way to mitigate risk and repair consumer confidence in banks. Their approach has now grown into a comprehensive strategic programme for achieving corporate sustainability. As one executive stated: 'Achieving sustainability is a never-ending journey, the moment you think you are there is probably when you are in most trouble.'[21] The bank's success at pursuing its incremental sustainability change strategy can be attributed to a variety of factors:

- The development and incorporation of a values and goals statement that also elaborates on how the process of change should be managed and the integration of this into the mission and strategy of the organization.
- The creation of a culture of constant innovation, including corporate sustainability and responsibility initiatives (for example, the development of green products; reduction of the organization's greenhouse gas emissions.
- The development of a work force that takes initiatives both to shape the emerging business environment and to adapt rapidly and responsively to changing market, social and ecological conditions.[22]

We focus here on planned approaches to change of the kind described by Porras and Silvers:

> Organizational change is typically triggered by a relevant environmental shift, that once sensed by the organization, leads to an intentionally generated response. This intentional response is planned organizational change and consists of four identifiable, interrelated components (a) a change intervention that alters (b) key organizational target variables and that then impacts on (c) individual organizational members and then . . . [results] in (d) organizational outcomes.[23]

In designing incremental change programmes, managers are faced by a variety of choices and options. They could attempt to pursue sustainability initiatives by developing corporate-wide programmes – based for instance on empowerment or the Natural Step[24] – or they could buy off-the-shelf programmes of the kind provided by consulting companies or tailor them in-house, or they could seek to encourage more organic, bottom-up initiatives where changes are initiated and trialled in pilot programmes in different parts of the organization.

These choices reflect the complexity of issues that managers face in implementing change programmes. One of these issues relates to the scope of the programme. The implementation of corporate-wide programmes can have a significant impact in raising awareness throughout the organization and lead to a variety of consistent initiatives. However, the broad scope of such programmes can also dilute valuable energies and disperse scarce resources. The result can be loss of momentum. By contrast, pilot programmes can work spectacularly because resources are focused and the scope is limited. But they may not be subsequently diffused through the organization. Packaged change programmes offer organizations quick access to tools and methods for implementing change. After all, why reinvent the wheel? But they may not meet the needs of a particular organization and those in the organization can lose the opportunity to develop skills in change design.

There is no one recipe for successful change: the approach must be carefully chosen on the basis of an analysis of the situation and the availability of resources; so we suggest here some principles in designing incremental change programmes. First, where possible, organizations should look internally for change agents. The knowledge and capabilities need to be internalized so that organizational learning takes place and skills are retained in house so that they can be used for future change programmes. If external experts are required, the organization should leverage their knowledge and capabilities and transfer these to internal change agents. Second, as much of the change programme as possible should be designed internally. If 'packaged programmes' are used, they need to be modified to suit the organization's unique culture and operating conditions. Change agents need a deep understanding and awareness of the culture of the organization before imposing a set of solutions on those who work there. Finally, significant outcomes can be achieved through small interventions. Donella Meadows states:

> Folks who do systems analysis have a great belief in 'leverage points'. These are places within a complex system (a corporation, an economy, a living body, a city, an ecosystem) where a small shift in one thing can produce big changes in everything.[25]

Applying the phase model to incremental change

Up to this point, we have discussed the need for incremental change and how it can be a powerful means to mobilize an organization's resources to achieve greater sustainability outcomes. In Chapter 1 we outlined a model of the phases of corporate sustainability. This model identified six phases in corporate progression towards full sustainability. These are:

- Rejection.
- Non-responsiveness.
- Compliance and beyond.
- Efficiency.
- Strategic proactivity.
- The sustaining corporation.

These phases emphasize that there is an enormous difference in the readiness of organizations to move to sustainable practices. Some firms are highly advanced in terms of having sustainable human resource practices; others have scarcely given them a thought. The same is true in the area of ecological sustainability: some firms are actively working towards practices that sustain and renew the environment while others continue to exploit the environment. Because traditionally the two kinds of sustainability have rarely been seen as connected, there can also be a lack of conjunction between an organization's current position on one dimension and on the other. The ideal of a fully sustaining corporation is outlined in Figure 7.1: the sustainability change matrix. The figure combines the scales of the two dimensions in the phases of corporate sustainability in a matrix. In the upper left-hand quadrant we have those organizations with relatively few human and ecological sustainable practices, being actively rejecting, indifferent or simply minimally compliant with both human and ecological sustainability standards. The goal is to move corporations to the lower right-hand quadrant, which represents varying degrees of active involvement on the base of efficiency, strategic advantage or fully sustaining practices.

Figure 7.1 outlines the incremental changes that organizations could take in shifting from an unsustainable to a sustainable corporation position. These represent 'ideal type' incremental changes. We have not documented here all other possible incremental change scenarios; for instance, those organizations that have already made substantial progress on either ecological or human sustainability (quadrants 2 and 3) may also be able to take more evolutionary and incremental paths to sustainability. In the next section we outline the benefits of engaging in incremental approaches to sustainability change.

Figure 7.1 *The sustainability change matrix: incremental paths*
Source: Adapted from D. Dunphy, J. Benveniste, A. Griffiths and P. Sutton, *Sustainability: The Corporate Challenge for the Twenty-first Century*, Sydney: Allen & Unwin, 2000, p. 256.

Benefits of incremental change

There are positive benefits for organizations that implement incremental changes. This section outlines a number of them.

The development of small wins

Whether planned or emergent, incremental change strategies allow organizations to achieve what Weick describes as small wins:

> A small win is a concrete, complete, implemented outcome of moderate importance. By itself, one small win may seem unimportant. A series of wins at small but significant tasks, however, reveals a pattern that may attract allies, deter opponents and lower resistance to subsequent proposals. Small wins are controllable opportunities that produce visible results.[26]

This strategy allows support to be built for the changes being implemented.

Take, for example, the case of Panasonic Matsushita. Its incremental change approach was built on the 'small wins' model of establishing the change programme's credibility. Initially, its approach to sustainability started out as a series of informal meetings between a group of managers who believed that the organization could achieve savings by reducing waste and energy use. Within five years this informal approach had developed into a planned and structured approach to pollution prevention through recycling, energy efficiency and supplier choice. In the process, the company made significant cost savings as well as process and quality improvements. Having successfully achieved the first goal, it has now implemented an environmental management system to assess, manage and minimize the impact of their business operations on the environment.[27]

Many of the efficiency gains achieved by firms such as Scandic, Ikea and Fuji Xerox relied initially upon achieving straightforward cost efficiencies: 'picking the low-hanging fruit'. These easily gained benefits contributed to building momentum and became the basis upon which later successes were built.

The concept of small wins as a strategy can be applied to ecological efficiencies, process improvements and the development of broader cultural changes (see Figure 7.2). Research shows that, even when companies start out with a pro-innovation bias in attempting to introduce eco-innovations, differences emerge between companies based on the ability of the change agent to draw isolated and scattered innovations into a coherent, integrated programme.[28] Where organizations successfully make links between small wins, they create an atmosphere of learning by doing. This contributes to their ability to wind back entrenched institutional practices and creates a dynamic for deep values-driven change. Integrated small wins become a means to generate systemic sustainability changes. Doppelt and Meadows, writing on the subject of change for sustainability, note that effective change requires a comprehensive understanding of organizational systems.[29] Furthermore, this research also shows that in those organizations where small wins weren't integrated they became encapsulated by the existing norms, behaviours and cognitive values of the organizational members and were easily undermined by forces opposed to change. In these cases the eco-innovations simply withered away.[30]

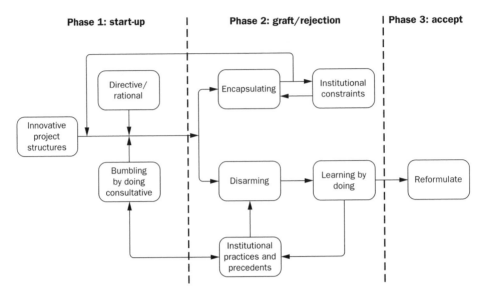

Figure 7.2 *Small wins*
Source: A. Griffiths and N. Haigh, 'Co-ordinating Small Wins as an Effective Mechanism for implementing Eco-innovations', best paper, Academy of Management conference 'Organizations and Natural Environment', New Orleans LA, 2004.

Capability development

Another benefit of many incremental change strategies is their ability to extend and develop new technical, operational and human capabilities within an organization. Technical capabilities are developed primarily through the introduction of new technologies and multi-skilling. Operational capabilities are developed by giving employees the technical skills and authority to make product and process improvements. Human capabilities are developed through up-skilling, knowledge development and empowerment.

We return to the case of Volvo, discussed in Chapter 6. Volvo's shift beyond compliance involved the development and integration of both ecological and human capabilities. This was achieved by the establishment of cross-functional project teams to work on corporate-wide key issues relating to sustainability; the implementation of broad communication and training programmes to educate employees and managers alike; and investment in R&D and technology. The performance of these programmes against sustainability goals was constantly reviewed, monitored and adjusted accordingly.[31]

Volvo executives were able to build on the existing corporate culture, which valued safety and social responsibility, by linking sustainability to their mission and values statements. Subsequently the programme focused on developing technical capabilities in product design, remanufacturing and recycling. These technical capabilities were embodied in the organization's standard operating and manufacturing procedures and policies. People capabilities were developed through team-working initiatives and the training of employees in sustainability awareness workshops, and were built on existing projects which had encouraged widespread employee participation.

Positive culture changes

Incremental change programmes are often focused on culture-building activities. In its steel operations One Steel implemented a pilot culture change programme to assist with the spin-off of its steel-making operations into a new business. It centred around story-telling and developing positive future images of where the steel-making business was heading. This was designed as a powerful yet incremental means to build on the existing corporate culture. Shanahan and Maria state that 'we know that story-telling – particularly when used in industries heavily entrenched in rigid mental models – can succeed in removing obstacles to strategy development and process improvement when other methods fail'.[32] Story-telling and other culture change programmes can open up lines of communication, create integration opportunities, commitment to new values and personal empowerment.[33] In *Dancing with the Tiger* Nattrass and Altomare highlight the importance of stories for creating and generating values change. 'Stories help us make sense out of our experience.'[34] They are an important component of values and culture change in an incremental approach.

Particular organizational cultures influence the uptake of innovative practices in different ways. Jones *et al.* found that corporate cultures with a 'human relations orientation' demonstrated higher readiness for change when it came to the implementation of a new information technology system. This was in direct contrast to those organizations that reported hierarchical command-and-control-style cultures. Furthermore, those organizations that had developed reshaping capabilities – that is, change competences – also showed greater readiness for change and higher use of the IT systems once they had been implemented.[35] Incremental changes that build positive culture and values can enhance an organization's readiness for change and acceptance of new practices. This was also the case at Scandic corporation, highlighted in Chapter 4. The successful redefinition of corporate values to 'profound caring' and the subsequent expression of this in greater stakeholder involvement and support depended on prior customer-orientated values.

Furthermore, there is a growing awareness of the importance of the understanding of subcultures within organizations and how these subcultures in turn understand issues associated with corporate sustainability. Recent research indicates that different groups across organizations and across levels within an organization may share similar values. although this research is in an early phase, it shows that these values strongly overlap with understanding of corporate sustainability. Figure 7.3 highlights the direct relationship between the organization's overall culture/values score – which is primarily bureaucratic and its understanding of corporate sustainability – which is dominated by an economic understanding. Furthermore, this leading research found that when this overall culture profile was broken down it resulted in the emergence of five distinct organizational 'subcultures'. Each of these subcultures corresponded with an almost identical plotting of understandings of corporate sustainability. One of the key implications of this path-breaking research is that, when it comes to incremental values-driven change, an understanding of a culture and the subcultures with an organization may be vital to tailoring effective incremental change processes to achieve greater sustainability outcomes and wider acceptance.[36]

Efficiency improvements

Incremental changes when implemented successfully can lead to improvements in operational performance. The drive towards eco-efficiency at Sony, for instance, has brought about improvements such as a 50 per cent improvement in the ratio of recycled parts and materials, a 50 per cent reduction in dismantling time and a 50 per cent reduction in the use of styrene foam.[37] These results came from implementing environmental management systems in manufacturing operations and the design of products. Operational efficiencies are not limited to changes in technical production systems. For instance, in a study of automobile manufacturing assembly plants, MacDuffie found

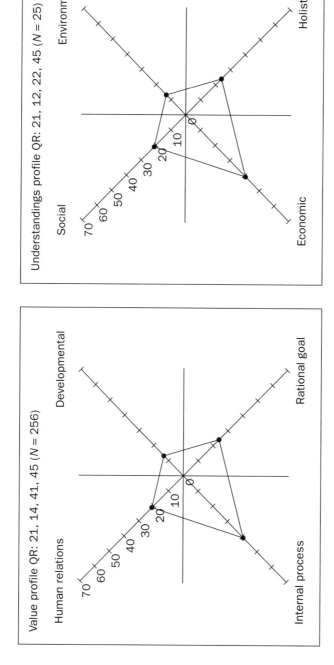

Figure 7.3 *Culture and corporate sustainability understanding profile for a transport company*

Source: M. Linnenlucke (2006).

that bundles of innovative HR policies – from selection, through multi-skilling, to job redesign and the introduction of teams – improved overall organizational performance. Furthermore, companies in which these bundles of HR practices were linked with the creation of flexible production systems outperformed traditional organizations where this link was missing.[38] Similarly, a study of steel finishing lines in the United States found that those organizations that used innovative work practices, including incentive pay, teams, flexible work arrangements, training and offering employment security, demonstrated higher levels of productivity than those organizations based on more traditional approaches.[39] These large empirical studies add weight to the thirty years of case studies, anecdotal evidence and broad industry surveys which have shown the benefits of such practices in creating high-performance organizations.[40]

Rockcote: the Nerang Design Centre

Rockcote is a small privately owned company that specializes in the generation of paints and architectural coatings for private and commercial use. Its 2005 design centre at Nerang, on the 'Gold Coast' in Australia, highlights the links between eco-efficiency improvements and human factors in establishing and making a creative, green design centre function. The Nerang Design Centre has quickly become an icon for green design in a commercial context. It has been created to exist in harmony with natural systems in order to optimize energy efficiency, water consumption, livability and profitability. The entire site is environmentally sustainable, the first of its kind in Australia.[41] The view taken by CEO Bob Cameron during the design process was 'it doesn't cost any more to do something properly in the first place'. All rainwater is collected in rain tanks for human consumption. Waste from toilets and sinks is treated on site through a series of ponds, aquatic plants and fish, then recycled using no fossil fuels. The building itself has been heavily insulated with clay and natural fibres, is situated on the site in such a way as to capture enough breeze and sunlight to render an air-conditioning system unnecessary, and utilizes natural light and ventilation to increase staff productivity. New technology has been implemented to sense the levels of natural light and brighten or dim the internal lights accordingly. Organic waste from the staff lunch room is composted on site. After hours, the showroom is made available free of charge for community functions, and the car park converts into a tennis court. The site is connected to mains water only to satisfy fire regulations, and more recently a solar power system has been implemented, enabling Rockcote to sell power back to the grid.[42] The entire design and operation of the Nerang Design Centre are a series of eco-innovations, all brought together to create an entirely sustainable development 'cutting edge, if not in the world, then certainly in Australia'.[43] The result is a commercial development operating 80 per cent cheaper than comparable traditional developments with an environment conducive to greater staff productivity and creativity.[44] It is an example of what can be achieved through incremental change that encourages the full participation of staff in all aspects of planning and execution.

New organizational structures

Incremental change strategies can be used to generate new organizational structures, systems and reporting relationships while maintaining the online operational capacity of the organization. For instance, STS redesigns which result in what are now known as 'high-performance work organizations' have generated a sophisticated methodology for the implementation and evaluation of team-based organizations. These new organizations have flatter reporting structures; are reliant upon the devolution of responsibility and autonomy; have shifted from control to commitment-based systems and changed the way that production is organized. Creating high-performance work organizations can take years, but many organizations in Europe, the United States and Australia have benefited from the use of such team-based approaches to change. They represent powerful successful models which can be emulated. Citing the work of Ostroff and Smith, Stace and Dunphy note that the concepts of team-based organizations can be used to enhance new organizational structures such as networks. These organizations demonstrate the following characteristics:[45]

- They organize around processes by linking work flows and relying on teams.[46]
- They keep hierarchies flat and remove the temptation to build control-oriented management systems.
- They assign ownership of processes and performance to teams.
- They link performance with customer satisfaction.
- They combine managerial and non-managerial activities to encourage self-management.
- They link customers and suppliers with teams.
- They focus on developing trust and competences.

Development of change competences

Incremental change programmes are an excellent vehicle to develop change agent skills and the change competences of managers and employees. For example, incremental change provides environmental managers not only with the technical and process skills required for further change but also the opportunity to develop important skills needed for building and maintaining coalitions, designing educational programmes, extending leadership skills for culture change and negotiating with community representatives.[47] Daily and Huang argue that successful EMS implementation requires cultural changes.[48] Change agents can use opportunities around incremental change to create cultures which empower employees as well as implementing team-working initiatives which support sustainability.

For example, Hewlett-Packard used the opportunity of its engagement with Corporate Social Responsibility to develop, build and extend its HR competences. As a direct result of harnessing diversity and unleashing the potential of its employees, HP has achieved remarkable success in its corporate sustainability programmes.

Benefits of incremental change

- *Development of small wins*. Small successes can be used to overcome areas of resistance and develop a powerful force for change.
- *Capability development*. Incremental changes can be used to develop human and technical competences.
- *Positive culture change*. Incremental change can modify values and build commitment through employee involvement and participation.
- *Efficiency improvements* can be generated as a consequence of making process improvements, changes to product or work design.
- Creation of *new organizational structures* based on teams, virtual teams and improvements in reporting systems and feedback loops.
- Development of *change competences*.

Potential pitfalls of incremental change

The first major pitfall to threaten organizations that are changing incrementally is misfit: moving out of alignment with the firm's dynamic market environment. To avoid this, organizations need constantly to monitor and evaluate their current environments and develop competences to anticipate future trends. Without such capabilities they can become vulnerable to what Strebel refers to as 'breakpoints': significant events that face organizations with a major environmental discontinuity such as loss of a major market or a new technology that makes the existing technology obsolete.[49] Confronted with a crisis of this kind, the advocacy of incremental changes is usually a form of organizational complacency and dysfunctionality. When organizations experience turbulent and transformed conditions, incremental changes will fail to realign them with the new environments. Under these conditions we advocate the use of transformational change strategies instead.

The gradualism of incremental changes means that they are susceptible to regression and abandonment, particularly if there is no clear link between the change programme and performance. Where success is not clearly defined, senior managers may withdraw their support from incremental changes and shift priorities for resources to other areas of organizational activity. Incremental changes do not usually occur in all parts of the organization at the same time or at the same pace. However, to attract continued managerial support, they must show significant performance improvements and clearly contribute to business results. Most of the cases that we have presented in this book demonstrate positive examples of successful change. However, not all cases have happy endings. In one energy company that we are familiar with the change agent responsible for implementing sustainability programmes within the organization found that her time was spread too thinly across a range of projects. Innovations that she had started foundered as she switched her attention to other projects. The lack of resources meant that she was unable to establish clear performance improvements beyond some compliance activities. As a result, momentum was lost and the change programme petered out.

Employee cynicism over the 'latest management fad' can be fatal to incremental change programmes. Employees and managers alike 'batten down the hatches' when senior executives launch the organization into the next alphabetically listed change programme. Abrahamson refers to 'permafrost' organizations[50] where change-fatigued middle managers block and actively resist initiatives from both below and above. Under these conditions, incremental change stands a significant chance of failure, disappearing like water into sand. A manufacturing organization that one of us researched, Bendix Mintex, had been through the 'alphabet soup' of change programmes. After many false starts it finally settled on a team-based approach to change. However, before this could succeed it needed to overcome employee cynicism about seeing the approach as just 'the latest fad'. It succeeded in overcoming the cynicism by including key opinion makers in the change process from redesign to implementation. Furthermore, it actively sought and encouraged employee suggestions on how the redesigned organization should work. By the time it began to implement the new redesign it had achieved a groundswell of support from the work force, who wanted to see their own ideas put into practice. It became a successful team-based organization.[51] Table 7.1 outlines major threats to the success of incremental change programmes and how these can be overcome. Table 7.1 outlines some issues specifically relating to incremental change. We have integrated some of Bob Doppelt's sustainability blunders and potential change solutions to dealing with these limitations of incremental change.

Table 7.1 *Overcoming limitations of incremental change*

Major issues	Action strategy
Lack of fit with external environment	Constant monitoring of the external environment of the firm and a preparedness to engage in transformational change if necessary
Decreasing managerial support for change programme	Demonstrate and promote performance improvements. Develop 'small wins' approach, market success in order to win management support
Change faddism	Maintain programme consistency and link the programme to overall corporate strategies and values statements
Lack of a clear vision and programme objectives	Outline clear goals and priorities – provide clear support and encouragement for small wins that align with these goals
Lack of learning mechanisms	Development of teams and processes whereby issues around incremental change success and failure can be drawn upon

Source: B. Doppelt, 'The seven sustainability blunders', *System Thinker*, June–July 2003, p. 3.

Major issues in the movement between phases

Moving from non-responsiveness to compliance

The organizations in most need of change are those in the rejection and non-responsiveness phases. In our view the movement from rejection (Phase 1) to compliance (Phase 2) is a transformational change of the kind we deal with in Chapter 8. So in this section we concentrate on the movement from non-responsiveness to compliance (Phase 2 to Phase 3). Non-responsive organizations tend to disregard the impact of their actions on the natural environment, the communities in which they are located and the value of their human capital. These corporations are economically, socially and ecologically blind or blinkered. In some cases, traditional values and a focus on operational and cost issues act as blinkers, resulting in a narrow view of what constitutes the firm's environment. Generally, business activities in these firms are concerned primarily with short-term profits to the detriment of broader societal and environmental responsibilities. This may be across all the organization's activities or in particular areas. For example, some corporations don't apply the same 'home base' standards to their activities in other parts of the world, particularly Third World regions and countries. For example, Esmeralda Explorations was the owner of the Baia Mare Aurul gold mine. When a tailings dam burst, spilling ninety-five tonnes of cyanide into the environment, it denied responsibility, claiming that there was no connection between the spill and the poisoning of the Lapus and Somes rivers in Romania and the Tisza in Hungary.[52] One doubts whether it would have made the same arguments in its home country. More recently Anvil Mining has been accused of assisting government forces in the Democratic Republic of Congo massacre villagers who were disrupting activities in the area of the company's mining operations. The company issued a press release denying any involvement. An independent report by the United Nations had found that the company had lent vehicles, drivers and logistical support to local troops and had paid local troops.[53] This issue was still to play out, with the company maintaining that it had done nothing wrong. Obviously, from these cases, significant challenges to the right to operate lie ahead for companies involved in such activities.

Non-responsive corporations are characterized by a blatant disregard for legislative and social standards. They may be willing to dump waste, fell old-growth forests, engage in poor OH&S standards and hide facts from the public about the damaging nature of their activities and/or products.

However, there are many examples of organizations, which once acted in this way, abandoning these approaches and supporting significant sustainability initiatives. Given the willingness of the board, CEO, senior managers and major financial investors, these organizations can make the shift from non-responsiveness to compliance using incremental change strategies. How is this to be achieved?

- Where there is organizational reluctance to initiate change, external pressure can be brought to bear on the organization through public protests, court action and third-party scrutiny or increasingly through pressure from investor funds. For instance, the Carbon Disclosure Project assesses the performance of companies on climate change issues and provides information to 155 investors with assets of US$21 trillion.[54] Increasingly investors are avoiding non-sustainable companies.
- By ensuring that someone with authority in the organization takes charge of the change process. Non-compliance can have major effects on the profitability, risk liability and reputation of the corporation. Consequently the change agent responsible for the shift needs to be a senior manager who reports direct to the CEO and has the power and authority to implement the changes. This should be someone with credibility and integrity who is respected throughout the organization.
- By making a comprehensive evaluation of legislative and commercial obligations. The survey should cover legislative requirement areas such as pollution, waste and licensing, mining and logging, and OH&S and other workplace codes. Similarly, the organization needs to develop an understanding of its insurance risks, potential liabilities and obligations to bodies such as securities commissions. Some international agencies refuse to lend capital for development projects in Third World countries if the corporations involved cannot demonstrate that they are attempting to build local capacity and meet sustainability expectations.
- By undertaking a review of existing operations to see whether and where they fail to comply with the legislative requirements. Areas requiring immediate action are then targeted and resources allocated. It may be necessary to design and run training programmes and management awareness sessions, to institute searches for new technologies and to establish measurement and reporting systems. In some cases, decisions may be made to disengage the company from activities that involve future risks or are not cost-effective to operate.
- By using the human resources system to link management performance with these new goals in order to ensure that programmatic

changes, such as OH&S initiatives, are accurately monitored and measured. Time lines and specified performance goals are set for the changes to be implemented. This phase requires standard project management skills. Managerial remuneration may also be linked with sustainability performance as a means of bootstrapping the organization's performance.

- By putting feedback loops in place in critical compliance areas to ensure that compliance is monitored and managers are rewarded according to their performance against these standards.
- By using external auditing bodies to review and monitor corporate progress against plans. This may also involve the use of international agencies, such as the International Standards Organization and its ISO 14000 series, as a basis for environmental management systems. A summary of moving from non-responsiveness to compliance is provided in the box.[55]

Pathways from non-responsiveness to compliance

- Appoint a senior manager with authority and reputation to implement the change process.
- Undertake an evaluation of the key legislative requirements.
- Review existing operations and identify areas for immediate attention.
- Align programmatic changes to goals.
- Create feedback loops in critical compliance areas.
- Use auditing bodies to assess compliance.

This approach to incremental change is unusual because it is directive in character. Transformational strategies are more often associated with a directive approach to change initiated by senior executives. However, in ensuring compliance, significant responsibility for shifting the organization and its operations lies with senior management, who must institute and support clearly defined standards and rules. While there is a directive element in this change process, this does not exclude employee participation in making compliance-related procedures succeed. The accumulating research evidence demonstrates that when employees are engaged on sustainability issues they make significant and valuable contributions to the development of eco-innovations.[56] An example of this comes from Interface, the carpet company, which has used incremental change processes and employee involvement to move a company whose products depended almost entirely on petroleum products. Its stylish Proscenium Collection uses a hybrid of polylactic acid (PLA) and nylon fibre. PLA is a bio-based, renewable resource made from maize and other plant materials. The starch portion of these non-food-grade agricultural products is converted to sugar and fermented to produce lactic acid. This is processed and polymerized to produce PLA, using 20–50 per cent less fossil fuel resources than traditional hydrocarbon resins. This means less greenhouse gases produced and also that the PLA can be naturally recycled.

Compliance with sustainable efficiency

For many corporations the incremental shift from compliance to efficiency is a natural extension of the capabilities, knowledge and practices developed in the earlier phase. For instance, compliance monitoring systems – particularly attempts to reduce emissions – often result in organizations also implementing process improvements and installing new technologies that enable the organization to move beyond compliance. Similarly, we find that organizations investing in compliance activities also start to invest in resources, specialist knowledge and skills (developing environmental managers, shifting from a narrow personnel focus to a broader HRM focus) and new technologies (monitoring systems; human resource information systems). For instance, at this stage there is usually a movement from personnel management to human resource management. Such a transition involves a shift in focus away from issues such as pay scales and legislative compliance activities towards the development of a more strategically oriented HR function that contributes to gaining competitive advantage.

What are the incremental steps involved in shifting organizations from compliance to efficiency?

- Efficiency programmes often start on the periphery of an organization as innovative line managers use their business units to experiment with such practices as job redesign, teamwork or reorganization of the supply chain. This often occurs in problem plants – the poor performers – and is part of a push to improve performance. Sometimes, however, efficiency programmes may be initiated by a senior manager or CEO who develops a particular commitment to sustainability, inspired by programmes such as the Natural Step. For instance, Interface's Australian operations went from being the 'worst performer' to being their No. 1 performing plant out of twenty-seven plants scattered around the world, largely because of the CEO's personal enthusiasm for sustainability.

- Learning from the pilot experiments is normally brought together and evaluated. Successes and failures are talked about and initiatives extended. Managers who lead the changes in these business units walk-the-talk. Their actions and commitment are matched by their willingness to utilize the knowledge of employees, question current organizational orthodoxies and push responsibility down the line. Robert Eckert, CEO of Mattel, attributes the company's turnaround, in part, to a 'walk-the-talk' approach that encouraged employee empowerment and contributed to human capital development.[57]

- In both HR and ecological areas, incremental change results in an increased emphasis on capability development. Typical initiatives include education programmes, cross-sectional problem-solving teams, reviews of barriers and enablers, and willingness to try new ideas and suggestions. Meanwhile successes are monitored in both a tangible form (costs; waste; quality) and in an intangible form (stories; shifts in culture and values). These shifts often become part of the organization's folklore and help employees develop a 'can do' attitude.

- We often notice that there is a point where the confidence-building activities, the devolution of authority, the education programmes and capability development all begin to crystallize. This becomes a critical leverage point. At this time there is the opportunity to shift the programme from a series of isolated small wins and grow more independent support for organization-wide change. It is important to seize the opportunity and provide the resources needed to significantly expand the programme.

When this critical mass for change is harnessed the programme develops its own momentum: for instance, efficiency gains are diffused to other parts of the organization. Problem areas outside the boundary of the business unit, such as product design and supply chains, now become open to influence and change. After the economic and other benefits of the efficiency changes have been demonstrated the programme is championed by senior management and extended throughout the organization. As this happens it is useful to dramatize and celebrate successes and reward key contributors to the change programmes. These steps are summarized in the box on the next page.

Steps in moving from compliance to sustainable efficiency

- Look for efficiency opportunities at the periphery of the organization or in poorly performing plants.
- Collate pilot projects' experiences and evaluate.
- Increase capability development.
- Monitor success and incorporate success stories into organizational folklore.
- Identify leverage points and generate critical mass support.
- Look for opportunities to create programme momentum.
- Identify and work on problem areas.
- Extend the programme with management support.

Efficiency to strategic proactivity

With each additional incremental step, organizations can build increasing depth of technical and human capabilities. We also see changes in the organization's culture, such as increasing employee commitment, and more indicators of its movement towards high-performance activities. There is often also a direct attempt to increase the diffusion of sustainability practices to suppliers and customers. For instance, in the HR area there is usually active recruitment and more retention of highly skilled people with strong sustainability values; challenging executive development programmes are developed and delivered and new opportunities created for exciting and meaningful careers (as has been seen in the HP and Rockcote cases). In the ecological area we see the emergence of strategic alliances with suppliers and customers and active engagement with community groups in the establishment of new products and services. This is exemplified by Scandic hotels, which promotes on its website the characteristics that suppliers should aspire to in order to help Scandic deliver on its own value and sustainability commitments.

Our case study analysis indicates that the following characteristics assist in shifting a firm from efficiency to strategy by incremental processes:

- Senior-level recognition that the efficiency gains achieved through value adding, and the capabilities developed along the way, are sufficiently valuable to be further integrated into the core strategic activities of the organization. For instance at BP Sir John Browne has played an integral role in setting targets and values for sustainability and linking them to BP's core business strategies; Chad Holliday, CEO, has played a similar role at Du Pont and Bill Ford as CEO and chairman at Ford Motor Company.

- The diffusion of strategic goals for sustainability to all key business units and managers within the organization. Along with that, responsibility for the attainment of sustainability goals is integrated into management reward and performance systems. For example, at Queensland Rail, sustainability was accepted as one of the five key strategic goals of the organization. Consequently, management performance and metric systems were changed to incorporate the attainment of corporate sustainability.
- Allocation of significant corporate resources into key areas such as research and development, knowledge management, alliance formation, industry networking and social partnerships. Toyota and Honda have both invested significantly in research and development pertaining to fuel cells, hybrid technologies and lightweight materials. Both these organizations are recognized as having distinct advantages over their US competitors in the 'greening of the automobile'.[58]
- Systematic exploration of opportunities for strategic alliances. However, by this time, suppliers are accountable for the impact of their products and processes on sustainability outcomes. Training and resources are provided to those willing to change.
- Accreditation systems such as EMS, TQEM, design for environment, teamwork, communities of practice and networking become common features of organizational life. Operational and efficiency gains are constantly improved upon and linked with strategic objectives.
- Finally, corporate strategies are constantly revisited in light of the performance of products and services; new directions are initiated; there is openness to third-party auditing and systematic assessment of the impact of the organization on communities. Shell's 2005 Sustainability Report, with its self-criticisms, and Interface's commitment to third-party auditing of its eco-products testify to the increasing importance of scrutiny of an organization's sustainability claims and its link with management strategy.

These steps are summarized in the box on page 252.

Steps in moving from efficiency to strategic proactivity

- Senior-level support built on the gains made in the efficiency stage.
- Diffusion of strategic goals relating to sustainability to all parts of the organization.
- Allocation of corporate resources to key areas.
- Identification of strategic alliances and other emerging opportunities.
- Use of accreditation programmes.
- Strategies revised in light of performance.

Strategic proactivity to the sustaining corporation

Incremental change can also facilitate the shift from strategic sustainability to the sustaining corporation phase. We view these changes as cumulative. In becoming sustaining corporations, organizations do not abandon the strategic approach or the capabilities that they have acquired and built as they moved through prior phases. Rather, the shift from strategic sustainability to the sustaining corporation requires an expansion and modification of the value base of the organization. In particular, we identify three key changes:

- Change programmes that focus on shifting the behaviours and values of organizational members. These are designed to produce extensive culture change. For instance, employees may be rewarded for undertaking community projects or taking an organizational sabbatical working on ecological issues. For example, since 1984 Patagonia, a successful manufacturer of outdoor equipment, has committed 10 per cent of its annual profits to grass-roots environmental groups and has adopted the following mission statement: 'Patagonia exists as a business to improve and implement solutions to environmental issues.' 'As an expression of its values-based culture Patagonia runs an internship programme for employees whereby they can work, fully paid, for up to two months in a non-profit environmental group of their choosing. Patagonia executives see these types of programmes as falling under the banner of their strategy – 'It's the right thing to do.'[59]
- The use of external parties to monitor, evaluate and encourage future performance: while not essential, this helps create momentum for further change. Third parties can also be used to challenge prevailing assumptions and organizational complacency. More important, the sustaining organization will start to challenge others within its industry

or supply chain to implement a broad sustainability agenda. For instance, Rockcote encourages and helps other organizations within its own geographical proximity engage in eco-initiatives. It has aligned itself with other eco-friendly companies to share resources and information and practical sustainability know-how. This is seen by all companies involved as a practical way of sharing information, learning by doing and removing the need for costly consultants.[60] As Bob Cameron, CEO of Rockcote, states, 'it would have taken us ages to figure out solutions to some of our waste water treatment issues . . . but when I saw what the others had done and saw the information that they compiled, it all made sense on how we should do it'.[61]

- A focus on design for environment, product and service innovation and the education of consumers and supply chain members on the role that they can play in creating viable alternative business models for sustainability and a sustainable society. Rockcote's Nerang Design Centre for example exposes visiting customers experientially to high-quality eco-design and eco-products – the centre itself is a visible demonstration of the economic, ecological and human value of moving to sustainability.

These steps are summarized in the box.

Steps in moving from strategic proactivity to the sustaining corporation

- Build on previous capabilities from efficiency and strategic stages.
- Focus on shifting behaviours and values to create large-scale cultural change.
- Use external parties to drive and challenge performance.
- Invest in innovation in product and process redesign and consumer education.
- Diffuse sustaining practices to others in the supply chain and other organizations interested in benchmarking.

Steps involved in incremental change

In the previous sections of this chapter we outlined some of the specific issues that organizations face when moving incrementally between the phases identified in Figure 7.1. In this section we round off this chapter by identifying eight generic steps involved in creating sustainable organizations through the use of incremental change strategies:

Step 1: begin with future workshops/search conferences. The incremental changes discussed in this chapter focus primarily on operational issues (such as product, process and people changes) and take place in strategic business units. However, starting change programmes at this level does not preclude having a vision or strategic direction. The cases of Scandic, Ikea and Patagonia all point to the importance of having a clear vision and strategic goals to move the organization or specific units forward. Future workshops and search conferences are tools that can be used to generate discussion, participation and commitment to the developing vision for sustainability and developing a plan for realizing the vision. They are also useful for identifying problem areas and potential strategic opportunities. Such events also act as leverage points to motivate and harness employee energy to the change.

Step 2: assess the organization's current position in relation to sustainability. This step addresses the questions: Where is the business unit currently in relation to sustainability practices? What are the barriers and enablers for making sustainability work? What influence will the existing corporate or unit culture have in facilitating or blocking sustainability initiatives? What are the activities that will need to be undertaken in order to shift the business unit from its present position to that outlined in the search conference? In some cases, such as Shell, assessing the current position also involves opening up the organization to external stakeholder evaluation and criticism. This stage also involves developing the business case for committing resources to sustainability.[62]

Step 3: Evaluate the type of change programme needed. This stage addresses the issue of the approach to be taken. Will the changes introduced be programmatic? That is, will the change programme seek coverage rather than depth – using change tools such as education programmes, the Natural Step workshops or competence training, or will the change approach encourage the emergence of organic innovations within identified business units? The choices made here will affect the types of change strategies used, on resource needs and expectations for performance. On the whole, we advocate progressing through organic innovations that are piloted and then diffused through a more programmatic approach, although the type of change programme needed may differ for different countries and potentially for different organizational subcultures. The multinational bank ING Group controls every aspect of its operations in the Netherlands through an environmental management system. This is more difficult in some countries; policies on investment concerning life sciences, coal energy and fur, for instance, are each considered separately.

Step 4: identify change agents. We shall comment in more detail on change agents in Chapter 9. However, change agents should be enthusiastic, knowledgeable about business processes and engender confidence and optimism. Furthermore, a team of change agents playing different facilitative, technical and coalition-building roles can have more impact than one change agent acting alone. For instance, at one manufacturing organization the implementation of world-class manufacturing involved the formation of a change unit in which a variety of roles were played. The role of the senior executive leading the team was that of the strategist/political operator. It was his role to garner senior support and protect the change programme in its infancy. The operations manager played a task-focused role: he designed and implemented the change programme. His activities were directive and he was responsible for maintaining the momentum of change. His directive style of leadership was complemented by the change facilitator, who concentrated on the social relations side of the change. The change facilitator was assisted by a shopfloor employee who was a key opinion maker. The change unit was coached by an external consultant who also played an important role in gathering information and providing a template for action and training. These roles were co-ordinated and influential in creating a successful multi-skilled unit that turned a brownfield manufacturing site into one that was competitive and world-class.

Step 5: pilot new practices and innovations. In incremental change programmes there is usually time to pilot test proposed changes. This allows competence deficiencies and operational problems to be identified and then addressed, rather like debugging a software program before its widespread adoption. Once the effectiveness of pilot programmes has been established, they can be used to build broader support throughout the organization. Pilot programmes are also an ideal way to test the appropriateness of the tools, and redesign techniques and forms of participation that will be used in the subsequent full-scale incremental change programme. They are also useful in estimating the resourcing that will be needed when the programme expands.

Step 6: harness further resources. When pilot programmes have been shown to be effective, diffusion of the changes requires access to further resources: time, money, people and management support. It is often best to start where people can readily be engaged and short-term wins can be achieved; later, areas of resistance within the organization need to be progressively incorporated into the programme. These areas may require a more intensive use of resources, particularly skilled change agents with high levels of interpersonal skills. If middle managers and supervisors are resistant to change, senior management support will be necessary to ensure that the programme is not sabotaged.

Step 7: communicate and extend the programme. The success of the pilot needs to be communicated throughout the organization and some of those involved in making the changes in the pilot situation used as change agents to initiate the changes elsewhere, working with line managers. At this stage it is important that the change programme doesn't just become a proliferation of largely unrelated initiatives in different operations. The answer to this, as Grayson and Hodges point out, is to ensure that the programme becomes 'built in' rather than 'bolted on' by integration at the strategic level.[63]

Step 8: align organizational systems. For the successful initiatives to turn into truly programmatic changes, operating systems, reward systems, information systems and reporting structures will need to be modified. These modifications should be designed to enhance the robustness of the change and to prevent regression in the pilot site and diffusion areas.[64] Without these broader changes, pilot sites can end up becoming 'islands of innovation in a sea of mediocrity'. As Shelton argues, they run the risk of 'hitting the green wall'.[65] The steps of incremental change are summarized in the box.[66]

Eight steps of incremental change

- Begin with future workshops/search conferences.
- Assess the organization's position.
- Evaluate the type of change programme needed.
- Identify change agents.
- Pilot new practices and innovations.
- Harness further resources.
- Communicate and extend the programme.
- Align organizational systems.

These eight generic steps by themselves do not guarantee the success of an incremental change programme. A great deal depends on the support given to the changes by senior management, readiness for change on the part of the work force and the skill of change agents. However, omitting one of these steps can seriously affect the potential success of the change programme. A fully fledged incremental change programme normally moves through all eight steps.

Conclusion

In this chapter we have outlined some of the key characteristics of successful incremental change programmes. We have noted that incremental change strategies are useful for organizations seeking to move between one phase of sustainability and the next. However, as we discussed earlier in this chapter, not all organizations will be able to move forward fast enough on the path to sustainability by using incremental change strategies. The next chapter outlines transformational change strategies – that is, strategies that change the mind sets, cultures, structures and products of organizations in radical ways to obtain sustainability outcomes.

Notes

1 Some of the key texts to have emerged that deal with sustainability-driven change in organizations adopt an incremental systems change perspective. See B. Doppelt, *Leading Change Toward Sustainability*, Sheffield: Greenleaf Publishing, 2003; B. Nattrass and M. Altomare, *Dancing with the Tiger: Learning Sustainability Step by Natural Step*, Gabriola Island BC: New Society Publishers, 2002.

2 D. Dunphy and A. Griffiths, *The Sustainable Corporation*, Sydney: Allen and Unwin, 1998, p. 56.

3 D. Dunphy and A. Griffiths, 'Corporate strategic change', in *International Encyclopedia of Business and Management*, London: Thomson Learning, 2002, pp. 1169–75.

4 A. Griffiths and D. Dunphy, 'Heresies to orthodoxies: organizational renewal in Australia 1966–1996', *Management Decision*, 2002, 40(1), 74–81.

5 M. Tushman and C. O'Reilly, 'Ambidextrous organizations: managing evolutionary and revolutionary change', *California Management Review*, 1996, 38(4), 8–30.

6 Nattrass and Altomare, *Dancing with the Tiger*.

7 R. Orsatto, 'The ecological modernisation of industry: a study of the European automobile field', doctoral thesis, University of Technology, Sydney, 2001, p. 35.

8 See, for instance, the work of D. Korten, *When Corporations Rule the World*, San Francisco: Berrett-Koehler, 1995; D. Korten, *The Post Corporate World*, San Francisco: Berrett-Koehler, 1999.

9 S. Hart and M. Milstein, 'Global sustainability and the creative destruction of industries', *Sloan Management Review*, 1999, 41(1), 23–33, esp. 24.

10 Ibid., p. 24.

11 A. Griffiths and M. Winn, 'Slack and Sustainability', paper presented to the Academy of Management conference, Hawaii, 2005.

12 M. Beer and N. Nohria, 'Cracking the code of change', *Harvard Business Review*, 2000, May–June, 133–41, esp. 133.

13 E. Abrahamson, 'Change without pain', *Harvard Business Review*, 2000, July–August, 75–9, esp. 75.

14 C. O. Reilly and M. Tushman, (2004) 'The ambidextrous organization', *Harvard Business Review*, 2004, April.

15 The Australian Business Roundtable on Climate Change warns that 'the longer we delay acting, the more expensive it becomes for business and for the wider Australian economy'. Australian Business Roundtable on Climate Change report *The Business Case for Early Action*, April 2006, p. 2. While the Millennium Ecosystem Assessment issued a stark warning: 'Human activity is putting such strain on the natural function of the Earth that the ability of the planet's ecosystems to sustain future generations can no longer be taken for granted . . . Nearly two-thirds of the services provided by nature to human kind are found to be in decline worldwide.' Millennium Ecosystem Assessment, statement from the board *Living Beyond our Means: Natural Assets and Human Well-being*, 2005, p. 2.

16 Readers who wish to understand in more detail the differences between incremental and transformational change can find excellent discussions and relevant research summaries in: B. Burnes, *Managing Change: A Strategic Approach to Organizational Dynamics*, 3rd edn, London: *Financial Times*/Prentice-Hall, 2000, pp. 253–8; I. Palmer, R. Dunford and G. Akin, *Managing Organizational Change: A Multiple Perspectives Approach*, New York: McGraw-Hill, 2006, pp. 74–86; D. Stace and D. Dunphy, *Beyond the Boundaries: Leading and Re-creating the Successful Enterprise*, 2nd edn, Sydney: McGraw-Hill, 2001, pp. 103–26.

17 D. Stace and D. Dunphy, *Beyond the Boundaries*, Sydney: McGraw-Hill, 2001, p. 64.

18 For further detail on the debates over planned versus emergent change, refer to B. Burnes, *Managing Change*, London: Pitman Publishing, 1996; K. Weick, 'Emergent change as a universal in organizations', in M. Beer, and N. Nohria, (eds) *Breaking the Code of Change*, Boston, Mass.: Harvard Business School Press, 2000; K. Weick and R. Quinn, 'Organizational change and development', *Annual Review of Psychology*, 1999, 50, 361–86.

19 Stace and Dunphy, *Beyond the Boundaries*, p. 110.
20 www.sustainability-indexes.com/htmle/indexes/djsiworld_supersectorleaders.html (accessed December 2005).
21 Quote from Noel Purcell, Westpac's group general manager for stakeholder communications; R. Kendall, 'Westpac now true CSR blue', *Ethical Investor*, 51, December–January 2005, 6.
22 Ibid., p. 111.
23 J. Porras and R. Silvers, 'Organization development and transformation', *Annual Review of Psychology*, 1991, 42, 51–78, esp. 82.
24 See the work of R. Henrik, H. Daly, P. Hawken and J. Holmbery, 'A compass for sustainable development', *International Journal of Sustainable Development and World Ecology*, 1991, 4, 79–92.
25 D. Meadows, 'Places to intervene in a system in increasing order of effectiveness', *Whole Earth*, 1997, Winter, 78–84, esp. 78.
26 K. Weick, 'Small wins: redefining the scale of social problems', *American Psychology*, 1984, 39(1), 40–9, esp. 43.
27 S. Benn, interview with D. Lett, Manager, Personnel and Administration, and A. Holmes, Supervisor – Local Purchasing, Panasonic Matsushita Pty Ltd, Penrith, Sydney, 29 August 2000.
28 A. Griffiths and N. Haigh, 'Co-ordinating Small Wins as an effective Mechanism for implementing Eco-innovations', best paper, Academy of Management conference 'Organizations and Natural Environment', New Orleans, LA, 2004.
29 B. Doppelt, *Leading Change toward Sustainability*, Sheffield: Greenleaf Publishing, 2003; Donella Meadows, 'Places to intervene in a system in increasing order of effectiveness', *Whole Earth*, 1997, winter, 78–84.
30 Griffiths and Haigh, 'Co-ordinating Small Wins'.
31 J. Maxwell, S. Rothenberg, F. Briscoe and I. Marcus, 'Green schemes: corporate environmental strategies and their implementation', *California Management Review*, 1997, 39(3), 118–34.
32 L. Rowledge, R. Barton and K. Brady, *Mapping the Journey*, Sheffield: Greenleaf Publishing, 1999. M. Shanahan and A. Maria, 'Creating change through strategic storytelling', *PRISM*, 1998, Q4, 99–108, esp. 100–1.
33 Ibid., 101.
34 Nattrass and Altomare, *Dancing with the Tiger*, p. 43.
35 R. Jones, N. Jimmieson, N. and A. Griffiths, 'The role of organizational culture and reshaping capabilities in creating readiness for change: implications for change implementation success, unpublished manuscript, School of Management, Queensland University of Technology, 2001.
36 M. Linnenlucke, 'Understanding Corporate Sustainability: A Quantitative Study about a single Organization', Master's report, Brisbane: University of Queensland Business School, Faculty of Business, Economics and Law, University of Queensland, 2006.

37 Rowledge *et al.*, *Mapping the Journey*, p. 136.

38 J. MacDuffie, 'Human resource bundles and manufacturing performance: organizational logic and flexible production systems in the world auto industry', *Industrial and Labor Relations Review*, 1995, 48(2), 197–221.

39 C. Ichniowski, K. Shaw and G. Prennushi, 'The effects of human resource management practices on productivity: a study of steel finishing lines', *American Economic Review*, 1997, June, 291–313.

40 For a review, see J. Pfeffer, *Competitive Advantage Through People*, Boston, Mass.: Harvard Business School Press, 1995.

41 M. Hele, 'Rockcote paints it green: solutions for water and waste', *Courier Mail*, 25 February 2005.

42 L. Moore, 'More than green', *Courier Mail*, 11 October 2002.

43 Ibid.

44 L. Pregelji, 'The Creativity and Innovation Process at Rockcote, Master of Technology and Innovation Management', case study, 2006; A. Griffiths, 'Rockcote: A Case Study in Eco-entrepreneurialism', case study, 2006, Brisbane: University of Queensland Business School.

45 Stace and Dunphy, *Beyond the Boundaries*, pp. 97–8, citing the work of Ostroff and Smith.

46 See B. Doppelt, *Leading Change toward Sustainability*, Sheffield: Greenleaf Publishing, 2003, pp. 114–15, for a commentary on the different roles that organization members can play in sustainability teams.

47 N. Roome, 'Developing environmental management strategies', *Business Strategy and the Environment*, 1992, 1(1), 11–23.

48 B. Daily and S. Huang, 'Achieving sustainability through attention to human resource factors in environmental management', *International Journal of Operations and Production Management*, 2001, 12, 1539–52.

49 P. Strebel, *Breakpoints: How Managers Exploit Radical Change*, Boston, Mass.: Harvard Business School Press, 1992.

50 Abrahamson, 'Change without pain', 76.

51 J. Mathews, A. Griffiths and N. Watson, *Socio-technical Redesign: The Case of Cellular Manufacturing at Bendix Mintex*, Industrial Relations Research Centre, UNSW Studies in Organizational Analysis and Innovation, University of New South Wales, 1993.

52 'Greenpeace warns of further water contamination in Romania and Hungary', press release 14 March 2000; 'Cyanide spill mine takes first step towards bankruptcy', Environment News Service, 16 March 2000.

53 United Nations Organization Mission in the Democratic Republic of Congo, *Report on the Conclusions of Summary Executions and other Violations of Human Rights committed by the FARDC in Kilwa on 15 October 2004*, 2005.

54 Innovest, Carbon Disclosure Project, Cleveland OH: Innovest Strategic Value Advisers, 2005. This figure quadruples the initial report of thirty-five investors with US$4.5 trillion in 2003.

55 R. Staub, 'Environmental auditing', in R Staub (ed.) *Environmental Management and Decision-making for Business*, New York: Palgrave Macmillan, 2005, pp. 263–70.

56 C. Ramus, 'Encouraging innovative environmental actions: what companies and managers must do', *Journal of World Business*, 2002, 37, 151–67.

57 R. Eckert, 'Where leadership starts', *Harvard Business Review*, 2001, November, 53–62.

58 D. Elliott, 'Would you buy a new car from this man?' *Time*, 30 January 2006.

59 Rowledge *et al.*, *Mapping the Journey*, p. 97.

60 Correspondence with Bob Cameron, CEO, Rockcote, 13 May 2006.

61 Ibid.

62 For a detailed outline of how this can be done see D. Grayson and A. Hodges, *Corporate Social Opportunity: Seven Steps to make Social Responsibility Work for your Business*, Sheffield: Greenleaf Publishing, 2004, pp. 101–39.

63 Ibid., p. 10.

64 R. Walton, 'The diffusion of new work structures: explaining why success didn't take', in P. Mirvis and D. Berg (eds) *Failures in Organization Development and Change*, New York: John Wiley, 1977, pp. 243–61.

65 R. Shelton, 'Hitting the green wall: why corporate programs get stalled', Corporate Environmental Strategy, 1994, 2(2), 5–12.

66 Interesting to note Donella Meadows identified nine steps, while Bob Doppelt identified seven steps. Our approach differs because we specifically identified the criteria and methods adopted by organizations involved in the roll-out of incremental change strategies. In other words, we identify change strategies that are situationally appropriate for incremental change. The approach taken by both Meadows and Doppelt is generically applied to incremental and transformational change approaches.

8 The transformational path

- Why transformational change?
- Step 1: know where you are now
- Step 2: develop the vision: the dream organization
- Step 3: identify the gap
- Step 4: assess the readiness for change
- Step 5: set the scene for action
- Step 6: secure basic compliance first
- Step 7: move beyond compliance
- Step 8: establish the performance criteria for 'compliance-plus'
- Step 9: launch and manage the transformational change programme
- Step 10: maintain the rage

Why transformational change?

For some organizations the move to sustainability can be incremental. As outlined in the last chapter, there are many organizations which touch the earth lightly and already contribute substantially to the health and welfare of their work force and the community. For these organizations, progress towards full sustainability can be a process of unspectacular but systematic and sustained development of awareness, policies and practices. These are the fortunate organizations.

There are many other organizations, however, that have been, or will soon be, subjected to unprecedented and unanticipated public pressure to make radical change. Why? Because some of their current policies or practices are revealed as plundering and polluting the planet, destroying the human capital assets of the organization or fracturing community relationships. We have given many examples throughout this book of organizations that have found themselves in such a situation and have had to respond by initiating radical, transformative change. In fact, some of today's leading corporate advocates of sustainability, whose managers have blazed a trail to sustainable practices, have been companies whose reputation suffered at some point because of unacceptable and unsustainable practices. For example, in the mid-1990s Shell faced a barrage of international criticism over its proposal to sink the redundant Brent Spar oil platform in the North Sea; this crisis was followed by more international criticism over its apparent support for a cruel dictatorship in Nigeria. Shell responded with a series of round-table meetings in fourteen locations throughout the world where it faced up to its severest critics for a frank exchange of views. As a result, it made a fundamental re-evaluation of its ethical position and business strategies, giving social and environmental sustainability issues a significant place in its core business strategies. On the other hand, Nike is a company that is still struggling to address issues around labour and human rights abuses. In these instances the 'third party' not-for-profit groups have extended their campaigns beyond their original targets to whole industry segments.[1]

We are moving into a period of history when organizations engaging in unsustainable operations will have their 'licence to operate' questioned by activist community groups or government watchdogs.[2] If organizations persist in these behaviours, they will be forced into crisis mode to extricate themselves, salvage their public image and retain market share. For instance, Monsanto's original drive to sustainability was undertaken to both strategically position itself out of low margin industries but also to respond to the increasing public concern and community activism over its polluting habits. The community is increasingly suspicious of 'greenwash' so the change has to be more than simply a cosmetic makeover. In Chapter 5 we saw that Monsanto failed to address these concerns expressed by peripheral stakeholders resulting in a perceptual gap between what the company was articulating and what the company was doing. This had extensive financial consequences for Monsanto. What is required sometimes is large-scale, transformative change: that is, a leap into a fundamental redefinition of the company or some significant aspect of it. This may involve developing a new definition of the business the company is in, a new strategic orientation or realignment, a new structure, a significant change in the workforce skill mix or profile and/or a substantive change in corporate culture.

To date we have talked about companies having choices. However, in some cases, such as extreme weather events, whose frequency and proximity seem related to climate change, some companies will have massive and transformative changes thrust upon them. These potentially could be disastrous for organizations. For instance, the New Orleans energy utility Entergy filed for bankruptcy protection following the near complete shutdown of its operations and revenue following Hurricane

Katrina. It was estimated that the company had lost its 337,000 electricity and natural gas customers and analysts predicted that, even as things improved, it was reasonable to expect that its future customer base could be smaller.[3] In the face of dramatic environmental discontinuities, managers must think about the forms of adaptive capacity they need to build into their organizations.

Other companies may choose to change transformationally even though they are not subjected to external pressures to do so. Some of these will be companies whose managers see the significant business opportunities that are emerging in sustainable development, and who wish to lead in taking up these opportunities. To do so they may have to reinvent the organization, for example by moving from manufacturing petroleum-based products to manufacturing and recycling products based on natural fibres while building a wholly new business operation that services and recycles. This is the story of DuPont, that has, since 1991 reclaimed more than 60 million lb of carpet. Some of the recycled content is used to manufacture products as diverse as carpet tiles and automobile parts.[4] However, central to DuPont's transformation has been the divestment of Conco and its shift towards life sciences investments.[5]

Other companies will be led by managers who are personally committed to contributing to a more sustainable world and who see their companies as instruments for accomplishing this. The move from a single-minded focus on creating short-term profits to embodying an ideological commitment to social justice and ecological diversity may also involve transformative change. The story of how Interface transformed its operations includes change of this kind as well.

We are addressing here what Robert Quinn refers to as 'deep change'. Quinn writes:

> 'Deep change differs from incremental change in that it requires new ways of thinking and behaving. It is change that is major in scope, discontinuous with the past and generally irreversible. The deep change effort distorts existing patterns of action and involves taking risks. Deep change means surrendering control'.[6]

Corporate transformations are not to be initiated lightly, for they are difficult to accomplish, often risky for the careers of the change agents involved and can have significant impacts on the lives of others, not all of which may be positive in the short term. In fact some have questioned whether it is possible to manage such change at all.[7] In our view, it is often possible to bring about transformational change, and we have documented many successful cases.[8] However, the magnitude of the task is often underestimated by managers, who consequently under-resource the process and fail to assemble the skills required to accomplish large-scale, fundamental change. On the other hand, while transformative change involves risk, there are times when failure to initiate transformative change results in the business being out of business. Not doing anything can be a greater risk than initiating transformational change. In the words of Hart and Milstein: 'Managers that treat sustainable development as an opportunity will drive the creative destruction process and build the foundation to compete in the twenty-first century'.[9]

Given the magnitude and urgency of the changes needed to bring about sustainability in society, we are confident that over the next few years many organizations will have to undergo corporate transformation. The good news is that many already have done so over the last quarter century due to the globalization of business, increasing competition and world economic recessions. Tough as these times have been, we have learned a great deal about how to reinvent organizations (and how not to). We can therefore draw on this experience and use what has been learned from it to manage the kind of transformational change needed to achieve full sustainability. In addition, we now know that 'long-living companies', that is, companies that survive for many years, undergo at least one significant period of transformational change and sometimes several. As mentioned earlier, de Geus has documented the histories of twenty-seven companies that lasted from 100 to 700 years – companies such as DuPont, Kodak, Mitsui, Sumitomo and Siemens.[10] Their ability to initiate and manage transformational change has been a major contributor to their longevity.

In addition, there is an increasing number of organizations whose basic corporate strategy is continually to transform or 'reinvent' themselves to maintain a competitive edge. Brown and Eisenhardt capture this well:

> For firms such as Intel, Wal-Mart, 3M, Hewlett-Packard and Gillette, the ability to change rapidly and continuously, especially in developing new products, is not only a core competence, it is also at the heart of their cultures. For these firms, change is not the rare, episodic phenomenon described by the punctuated equilibrium model but, rather, it is endemic to the way these organizations compete.[11]

Those organizations that see the development of new sustainable technologies, processes and products as central to their strategic success may choose to use continuous transformational change as a way of dominating their emerging markets.

This chapter outlines the practical process by which change agents can reinvent and reconstruct organizations into responsible instruments for creating products and services that contribute to a fulfilling life on a healthy planet. In the process, this makes a significant contribution to their own financial success and sustainability as viable organizations.

So how is transformative change initiated and effectively implemented? We outline the steps involved in the process and give concrete examples of successes and failures.

Step 1: know where you are now

Transformative change involves reinventing the organization – creating a compelling image of a desirable future organization dramatically different from the current one. But before charging off into the future, it is important to know the starting point: the organization as it is now. This is not a minor task, particularly in a large, complex company. It is easy to assume that the organization's current strategic identity is known and understood – after all, many people in the organization may have been around for years. Yet everyone in an organization has a different experience of it – organizations are not primarily buildings, equipment, finance and organization charts. Rather they are constructs in the minds of those who work in and with them, who buy from them and supply to them. They are primarily subjective realities, images that have been forged from individual and collective experience over time, and these subjective realities are usually partial and fragmentary and differ widely from one person to another. It is not enough to create a vision of the future and build an informed commitment to it. It is necessary first to build a shared understanding of the organization's current reality and of the need to radically shift that reality.

As Lynda Gratton notes:

> Working at the level of meaning in an organization requires a new way of thinking. To understand meaning it is not sufficient to simply consider what the organization is doing with regard to its tasks, the reporting structure or policy statements. We have to understand how the organization is perceived by its individual members. Working at the level of the 'unwritten rules of the game' provides us with such an

opportunity. This level of analysis begins to answer questions about what is important around the organization, what people have to do to get on, what really motivates and excites individuals, and which factors send the most positive messages.[12]

So up front of any transformative change programme we must assess the current reality. How?

There are two basic sources for constructing a shared view of the organization's current situation. The first source is carefully chosen members of the organization, including preferably some who have left. What can be gained from this source is a précis of the history of the organization, an outline of its defining formative moments. How did it come to be what it is? Who played key roles? To what extent were issues of sustainability taken into account along the way? The other source consists of representatives of key stakeholders – customers and suppliers, for example – who have dealt with the organization throughout its history. What is their experience of the organization? Have their expectations, particularly around sustainability (for example, pesticide-free food products), been met in the past? Are they being met now? To what extent are they expecting sustainable practices? Even if they are not, how would they respond to the development of such products and services?

There are various ways in which this information can be elicited; for example, through surveys, interviews, focus groups, and analysis of organizational and community records. Sometimes valuable information about the expectations of external stakeholders can be gleaned from members of the organization who have roles that require regular contact with a key stakeholder group. For example, we were working with a port authority to identify key stakeholders and their expectations. The CEO mentioned the fishermen and their reaction when the authority closed off access to the authority's wharves where tugs were moored. The move was made because of persistent vandalism to the tugs while they lay beside the wharves. After protests from the fishermen at the closure of the wharves to the public, the authority built a new wharf, at considerable expense, from which boat owners could operate. This, the CEO thought, had resolved the issue. 'For the boat owners,' remarked the head of security, 'but not for all the fishermen whose equipment was only rods and hand lines. They're still mad as hell about being excluded from their favourite fishing sites.' Most organizations have a wealth of information about external stakeholder attitudes which is not accessed, integrated and assessed by the senior executive team, let alone made known throughout the organization as part of creating the consensual reality needed to launch a change programme.

An important part of assessing current reality is to identify the core cultural values of the organization and the entrenched behavioural *mores* that control much of day-to-day behaviour in the organization. Here a trained outsider can often make the most useful contribution by focusing a fresh independent eye on the customary ways members of the organization undertake everyday business. The best observer is someone who is sensitive to the differences that often exist between espoused and enacted values – what people say they support versus what they actually do. Managers, for example, often express the view that 'people are our major asset' but their actual human resource practices may not reflect this stated belief. What are the prevailing views on sustainability issues held by the dominant coalition and other key groups such as trade union members, salespeople, maintenance workers, and research and development staff? What is the result, in practical terms, for the welfare of the work force, for the community, for the environment?

'Telling it the way it is' can be confronting for many members of the organization. Some organizational members will have a strong personal stake in preserving fictional views of the organization's current reality, for their own identities are bound up in maintaining the fiction. For example, they may not welcome a realistic assessment of the organization's impact on the environment. They may seek to 'shoot the messenger' who brings the disconfirming views. Remember the strenuous action of cigarette manufacturers who sought to disconfirm scientific evidence of the link between smoking and cancer. We emphasize strongly here that the basis for effective transformational change is widespread consensual agreement on the current organizational reality. It is necessary to be honest, sometimes brutally honest, to bring this about. It is easier to achieve when members of the dominant elite(s) are open to acknowledge different viewpoints and willing to absorb new information even when it challenges their traditional views. In fostering this openness, the credibility of the source of such information can also make a critical difference: respected external change agents with authority and expertise are more likely to be heard than insiders or outsiders without these attributes. A combination of confrontation by concerned community groups and, in parallel, a significant challenge from one or more sources whom executives respect and trust can provide the jolt needed to create the initial momentum for change.

In this regard, Byong-Wook Lee outlines some of the prevailing assumptions about waste in a Korean steel producing operation. These assumptions had to be confronted before waste and the associated pollution could be significantly reduced. The commonly held views were that 'change of waste management is expected to have very limited effect upon the company's financial performance' and that 'there is little room to reduce wastes through changes in the steel making process'.[13] Neither view was accurate, but the beliefs were deeply entrenched in the traditional culture of the organization. Shell uses a panel of international experts to critically evaluate its sustainability report as a means of challenging the company to do better.[14]

Step 2: develop the vision: the dream organization

Transformative change is an opportunity to rethink the *raison d'être* of the organization. Organizations are organic entities, social systems, which take on a life of their own often independent of those who brought them into being. They are shaped initially by the purposes of their founders but modified by external social pressures, by momentous and sometimes unanticipated events. Organizations sometimes actively shape the economic, physical and social environments in which they operate; they both shape and are shaped by these forces. They sometimes lead changes in their environments; more often they lag behind.

Organizations are, however, human creations, held in place by the values and actions of those in and around them. What has been created by human thought and action can also be recreated. However, to use an analogy, remanufacturing is a different process from manufacturing. In remanufacturing the physical basis of metals, for example, may have been changed by heat, vibration and wear. In remanufacturing, therefore, different processes have to be invented to produce the same or similar outcomes that result from manufacturing from raw materials. The same is true of transformative change: changing an organization that has already developed a history and a culture requires a different approach from creating a new organization. We are intervening in a system that has already developed powerful properties and processes of its own and these processes are usually deeply embedded in the minds, emotions and lives of the members of the organization and its external stakeholders. Changing the organization involves changing those in it, often including ourselves; it often also involves changing the expectations of those outside.

The first step in transforming an organization is to creatively imagine one or more future realities (scenarios) that the organization will face. The future is usually three to ten years out – the time chosen depends fundamentally on an estimate of how long it will take investments made now, in capital, human and technical abilities, to be realized. This scenario planning begins with an identification of: (1) the major current trends that are likely to affect the future viability, success and sustainable contribution of the organization; and (2) who the critical stakeholders are likely to be in the future, for they may be different from those the organization relates to now. Scenario planning of this type first emerged in the Royal Dutch Shell group in the 1970s and has since been elaborated and widely used under the general heading of 'strategic scenarios analysis'.[15] It is widely used: for example, the US power industry has created scenarios that apply to the development of industry technology in a world experiencing climate change and resource uncertainty.[16]

In constructing future scenarios, it is neither necessary nor wise to eliminate alternative scenarios for one 'most likely' scenario. Rather, a vision may be elaborated of the most likely scenario but parallel visions roughed out for 'best case' and 'worst case' scenarios. The purpose of the exercise is not simply to create a strategy for the future but also to create a purposeful process of engaging people inside and outside the organization in scoping out possible new paths ahead – to engage them in a critical debate about possible alternative futures. The aim is to build the commitment of all critical stakeholders to a challenging new future role for the organization.[17] At the same time, it is important to avoid locking the organization into an irrevocable path to a future that may never eventuate. The organization needs to be proactive, to create direction and momentum but also to retain the flexibility to adapt to unanticipated developments.

A critical part of this process of strategic realignment is to move from an identification of key future stakeholders to an imaginative construction of how their expectations may affect the organization in the future. This is an opportunity to engage these stakeholders in a dialogue about how they view their future – to give them voice. It is important also that as many members of the organization as possible are in a position to hear for themselves these voices from the stakeholders or their representatives. For example, Ford is in the process of transforming itself once again. This first occurred in the mid-1980s, in response to intense quality-oriented competition primarily from Japanese automotive manufacturers and their associated lean production systems. More recently the company is responding to further competitive threats from low-cost manufacturers and rising energy costs that are forcing consumers to more environmentally friendly and smaller cars. It is estimated that this new transformation will result in the closure of ten out of its forty-three plants in the United States with a loss of 123,000 jobs. However, it is doing this in order to deal with the combined effects of competitive pressures and poor financial performance. However, Bill Ford, the company chairman, is using this transformation as an opportunity for Ford to become more innovative in its product development and more sustainability oriented.[18]

This exercise leads into a definition of the most critical issues facing the organization. The natural next step is to ask: What will these anticipated changes mean for our organization? What problems will we face? What opportunities will be available to us? What values will we stand for?

These questions centre on defining a new identity for the organization and developing an innovative strategic intent to guide the organization in its future decision making. An important facet of this process is defining a set of core values in which human and ecological sustainability have a central place. For example, the Co-operative Bank in the United Kingdom has a history of pioneering ethical business practices and instituting community-minded policies. In its 1998 *Partnership Report* the bank extended its list of key stakeholders beyond shareholders, suppliers, customers, staff and their families to include local communities, national and international society and future generations. The bank aims to deliver 'value' to each of these stakeholders – value as defined by the group itself and not by the bank. As a result, for example, the bank does not invest in firms that violate human rights. It also operates a credit card scheme where a proportion of profit made from money spent by customers on their cards is donated to organizations such as Amnesty International and Greenpeace.[19]

These core values also define how the organization will measure performance in the future. Stace and Dunphy express the change occurring in this area as follows:

> As the era of industrial capitalism recedes, it is evident that the strategic benchmarks of organizations are changing. In the classical era of industrial capitalism, strategic benchmarks were nearly all expressed in financial or market terms: the typical measures were net profit, return on investment, return on earnings and market share. Organizations compared themselves and were driven by these or

similar ratios. It was as if the unwritten law of each organization was to become the biggest and most profitable, quite often by immolating competitors. Today we are witnessing a sea change. Why? Because shareholders are not the only organizational constituents of the firm: stakeholders, customers, network and alliance partners are just as important.[20]

As noted elsewhere in the book, numerous organizations are now adopting triple bottom line performance criteria or comparable approaches that reflect a significant broadening of values and acceptance of a multiple stakeholder approach. Involving forward-thinking stakeholders in the process of renewing the corporate vision and strategic intent is an important part of building 'relationship capital'. Creating an engaging dialogue with key stakeholders ensures that their interests are taken into account and that they know this. It also enlists their active support for the emerging changes in the organization's operations.

The central challenge of transformative change is to unleash the imagination of organizational members and stakeholders so that they collaborate in creating a vision that breaks out of existing cultural assumptions to create a prototype for a truly sustainable and sustaining organization. Whereas incremental change can often be successfully generated and led entirely by people internal to the organization, transformative change almost always needs input from outsiders. The outsiders need to be informed, radical, lateral thinkers who can and will challenge existing assumptions about the current organizational platen and accepted best practice. For example, Placer Dome, an international mining company, invited major critics of its environmental and community relations practices (for example, Greenpeace) to examine, critique and propose new policies and procedures acceptable to them.[21]

The vision must be spelled out as clearly as possible and personally endorsed by senior management. However, at this stage it represents a new identity, a change of direction, an idea in process to be explored, tested and progressively given shape through future action. It must also be formulated in a way that speaks to the hearts and minds of the key players in the organization and to stakeholders whose support will be needed for it to be realized. It has to have a clear relationship to the core business strategies of the organization. Ideally the essence of the new identity can be expressed simply and directly, for example, BP = Beyond Petroleum, signifying that the company is repositioning itself to phase out its dependence on petroleum and to become a significant player in the development of alternative energy sources.

Step 3: identify the gap

Having reached this point, now is the time to pull back from the dream and to create a realistic assessment of the gap between the organization's current situation and where the new vision seeks to position itself in the future. The Corporate Sustainability Matrix around which this book is constructed provides a way of estimating and describing the gap as well as indicating how to move forward. To do this, you need to work independently through the human sustainability column and the ecological column – an organization may be at a different stage in each of these areas (see figure 8.1). It is possible for the same organization to have a highly strategic approach to human sustainability (Phase 5) but to be lagging in terms of compliance in the ecological area (Phase 2) – for example, a mining company which has first-rate human resource policies but which has environmentally destructive operations.

The outputs of steps 2 and 3 above supply the information needed to position, in the matrix, where the organization is now and where it aspires to be, and over what time span. The differences between current and envisioned future positions in the matrix define the gap to be bridged. Let's take the case of a bank, for example, which has systematically built its HR strategies over a ten-year period, using them to attract and retain some of the best talent in the industry. The bank has also been concerned about its contribution to the community and also used its community relations to support its progressive, 'concerned and caring' image. This places it in Phase 5, strategic sustainability (HS5), in the area of human sustainability. However, it has given little thought to its environmental impact. It uses huge amounts of paper, most of which is not separated for recycling. It constantly updates its computers, printers and so on, but commits them by truckloads to landfill. It is discussing developments in the ethical investment fund area but has not yet launched such a fund or developed an alliance with another financial institution that has. This places it, for ecological sustainability, in Phase 2, non-responsiveness (ES2). So its overall position on the Sustainability Change Matrix, Figure 8.1, is at point A. Now it aspires to be a leader in the introduction of both human and ecological sustainability practices by moving towards HS6 and ES6. Clearly it needs, at the most, incremental change in the human sustainability area. But its transformational change programme needs to centre on ecological sustainability, where it has a lot of ground to make up before it reaches its ideal position at or near point B. The gap between the current phase and the desired future phase defines the bridge the organization must cross in order to emerge transformed.

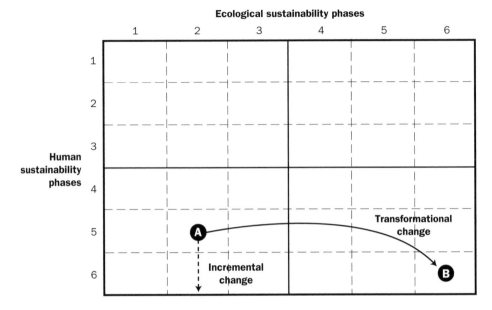

Figure 8.1 *Bridging the gap: what kind of change?*
Source: Adapted from D. Dunphy, J. Benveniste, A. Griffiths and P. Sutton, *Sustainability: The Corporate Challenge for the Twenty-first Century*, Sydney: Allen & Unwin, 2000, p. 256.

If the organization is complex, having divisions and units with differentiated operations, market environments and cultures, the process of positioning on the matrix may need to be analysed for each differentiated unit. This implies that the organization may have to pursue a complex change strategy that is a mix of both incremental and transformative change, depending on the current character of the sub-units. The more differentiated the change strategy in this regard, the higher will be the cost of co-ordinating across ongoing strands of the change programme. Resources, human and financial, need to be allocated to ensure that the various change initiatives move the organization as a whole on its chosen trajectory rather than spinning off on their own orbits.

The most obvious output of this stage of the design process is a realistic assessment of the nature of the gap to be bridged – the gap between the organization's current commitment to and performance on key sustainability indicators and the new vision of the future. This gap may be substantially different for human and ecological sustainability and may also differ from one part of the organization's operations to another.

If the process has been well managed to this point, an important secondary output is that commitment to change is already building among key opinion leaders within the organization and significant external stakeholders. Transformative change is always a political process and a central task of change agents is to build active support among constituent groups, or at least receive tacit acceptance of the desired changes. This is not always possible: there are usually individuals and groups who have a significant stake in the existing order, the *status quo*, and whose interests are threatened by change. It would be naive not to expect active and passive resistance from them. What is often harder for change agents to accept, however, is the resistance that often comes from some of those who are disaffected from the *status quo* and who stand to *benefit* from the proposed changes. Some people cannot project themselves into a future world, cannot assess realistically how their interests will be served by change, or actually prefer to remain locked in, complaining, to the security of a known if debilitating role rather than break the chain and be free. We cannot make people change; we can only provide opportunities for them to change themselves.

Step 4: assess the readiness for change

For those who have been intensely involved in the diagnostic process described in steps 2 and 3 it is easy to assume that the organization as a whole is poised and ready for change, or that, if there are points of resistance, these will simply fade away as the change proceeds. This is usually far from the truth. Planning change is the easy part; intervening in an ongoing system that is alive, has its own compelling logic and of which we are only a small part is a huge challenge. Even formal authority has limited validity in a transformative change process. Ordering people to change is seldom effective; change by memorandum and edict usually fails. Leadership, not management, is the critical element in transformative change. Leadership at all levels is vital in creating the bursts of energy that must spark responses in opinion leaders and build momentum for change. This is an issue we will deal with in more detail in the final chapter.

Transformative change may involve authoritative action, even coercion, but its success depends ultimately on emotional contagion across the living networks of human relationships that make up an organization. There must be a compelling intellectual agenda for change, but that is not enough to transform deeply entrenched behavioural patterns built up over years of repetitive action. People are more than minds; they have hearts and spirits as well and the agenda for change must also appeal to people at emotional and spiritual levels. The sustainability agenda has the potential to do this. For example, most parents care about the world their children and grandchildren will inherit. Most people want to work for organizations that are seen to be making a contribution to community life. We seek meaning and purpose in our lives: the great opportunity that faces managers and change agents in the move to sustainability is to actualize the opportunity this represents to enhance the sense of meaning people derive from coming to work each day. A transformative change programme can catalyse meaning and provide opportunities for the development of wholeness through purposive and fulfilling work.

As Debashis Chatterjee points out: 'Organizations are not merely structures of units and departments but living fields of creative intelligence of the people who constitute the organization.'[22]

However, we caution change agents about the 'one size fits all' approach to selling and motivating for sustainability-driven transformation. In our research and consulting experience, we have identified at least four different sustainability change drivers. These include:

- *The emotional pitch* (mentioned above). This appeals to people's need and desire to leave the world a better place for their children and future generations. However, the message may not appeal to all stakeholders and not generate the conditions for change readiness.
- *The financial risk pitch*. This often appeals to senior executives and argues a case for change readiness based on the risk of losing capital and reputation.
- *The classic business case for sustainability*. This is built on the premise of delivering measurable benefits such as operational efficiencies (see Chapter 4).
- *Opportunity case*. This case outlines the prospective opportunities that become available for organizations when they adopt a different mind set on sustainability issues (see Chapter 5).

The fourth step involves identifying the important internal and external organizational stakeholders whose attitudes and actions could affect the success of the proposed change programme, and working out how their interests may be affected by the changes. It may be appropriate to consult them beforehand if this has not already happened. Again, where possible, the change programme should be modified to ensure that the interests of as many key players as possible are served by the unfolding programme of change. However, in transformative change there are usually some groups whose entrenched interests will be threatened. If this is the case, positive alternatives can sometimes be developed to reduce the win–lose nature of the situation. If not, then conflict can be expected and strategies developed to minimize the threat their opposition will represent for the repositioning of the organization. We stress that transformative change is a political process characterized by conflict and power plays. Those initiating the change need to develop a clear understanding of the sources of their authority and power to initiate and carry through the desired changes, build political alliances to support their initiatives and anticipate potential sources of opposition and indifference. Sustainability is a relatively new ideology and support for it cannot be assumed but needs to be won progressively.

Step 5: set the scene for action

There are three additional issues that need to be addressed in creating a base for effective action: awareness of the need for change; identifying change leaders; and assembling the resources needed for the change programme.

Before change can happen, those in the organization must be aware of the need to change. In creating an awareness of the need to change, it makes sense to start where there is the most potential energy for change, that is, with those who are already aware of and committed to the changes. In today's organizations there are usually articulate advocates of sustainability who understand at least some of the key issues and who are impatient for change. There are also others who are aware but tend to be 'covert' believers, less articulate but waiting for encouragement and clear opportunities before becoming involved. The awareness-building process can start by bringing these people together and identifying the potential contributions they can make to the change process both individually and collectively. One of their most important resources will be the informal networks of others in the organization whom they can influence, so creating a process by which the 'ripples' of awareness can spread out through the natural links between people in the organization. In the early 1990s, for example, Scandic Hotels, the hotel chain in Scandinavia we discussed earlier, embarked on a change programme to improve the environmental and economic performance of all its hotels. In the first year alone, employees identified more than 1,500 potential innovations which resulted in significant savings and reduced the hotels' environmental impact. In 1997 it was rated in the top 100 most desirable companies to work for in Sweden and successfully attracted large numbers of environmentally conscious guests.[23] By 2003 Scandic had trained over 9,000 employees in sustainability awareness programmes as a way of institutionalizing sustainability in the culture of the organization.

Another important step in building awareness is to open windows on the world and on the future for those in the organization. The more those in the organization can be given access to leading thinkers and organizational practices in corporate sustainability the more compelling the case for sustainability becomes and the more engaged they will be. Lectures, seminars, site visits, articles, videos and books can all help build a compelling case for change. They are an important part of creating an intellectual agenda for the change programme.

But effective change programmes require leadership and resources as well as ideas. The next task therefore is to identify change leaders at all levels of the organization, to bring them together around creating a practical agenda for change and to win their commitment to make the change happen. This team (or partnership of several teams) will become the guiding coalition driving the change programme. To be effective, this group needs to have representatives of all key power groups, formal or informal, in the organization that have the capability to make the programme succeed or fail. It needs to include at least one member of the top team so that its work is linked with the core business strategies of the organization. The change leaders include those who have the requisite technical knowledge in areas such as human resource management, corporate social responsibility and the natural environment. They also need to have the EQ (emotional intelligence) skills required to work effectively with people and the SQ (spiritual intelligence) skills needed to provide the wisdom to make sound choices in the face of complex problems.[24] We shall discuss the role and relevance of these factors in more detail in Chapter 9.

However, even the best leaders cannot effect large-scale change without the necessary resources of time, personnel support and finance. Some of the best-planned change programmes fail because senior executives believe that key personnel can simply act as change agents in their 'spare time' and that change programmes do not need the kinds of resources that would be considered essential to a well run operational task of similar magnitude. Managing a large-scale organizational change programme is equivalent to an engineering project such as creating a new mine, building a skyscraper or installing an organization-wide IT system. Because there may be no visible end product, justifying the time involved and the provision of the necessary resources often demands building a convincing case for equivalent support.

If enthusiasm has been engendered for change, those who assume leadership can readily underestimate the time needed for deep change. Lynda Gratton, through UK-based Leading Edge research consortium, has had the opportunity to monitor several transformational change processes in leading companies. One of the companies studied was Glaxo Wellcome, the world's largest drug company by sales. Their position was challenged because of cost cutting in drug purchases and the introduction of 'managed care'. In 1988 Glaxo chairman Richard Sykes and his senior team reviewed their business strategy, deciding to move away from a single product focus to the concept of disease management, closer partnerships with their customers and speedier delivery of drugs. Gratton details how it took two years of intensive targeted activity to transform the company's functional, hierarchical structure to a process-driven, customer-focused culture with effective multidisciplinary teams. Only then, two years later, did the company begin to pick up the performance benefits it had aspired to; over this period it also created a stable of new drugs to fuel its continuing success in the future. But it was really the late 1990s before the new culture they had envisaged ten years earlier was hard and soft-wired into the organization and the benefits were fully realized. Deep change takes real time.

While incremental change can often be effectively undertaken with resources internal to the organization, transformative change usually requires the use of competent, qualified and experienced external consultants. Cultural shifts require a rethinking of cherished assumptions, the challenging of existing patterns of behaviour and the generation of novel alternatives. In this process, it is valuable to have the assistance of parties who have not been socialized into the current corporate culture and who have moved across a variety of organizations in different industries. Organizations undergoing cultural change have characteristics of both chaos and order, and this is becoming a normal pattern of corporate change in a much more dynamic and unpredictable world.[25]

Step 6: secure basic compliance first

We want to stress here that securing compliance with legal requirements and the legitimate expectations of stakeholders is the necessary base from which transformational change to more advanced stages must be made. No matter how urgent the need to move the organization forward to other stages of sustainability, it is dangerous to skip this stage – dangerous because failure to comply with legal requirements for health and safety, for example, could lead to costly lawsuits and a damaged corporate reputation. In the United States Honda had to pay US$267 to settle claims that it disconnected pollution monitoring equipment on 1.6 million cars. They contravened America's Clean Air Act and the fine was their reminder that the US government is now taking air pollution seriously.[26]

Honda is also taking pollution and climate change issues seriously. In 2004 Honda was awarded Greenest Automaker Award. It is worth quoting the Research Director of the Union of Concerned Scientists on the contrasting performances of Honda and GM:

> Honda is in a class of its own when it comes to producing clean cars and trucks . . . General Motors on the other hand is stuck in reverse. GM has spent countless dollars in advertising trying to create a green image, but as the only automaker to move backwards on both smog and carbon dioxide, its rhetoric doesn't match reality.[27]

It is not only dangerous to skip this stage but also irresponsible because the health and safety of employees, of the community and the environment are the first responsibility of any organization in the twenty-first century. In addition, transformational change inevitably creates disorder that can increase the risk of non-compliance. Consequently, it is important to create clear guidelines for compliance first and to build a tight control system that is actively maintained at a grass-roots level. This needs to be backed up by clear managerial accountability to hold compliance in place when everything else is changing. It is vital to ensure that compliance norms are internalized and to create a working set of operational procedures to reduce corporate risk to a minimum. Contingency plans for damage control also need to be in place in case the compliance procedures fail (for example, in a mining operation, a tailings dam collapses in an unprecedented downpour despite well thought out measures to prevent it).

It is not only compliance with legislation that is important: as we pointed out in Chapter 4, companies must also meet the strong expectations of stakeholders even if these do not have legal standing. For example, Monsanto set out to model sustainable development but experienced global outrage when it developed genetically modified seeds that would not reproduce themselves; it meant that farmers would have to buy new seeds from Monsanto every year.[28]

Compliance is the base platform on which sustainability can be built. We outline here the necessary tasks to be performed in achieving compliance:

- Identify potential risks through undertaking a risk analysis.
- Establish the priorities for risk reduction.
- Decide who will take charge of the compliance generating process, keeping in mind that this is an opportunity to begin to identify and develop change leaders for later stages in the path to sustainability. Create a task force to plan and guide the process.
- Estimate the resources needed to achieve compliance and assemble these resources.
- Develop a co-ordination and communication plan that links line and staff responsibilities.
- Set criteria for success and construct an ambitious schedule for completion.
- Establish a monitoring and review process that is understood, transparent and widely reported.

In a transformational change process the priority is to achieve compliance effectively and rapidly. This can be accomplished by creating a number of task forces in important areas of sustainability such as OHS, EEO, water and energy conservation, and then having these task forces operate in parallel. (In an incremental change programme, these key compliance areas might be tackled sequentially.) The cost of organizing in parallel lies in the need for greater co-ordination across the teams to ensure that the end result is a well integrated and mutually consistent set of policies and procedures. Therefore there is a need for an effective liaison role in linking the teams together as they work on their focal issues.

Step 7: move beyond compliance

With an effective compliance base in place, it is time to put the organization into fast forward mode. At this point it is useful to return to the sustainability matrix and to confirm the decision, made in step 1 above, to move towards either the phase of 'strategic sustainability' or to 'the sustaining corporation' (see Figure 8.1). In addition, the gap between where the organization is now and where it aspires to be needs to be reviewed. Now is the time also to outline the major steps through which the change programme should move and the time frame for this.

The resulting change programme must be challenging but achievable. For example, if significant cultural change is needed, then the schedule would normally cover three to five years.

There are two possible transformational change paths to take at this point: either to attempt to take the organization in a leap forward to Phase 5, strategic proactivity, or to Phase 6, the sustaining corporation. Obviously the latter is the goal involving the biggest stretch but both involve moving rapidly through Phase 4, efficiency. This has significant implications; for instance, it may be possible to pick up some of the key achievements of the efficiency phase along the way but there is a real risk that transformational change of this order will actually work against making efficiency gains, at least in the short term. The speed and extent of large-scale transformational change often brings significant inefficiencies because of the level of disorganization involved. Similarly, the larger leap from the compliance phase to the sustaining corporation runs the additional risk of losing some of the advantages to be gained in the strategic proactivity phase. It is possible to lose strategic focus and direction and so place the sustainability of the organization itself at risk. It seems that this is what happened at Monsanto.

We wish to stress that transformational change, unlike most incremental change, involves significant risks. These risks should not be taken lightly as they can endanger the viability of the firm itself and can damage the careers of many involved. There are situations, however, when the risks are warranted: for example, when the core business of the organization is clearly no longer ethical (cigarette companies), when the firm's production processes need to be completely replaced because they are dangerous to the work force and society (organochlorines) or when there is a significant strategic opportunity that demands major reorganization (alternative energy generation).

The critical questions to be answered in this step are: Where are we going in terms of sustainability? How fast must we make the changes? Can we assemble the resources needed to make this schedule realistic? Where are the critical gaps in our expertise that we must fill? Where is the most resistance likely to occur? How will we know we are succeeding?

The answers to these questions form the outline of the emergent change programme. Other useful questions are: Can we identify positive models for the changes we need to make – either within our own organization or in other organizations? What other organizations have attempted to travel this path? Can we access them and assess their level of success? Were their attempts successful or unsuccessful? Where they were successful, what can we learn from their achievements? Where they were unsuccessful, what can we learn from their mistakes? Site visits are often useful in making these assessments and maximizing learning from the experience of others.

In drawing up the programme for change it is vital to ensure that the sustainability goals adopted are integral to the overall business plan for the organization. Sustainability must be a business imperative, not simply an add-on or option. In transformational change, sustainability initiatives can contribute significantly to business performance, particularly to future corporate repositioning. Weizacker *et al.* give a multitude of examples of companies that have dramatically reduced their use of resources and at the same time significantly increased their profitability.[29] In addition, sustainability initiatives can be important in securing the support of key stakeholder groups for the organization's strategy of repositioning itself in new markets. However, other stakeholders may perceive some sustainability initiatives as a threat to their interests. For example, suppliers who find their materials or products bypassed for others with more sustainable characteristics may be alarmed to see their business being diminished. As stated before, transformational change is always a political process. It is important therefore to understand which stakeholders will be important for success and to attempt to secure their support or, if necessary, neutralize their opposition.

The questions to answer at this stage are: Where will this change programme or its outcomes add value for this particular group of stakeholders? How could it diminish value, as the stakeholder perceives it? How can the positive value proposition be most effectively communicated to each stakeholder group? How can any negative perceptions be managed to ensure that the programme of change is not undermined by any resulting opposition?

Step 8: establish the performance criteria for 'compliance-plus'

If the change programme is to be seen to contribute significantly to the core business of the organization and to the well-being of the community and the environment, then we need to define the criteria for performance. How shall we judge whether the programme is successful? What performance criteria shall we use for this?

There are two kinds of performance criteria to use; the first is 'output criteria'. What are the outputs we are seeking in terms of such factors as decreased waste or community contribution? The second kind of performance criteria is 'process criteria'. What characteristics of the process of change are we seeking to create (for example, the progressive engagement of key interest groups in the change programme or a more collaborative set of relationships between different organizational units)?

Many change programmes fail to define performance criteria at all and, as a result, they falter or fail. If we don't know what we are trying to achieve or fail to reach agreement on the goals of change, confusion and chaos will reign. Most successful change programmes define output criteria and this helps keep them on track. But in our experience few change programmes define process criteria. However, the quality of the developing change process can be critical in achieving sustainable performance. There is a tendency in transformative change programmes to sacrifice the quality of the change process in the interests of achieving the desired performance outputs quickly. The result can be resentment, cynicism and a failure of key groups to engage and commit to longer-term performance.

Output criteria relate to the following kinds of performance for existing products and services:

● Reduced costs, increased profitability.
● Added quality.
● Innovation, flexibility and speed of initiation and response to market shifts.
● Increased market share.

In addition, other criteria may relate to the process of strategically repositioning the organization:

● Entry to new markets.
● Development of new products and services.

- Industry leadership.
- Enhanced public profile and reputation.
- Creation of a new industry.

Beyond these traditional measures of effective business performance, other criteria might be:

- Elimination of waste and sources of pollution.
- Building work force ability to contribute to the development of sustainable operations.
- Building work force commitment to continue to build the company's future sustainability performance.
- Development of new environmentally beneficial production processes.
- Contributing to strengthening community relationships.
- Increasing stakeholder support, including licence to operate and increased trust.
- Significantly reducing the organization's ecological footprint.

These outputs may significantly increase the real wealth of the organization. An important issue to be decided early in the change programme is, therefore, how these benefits are to be distributed among the organization's stakeholders. The traditional answer for a listed company is that the increased wealth would be divided between the shareholders and reinvestment in the company's future growth, usually in the form of capital assets. In the new world of business that we have been describing, capital assets are becoming less important than intellectual capital and stakeholder relationships assume greater significance. Therefore the increased wealth represents an opportunity to invest in the further development of the abilities of employees and in strengthening key stakeholder relationships rather than increased investment in buildings and hardware. This is the route followed by organizations such as HP, Scandic and Westpac and is central to how they generate added value through sustainability initiatives.

Process criteria are ways of assessing whether the change process itself is generating the quality of relationships and capabilities needed to sustain future change. Criteria that may be used here include:

- Progressive engagement of key individuals and groups, both internally and externally.
- Development of concrete, actionable plans for delivery of the outputs above.
- Progressive development of skilled and committed change leaders at all levels.

- A climate of trust and more collaborative relationships between organizational subunits.
- A culture of non-defensive learning.

An important issue to be addressed in regard to process quality is the style of change leadership that will be adopted to bring about the desired transformation. Research on change programmes shows that as the scale and speed of change increase there is a shift to more directive styles of leadership.[30] In addition, the research also shows that the majority of organizational members understand the necessity for this and support it. So in large-scale transformational change it is not necessary or appropriate for all decisions to be made participatively. The executive team needs to decide early in the change programme what issues will be dealt with by executive decision and are therefore non-negotiable. Safety, for example, is generally regarded as a non-negotiable value. Similarly, the team should decide what kinds of decisions will be made participatively, that is, where individuals, groups, stakeholders or their representatives will be encouraged to participate, influence or determine outcomes. The rationale for this decision-making approach needs to be clearly understood throughout the organization.

However, if management is to take a decisive lead their actions must consistently model their rhetoric. As Alan Pears has pointed out, it is important for senior managers to set visible examples: 'Where senior managers drive fuel-guzzlers and insist that reports be submitted on non-recycled paper printed single-sided, it is difficult for staff to believe the organization is serious about larger environmental issues.'[31]

Step 9: launch and manage the transformational change programme

The reader may be wondering whether we would ever get to this point, that is, of doing what we set out to do. Is all this taxing groundwork necessary? Why not simply get on with it and launch the change programme in the first place? We can only reiterate that launching transformative change programmes is a risky endeavour and that a great deal of the success comes from careful preparation in advance. While this preparation consumes time, it can be carried out efficiently and significantly raises the chances of a successful outcome. Managing a change programme has some similarity to painting a house: a large part of the business of doing a first-rate job lies in the careful preparation of surfaces and selection of the appropriate paints. The painting is the easier part.

There is an extensive literature on how to conduct successful change programmes. We do not intend to cover this in any detail but refer the reader who is unfamiliar with the literature to read selectively from the list we provide (see 'Further reading', pp. 335–6). Here we shall simply outline some of the key steps in a programme designed to move the organization rapidly along the path to sustainability:

- Create and communicate the main focus of the programme so that all in the organization understand the direction and rationale for change (for example, BP: Beyond Petroleum; S. C. Johnson: A family company; Honda: The power of dreams).
- Map the main sub-projects in sufficient detail to clarify for change agents how the change is expected to happen, ensuring that the link to business strategies is clear.
- Build a network of change agents (line and staff personnel, internal and external consultants); break the overall change programme down into projects that can be handled by multidisciplinary task forces led by these change agents.
- Establish a change co-ordination team consisting of executives and other strategically located change agents; clarify authority for decision making and accountabilities against goals and time lines; pay particular attention to the roles of front-line supervisors and ensure that they have a clear role to play.
- Monitor the emerging trajectory of change and remediate where necessary. The monitoring should be of both output and process performance criteria; seek and respond to grass-roots feedback.
- Create and celebrate early wins and publicly reward those responsible for them.
- Progressively enlarge the sphere of engagement – go with the energy; remember that opposition is a natural part of the engagement process. (Apathy and cynicism are more serious threats.)
- Create momentum, feeding in resources where necessary.
- Communicate and dramatize success; foster transparency and truth.
- Ensure that, as the capabilities for organizational reshaping develop, they are reinforced and progressively translated into intellectual capital.
- As change goals are reached, consolidate them in new operational systems under the control of committed and competent operational managers (not change agents) and operational teams.

- Ensure that the operational managers achieve efficiencies as the new systems are debugged and routinized.
- Check that key stakeholders perceive that the promised value propositions are being delivered; consolidate their support.
- Build reward systems that reinforce and renew the core values of the new culture and reinforce the behaviours that support the emerging system. These behaviours then become the cultural norms supporting the next stage of sustainability development. It is vital that achievement of sustainability outcomes is a major criterion in staff assessment for career advancement.

Step 10: maintain the rage

In a dynamic world, change is an ongoing process. When the goals have been achieved, the change process may become incremental rather than transformative, but change continues. Organizations ossify unless they continue to change with their environments. Therefore it is essential to continue the process of environmental monitoring and identification of emerging stakeholder interests around issues of sustainability. The organizational members need to ensure that the organization maintains its leading-edge position; it is easy to fall behind the leading edge through becoming complacent.

Those organizations that move to the stage of becoming sustaining corporations can improve their performance even further by contributing to a growing industrial ecology. An industrial ecology is an active network of organizations for exchanging ideas, products and services in sustainable ways. The best-known example of this is an eco-industrial park in the town of Kalundborg in Denmark. Several companies in the town created a system of exchange whereby the by-products ('wastes') from one company's operation became a resource or raw material for another.[32] Networks and alliances of organizations like this, working actively to promote and model sustainable practices, are epicentres for the development of the new sustainable economy. As their success becomes apparent they contribute to a developing climate of political and community support for the enhancement of human capability and environmental regeneration. Any optimistic scenario for the future depends on widespread transformational change designed to bring about a different form of economy from that existing today. Networks of transformed organizations are a major dynamic for transforming the economy as a whole.

In the box, we have outlined ten steps to creating a successful transformational change programme. These steps are distilled from the experience of many change agents working on a range of transformational change programmes and adapted to the task of moving organizations rapidly towards sustainability. They are a useful guide but in reality, as we have noted, the change process will be more chaotic than this indicates. Nevertheless, the steps can help us assess our progress in managing change and they set a direction to work towards. Leadership is the decisive factor that determines whether we succeed, and we turn to that next in Chapter 9.

Ten steps to creating a successful transformational change programme

1   Know where you are now.
2   Develop the vision – the dream organization.
3   Identify the gap.
4   Assess the readiness for change.
5   Set the scene for action.
6   Secure basic compliance first.
7   Move beyond compliance.
8   Establish the performance criteria for 'compliance plus'.
9   Launch and manage the transformational change programme.
10 Maintain the rage.

Notes

1   Consider the campaign under way by Oxfam with its Nikewatch site and the broadening of its campaign on the abuse of human rights and labour conditions to the sportswear manufacturing industry in general.
2   J. Elkington, *Cannibals with Forks: The Triple Bottom Line of the 21st Century Business*, Oxford: Capstone, 1999. United Nations Mission to Democratic Republic of Congo (2005) Report on the conclusions of the special investigation into allegations of summary executions and other violations of human rights committed by the FARDC in Kilwa on 15 October 2005.
3   M. O'Driscoll, 'Entergy reeling after Katrina, Rita', *Greenwire*, 26 September 2005.
4   www.bsdglobal.com/viewcasestudy:DuPont (accessed 13 March 2006).

5 S. Hart and M. Milstein, 'Global sustainability and the creative destruction of industries', *Sloan Management Review*, 1999, 41, fall, 1–11.

6 R. Quinn, *Deep Change: Discovering the Leader Within*, San Francisco: Jossey-Bass, 1996, p. 3.

7 I. Palmer and R. Dunford, 'Who says change can be managed? Positions, perspectives and problematics', unpublished paper presented at the International Research Workshop 'New Ways of Thinking about Organizational Change: Discourses, Strategies, Processes, Forms', University of Sydney, 26–27 Nov. 2001.

8 D. Dunphy and D. Stace, *Under New Management: Australian Organizations in Transition*, Sydney: McGraw-Hill, 1990; D. Stace and D. Dunphy, *Beyond the Boundaries: Leading and Re-creating the Successful Enterprise*, 2nd edn, Sydney: McGraw-Hill, 2001.

9 Ibid., 32.

10 A. de Geus, 'The living company', *Harvard Business Review*, 1997, March–April, 51–9.

11 S. L. Brown and K. M. Eisenhardt, 'The art of continuous change: linking complexity theory and time-paced evolution in relentlessly shifting organizations', *Administrative Science Quarterly*, 1997, 42, March, 1–34, esp. p. 1.

12 L. Gratton, *Living Strategy: Putting People at the Heart of Corporate Purpose*, London: Financial Times/Prentice-Hall, 2000, p. 18.

13 Byong-Wook Lee, 'Waste costing for a Korean steel producer', in K. Green, P. Groenewegen and P.S. Hoffman (eds) *Ahead of the Curve: Cases of Innovation in Environmental Management*, Dordrecht, Netherlands: Kluwer Academic Publishers, 2001, esp. pp. 63–7, 71.

14 Shell sustainability report (2005).

15 Stace and Dunphy, *Beyond the Boundaries*, pp. 71–3.

16 Electric Power Research Institute, 'Program on Technology Innovation: Electric Power Industry Technology Scenarios', report prepared for Global Business Networks, 2005.

17 L. Gratton, *Living Strategy*.

18 D. Elliot, 'Can this man save the American auto industry?' *Time*, 30 January 2006, 38–48.

19 J. Benveniste, 'Quality of work, home and family life', in D. Dunphy, J. Benveniste, A. Griffiths and P. Sutton (eds) *Sustainability: The Corporate Challenge of the 21st Century*, Sydney: Allen and Unwin, 2000, pp. 102–23, esp. p. 117.

20 Stace and Dunphy, *Beyond the Boundaries*, p. 83.

21 J. Benveniste and D. Dunphy, *The Path Towards Sustainability: A Case Study of Placer Dome Asia Pacific*, Centre for Corporate Change, Australian Graduate School of Management, University of New South Wales, 1999.

22 D. Chatterjee, *Leading Consciously: A Pilgrimage Towards Self Mastery*, Oxford: Viva Books and Butterworth-Heinemann, 1999, p. 39.

23 B. Smith and J. Yanowitz, 'Sustainable innovation and change: the learning-based path to growth', *Prism*, 1998, 4th quarter, 35–45.

24 D. Goleman, *Emotional Intelligence*, New York: Bantam Books, 1996; D. Zohar and I. Marshall, *Spiritual Intelligence: The Ultimate Intelligence*, London: Bloomsbury, 2000.

25 See D. Hock, *Birth of the Chaordic Age*, San Francisco: Barrett-Koehler, 1999.

26 C. Handy, *The Elephant and the Flea: Looking Backwards to the Future*, London: Random House, 2000, p. 82.

27 Greenbiz.com, 'Honda greenest auto maker, GM tumbles to worst overall', 2004 (accessed 22 May 2006).

28 Ibid.

29 E. von Weizacker, A. B. Lovins and L. H. Lovins, *Factor 4: Doubling Wealth – Halving Resource Use*, Sydney: Allen and Unwin, 1997.

30 Stace and Dunphy, *Beyond the Boundaries*, pp. 106–18.

31 A. Pears, 'Towards ecological sustainability: technologies and processes', in D. Dunphy, J. Benveniste, A. Griffiths and P. Sutton (eds) *Sustainability: The Corporate Challenge of the 21st Century*, Sydney: Allen and Unwin, 2000, pp. 167–90, esp. p. 183.

32 H. Tibbs, 'Industrial ecology: an environmental agenda for industry', *Whole Earth Review*, 1995, September–October, 120–34.

9 Leading towards sustainability

- Facing up to the future
- Key factors in change-agent competence
- Achieving mastery
- Starting with self-leadership
- Seeking cosmocentric consciousness
- Building or assembling the skills needed for diagnosis and action
- Creating dialogue and shared scenarios
- Identifying and dealing with resistance to change
- Who are the leaders/change agents?
- Building alliances of change agents
- Constructing the sustainability agenda
- Achieving ecological sustainability

Facing up to the future

Leadership is the creation of new realities. In this final chapter we discuss the leadership of change and the roles that different kinds of change agents can play in constructing the new reality of the sustainable corporation. Transforming the way we do business is no minor task and will require the inspiration, energies and skills of more people than are currently engaged in the task. If we are to create a sustainable world, we need many more effective leaders.

In raising the issue of change leadership we cannot ignore how much easier it is to accept the *status quo*, to respond to our fear of change and our desire for certainty, to opt out rather than to engage actively in attempting to change the organizational world. Most of us, if we are honest, would rather let someone else lead in this kind of endeavour. Change of the order we are advocating here threatens us with uncertainty and chaos. It is much easier to hold on to traditional ways of doing things and to accept the leadership of others who don't question the *status quo*. The past, because of its familiarity, seems to offer us security – more security, at least, than a divergent and uncharted future. However, as we have argued throughout this book, many past practices are unsustainable. If we want the world we know and love to survive, we must change it. If we are to survive and thrive ourselves, we too must change. To change, however, requires the rawest kind of courage.

Choosing to lead change similarly involves courage, risk taking and the development of high levels of skill. These are the focus of our discussion in this chapter. The chapter is also designed to help you answer some basic questions about your own potential role as a leader of sustainable change:

- How do I equip myself to be an effective leader?
- Where shall I start?
- Who can I work with to have the most impact?

> We are entering an era, I believe, when world class enterprises will build . . . sophistication in understanding and tapping the intelligence and spirit of human beings.
>
> (P. Senge)[1]

Key factors in change-agent competence

What do we need to be effective change leaders? We need clarity of vision, knowledge of what we wish to change and the skills to implement the changes. But none of these can be fully effective without maturity and wisdom. In the end it is who we are, not what we know or can do, that makes the crucial difference in effecting organizational change. Ideally change agents need the following characteristics – but note any provisos that follow.

Goal clarity

'I know what outcomes I want to produce.' Yes, we do need to know what we want to achieve, but our understanding of the goal doesn't have to be precise when we begin. What we need is a 'strategic intent', a direction, a deep, intuitive response to the organizational situation in which we find ourselves, an aspiration to nudge our organizational world a little closer to the ideal of sustainability. This aspiration does not necessarily require transformative leadership, but it does entail a clear understanding of core values and core purpose.[2] For instance, at Insurance Australia Group (IAG), Australia's largest insurance group, the CEO, Mike Hawker, has defined corporate social responsibility as a core value and sustainability as a shared purpose across the organization. At IAG sustainability is defined as being about ensuring the organization is around in the future for its customers, employees, community and shareholders. That involves:

- *Economic* sustainability: building value for shareholders.
- *Human* sustainability: safety, work–life balance, diversity.
- *Environmental* sustainability: advocating climate change, reducing impact on environment.
- *Social* sustainability: reducing risk in the community such as crime, fires, car accidents, etc.[3]

Role clarity

'I know what to do to produce change.' Of course, when we start, we often do not know what to do. We may not have a clue about what to do to make change happen. This is a paradox we face as change agents – we need to find a viable and effective role to play in midwifing the future but everything seems to conspire to block us. Nike, for instance, initially floundered in finding its response to the boycotts and activism associated with poor working conditions in subcontractor factories in developing countries such as Vietnam. However, in 1998 Nike established a global corporate responsibility function and created the specific role of Vice-president of Corporate Responsibility, covering areas such as labour compliance, global community affairs, stakeholder engagement and corporate responsibility strategic planning and business integration. Tangible sustainability outcomes for Nike include an environmental sustainability policy and initiatives. These initiatives were targeted to give 3 per cent of the company's pre-tax income to communities around the globe (US$37.3 million in cash and product in fiscal year 2004); it also developed an internal and external contract factory monitoring programme; and integrated corporate responsibility more tightly into the business.[4]

Similarly, at Hewlett-Packard, Environmental Product Stewards are responsible for incorporating design within manufacturing centres and design teams. These stewards are charged with the specific role of taking the Hewlett-Packard *Design for Environment* guidelines to the practical level.[5]

Relevant knowledge

'I have or can access the knowledge required to produce the outcomes I want.' Corporate change processes demand depth of knowledge, and in the area of sustainability that knowledge is often not gained easily. Sustainability cuts right across traditional disciplinary boundaries. In a particular project, for example, we may need knowledge of the political processes of the organization, technical knowledge about energy conservation, water purification, chemical pollutants, and knowledge about the attitudes of key external stakeholders. It would be an unusual person who had this knowledge at the beginning of a change programme. But we don't need all the knowledge before we start; we can acquire it as we go along, in partnership with others more knowledgeable than ourselves in some of these areas.

Nike is a firm which illustrates this principle of learning as we go. Mark Parker and Charlie Denson, co-presidents of Nike's brand, can state that its decade-long journey in understanding its impact has enabled the firm to clearly enunciate its three-pronged strategic goals:

- To use sport as a tool for positive social change and campaign to turn sport and physical activity into a fundamental right for every young person.
- To effect positive, systemic change in working conditions within the footwear, apparel and equipment industries.
- To create innovative and sustainable products.[6]

Relevant competences and resources

'I have or can assemble the skills and resources to make it happen.' Again, we may not have the skills we need when we first take up a role as an organizational change agent. Acquiring skills is a lifetime endeavour. So we need to be realistic about the skills we have and start the change process in a way that builds on our current skill level. However, the only effective way to learn skills is through experimentation and practice. To acquire them, we take faltering steps at first but, with practice, our steps become firm and purposeful. Mentors and models help, so, if we are relatively unskilled, another criterion of where to start the change process is to find others who have the necessary skills and work with them. To begin, we need only a sub-set of the skills demanded by the full change programme and, if we work with others, we do not need the full repertoire of skills ourselves.

Self-esteem

'I believe I can do it.' Sometimes this one is the toughest call of all, but a passionate belief in the profound importance of the change we are initiating is a great help. Being a change agent is not for the faint-hearted. Emotional resilience is a fundamental requirement. We are often called on to persist in the face of adversity, derision, contempt and anger. Changing entrenched power structures can be a career-threatening experience. But then, abandoning the cause of sustainability is a planet-threatening experience. If we choose to undergo some adversity, at least in the end we have the satisfaction of knowing that we stand for life, for hope, for a viable future for us all.

If we believed we need the five characteristics so starkly listed above without the added provisos we would never start to try to change corporations. These are ideals to be worked towards; they set a direction for our learning – they are not the starting line we must cross to begin. They define mastery in this field and we discuss below the path to mastery – it is a long path and we learn primarily by doing. If we choose well, we also learn by apprenticeship to others more experienced and skilled than ourselves and by finding models and mentors. But definitely by doing.

We need to learn to live with ambiguity and a degree of chaos. Managing corporate change is rather like white-water rafting or surfing. The first lesson is not to try to control the environment but to move with it. Like rafting or surfing, success in change leadership comes from being willing to change our internal psychological world.

Achieving mastery

But that's only Change Leadership 101. As in any field of serious endeavour, learning of this kind is a lifetime commitment. We start as novices and may achieve mastery but that takes effort, time and commitment. Table 9.1 outlines the stages in achieving mastery as a change agent. Moving through these stages opens us to a series of opportunities rather than problems.

Chatterjee writes eloquently of the need for change agents to develop personal mastery:

Personal mastery is a journey towards a destination we may call an *integral being*. Integral beings experience a life of oneness with themselves and their universe. They act from the wholeness of this experience. There is harmony and a unique synchronicity between their beliefs and their actions. Their bodies, minds, and senses orchestrate themselves to the effortless rhythms of the universe.[7]

Similarly Handy talks of change agents as 'alchemists' who don't react to events but shape them. He characterizes them as passionate about what they are doing because they have a conviction of its importance. He also sees them as being able to leap beyond the rational and logical and stick with their dream, if necessary against the 'evidence'.[8] In fact they are changing the world as they go, building excitement and momentum. Like water finding its way down a hillside, they simply go round obstacles and dissolve resistance.

Table 9.1 *Stages in achieving change-agent mastery*

1 Novice: learning the 'rules'
We seek clear guidelines for how to act in different situations; for example, many novices are drawn to the Natural Step programmes, which offer simple rules for instituting sustainable practices. We seek the codified knowledge of others who have done it.

2 Advanced beginner: beyond rules to strategies
We realize that in many situations the rules don't work. Making change is more complex than we thought. Rules become more blurred and evolve into thoughtful strategies.

3 Competence: disciplined effectiveness
We develop a 'feel' for the complexity of change, select cues and respond to them on the basis of our accumulating experience. Our knowledge now is more tacit; our strategies are now evolving to include deeper levels of awareness.

4 Proficiency: fluid, effortless performance
We have internalized the strategies and they are backed up with high levels of skill. Intuition now dominates and reason is secondary.

5 Mastery: acting from our deepest intuition with confidence and flow
We become one with the changes we are making and are changing ourselves and our organizational world at the same time. Our inner and outer worlds are one. What we do often seems effortless and spontaneous.

Starting with self-leadership

Being a change agent means living in and between two worlds. One is the world of inner experience, of personal meaning, of selfhood. The other is the outer world of action. The inner world is the real challenge for change agents. Paradoxically the secret to changing the world about us is discovered only within ourselves. Mahatma Gandhi had a very clear idea about where his leadership began. He said: 'I must first be the change I want to bring about in my world.'[9] Our ability to model in our own lives – in our attitudes, words and actions – the changes we wish to bring about: this is the most powerful intervention we ever make. Our integrity is the test of the worth of what we advocate. After all, if we cannot bring about the changes within ourselves, do we have the right to ask others to make these changes? And if we cannot make the changes ourselves, what chance do we have of success in changing others?

Quinn writes of how important it is for organizational change agents to make deep change at the personal level: 'To make deep personal change is to develop a new paradigm, a new self, one that is more effectively aligned with today's realities.'[10] He sees a vital link in our ability to make deep change within ourselves and the effective leadership of organizational change. Leaders who are prepared to make deep change within themselves, in Quinn's view, make transformative organizational change possible.

Recent research on leadership effectiveness reinforces the notion that change leadership requires particular kinds of psychological strengths. In particular, Luthans draws on developments in positive psychology – a field which emphasizes building on people's personal strengths rather than focusing on their weaknesses. He reviews research into the contribution of personal strengths to performance improvement in the workplace. He finds that these characteristics include 'realistic hope, optimism, subjective wellbeing/happiness and emotional intelligence'.[11] These are, of course, the characteristics of mature, emotionally healthy human beings as well as effective change agents.

Through reviewing the change agent literature and discussions with change practitioners Dunphy has identified the following as important personal characteristics for change agents:

● Personal resilience and persistence.
● Realistic self-esteem, self-direction and initiative.
● Tolerance of ambiguity.

- Flexibility and adaptability.
- A clear focus.
- Enthusiasm and motivation.
- The ability to inspire others.
- Political awareness and sensitivity.
- Empathy.
- A sense of humour.
- A helicopter view.
- Commitment to continuous learning.[12]

We all fall short of this ideal, of course, but attempting change leadership is one way to acquire these characteristics.

Seeking cosmocentric consciousness

In bringing about deep change leading to sustainability the old Newtonian world view of a mechanistic, atomized universe doesn't help; nor does the 'objectivist' stance, so deeply inculcated by a traditional scientific world view, based on the myth that knowledge is created by scientists who stand outside the universe they are studying.

Chatterjee draws on Indian spiritual tradition in describing the importance of meditation in helping us relinquish both our belief that the world is made up of discrete objects and the egocentricity associated with this belief. In his view, we can progress from being egocentric personalities attached to material objects to cosmocentric individuals in a harmonious relationship with nature. The egocentric person feels empowered by the objects he or she can possess. By contrast, cosmocentric consciousness frees us from the clutter of objects and possessions so that the universal consciousness that flows through the entire universe also flows through us.[13] Albert Einstein wrote eloquently in the same vein:

> A human being is part of the whole, called by us the Universe, a part limited in time and space. He experiences himself, his thoughts and feelings, as something separated from the rest – a kind of optical delusion of his consciousness. This delusion is a kind of prison, restricting us to our personal desires and to affection for a few persons nearest to us. Our task must be to free from this prison by widening our circle of compassion to embrace all living creatures and the whole of nature in its beauty.[14]

Organizations too have their collective consciousness. Quinn writes of the change agent listening to the inner voice of the organization which calls for the realignment of internal values and external realities. He regards the inner voice of the organization as 'the most potent source of power in the organization':[15] 'Preparation, reflection, and courage are needed to hear the inner voice. The inner voice will provide direction if people have the courage to listen and the commitment to change.'[16] In our view, responding to the inner voice includes voicing the unspeakable – speaking for the interpersonal underworld that exists in most organizations but fails to gain official recognition. This is the world of collective fear and despair, of latent rebellion, of long-remembered anger, of irreverent humour and cynicism. Giving voice to these aspects of the organization's life is often like pointing out that the emperor has no clothes. This is also the world of high dreams and ideals: people's hopes and yearnings for more fulfilling and meaningful work. These aspirations have often been submerged by disappointment and discouraging experiences but can rise to the surface again with compelling power.

To develop cosmocentric consciousness is to care, and caring is an important part of effective leadership. Effective change leaders are passionate about the changes they support; their actions are value-driven. They care about the environment; they care about the community; they care about the individuals with whom they work.

Empathy, caring and love are not popular terms in the current managerial vocabulary. They are, however, words we can dare to speak and to live. Professor Leo Buscaglia, an outstanding academic educator, recounts how deans from other schools would call to invite him to give a visiting lecture. They would eventually ask him for the title of his lecture and, when he said 'Love', there would be an embarrassed silence on the other end of the phone, followed by a remark like 'Could you make that Love comma As A Behavior Modifier?'[17]

True knowledge of the world and of others comes from empathetic understanding, not cold objectivity. Love is the matrix from which community is born; love creates the 'we' from the 'I'. From conception to old age, maturity and health are products of supportive social relations. Without empathy, caring, compassion, respect, tolerance and love, organizations cease to be communities, trust dissolves and all relationships become calculative. As we have discussed earlier in this book, the nature of modern organizations means that they don't operate effectively without trust. But trust does not grow automatically; in organizational life, it is built consciously, purposefully over time by those who care.

Cosmocentric consciousness, or spiritual intelligence, helps us connect with the emerging forms of the future.[18] Without this kind of consciousness it is hard to find the future – with it, the future seems inescapable. The future is within us and around us. Its shape is already coalescing in our dreams.

Building or assembling the skills needed for diagnosis and action

Self-leadership is necessary, but it is not enough. As well as self-knowledge and an empathetic understanding of others, effective change leaders need skills.

First on the list are skills associated with effective diagnosis. If we are to attempt to change an organization we must first understand where the organization is on the path to sustainability and where it needs to go. Making the right diagnosis is as important in achieving organizational well-being as it is in achieving individual physical health. One of the major challenges for organizational change agents is that they usually have to make the analysis themselves and they have to do it on the run and *in situ*. It would be nice if our organizational change efforts began with a neatly packaged Harvard Business School case analysis, but unfortunately they don't.

If we work in the organization, then we are part of what we are analysing. Our viewpoint will be biased by the position we occupy – the view from below is always different, for example, from the view from above; the industrial engineer's view is different from that of the salesperson in the field. On the other hand, if we are external to the organization – for example, a consultant – we may have a more open mind; but we don't have the advantage of inside information. Whatever our role, as we start actively to find out more about the organization, looking at records, interviewing personnel and so on, we are already intervening in the ongoing system.

So we are studying a dynamic system of which we are part or become a part as we study it. We can't put it in a laboratory, take it apart and analyse it under a microscope. All we can do is immerse ourselves in it, understand that our own view will be biased and try to offset that by empathetic identification with others who occupy very different positions. We can also gather data that can expand or contradict our biases. Moving around the organization helps, as do cultivating an open mind, observing and listening. The skills of action research are the most useful. In some cases we may wish to add more formal means of analysis such as surveys and financial analysis. These can help but are no substitute for being there with full awareness.

More specifically the action research and diagnostic skills we need are:

- *A well developed systematic theoretical position*, a framework or multiple frameworks, that is, a model of how organizations operate which helps us select the kind of data that are useful for understanding and for future action. This model is always partial and limited and so we must be open to revising it on the basis of experience.
- *A model of the ideal sustainable organization* combined with openness to others' ideal models. The future is mostly a collective creation, emerging from the active dialogue and interaction of interested parties. We need to be as clear as we can on what we want so that we can engage fully with others in that dialogue; but we need to be open to any emerging shared vision. Of course, there may be competing visions and resistance to visions in general: conflict is simply an element of the unfolding drama through which the future is defined; conflict is a signal that something important is at stake; it is a measure of progress on the path, not the end of the path.
- *The ability to question and listen to others* for factual, value-based and emotive information; all three kinds of information are useful. Moving to sustainability necessarily involves values and emotions as well as facts.
- *The ability to use varied data sources and methods of analysis*, to apply critical insight and make balanced judgements. If we want to make a map, it is useful to view the landscape from different viewpoints – triangulation increases accuracy.
- *The ability to convey a concise diagnosis* to others in their terms. The emerging field of sustainability studies is already developing its own language – professional and technical jargon. Some of this is useful as shorthand and for technical precision. But if we are to influence others, we need to be able to translate what is important into the everyday language of the workplace.
- *The ability to monitor and evaluate the change process*. The process of diagnosis does not stop when the action begins. Diagnosis becomes even more crucial in checking whether we are achieving what we set out to achieve and whether we need to change the path we travel along as we reach a fuller understanding of where we need to go.

Diagnostic skills help define the path to sustainability. Moving down that path requires change agents to develop other skill sets too, particularly the skills of effective communication, of managing stakeholder relationships and project management:

- *Skills of effective communication:* willingness to listen and ask skilful questions; the ability to adopt multiple viewpoints; the commitment to keep people informed and 'in the picture'; the ability to communicate clearly and simply with others in speech and writing; the ability to use images and emotions as well as facts in communicating with others.
- *Skills of managing stakeholder relationships:* direction setting (visioning) and defining the scope of responsibilities for parts of the vision; influencing and networking; delegating; developing, mentoring and coaching others; performance management and monitoring; team building.
- *Skills of project management:* making and taking opportunities; updating technical and organizational knowledge; problem solving; resourcing.

Relevant to each of these skills sets are communication skills that can convey the value proposition of sustainability to different stakeholders. For instance, IAG's CEO, Mike Hawker, demonstrates his skilled role in communicating sustainability both in terms of a core organizational value for all stakeholders and in terms of a value proposition to customers:

> The bigger the organization the more important it is to have a set of control structures to ensure that you are consistent in what you do and the two control structures that work are firstly values (a set of corporate values that don't change, they stand the test of time and the values describe the nature of people in the organization and describe how people will act). And the second one is a clear understanding throughout the organization of what it is you offer as a value proposition (purpose) to your customer. We think that the only way you get the consistent delivery is through a control mechanism which is value based and purpose based.[19]

Figure 9.1 summarizes our analysis of the skills needed to become an effective change agent. These skills will be in great demand as more organizations embrace what Hirsh and Sheldrake refer to as 'inclusive leadership'.[20] Inclusive leadership, as they define it, derives from adopting the stakeholder perspective on organizations. It involves managers developing and maintaining an interactive exchange with all those who have a stake in the organization: investors, employees,

Figure 9.1 *Skills of effective change agents*

suppliers, customers, the community, and representatives of the environment and future generations. Organizations need to perform instrumental tasks and to reach financial objectives. But this is most effectively achieved by creating a wider set of outcomes that meet the needs of key stakeholders.[21] The skills of relationship building will be particularly critical as organizations move forward on the path to sustainability.

Creating dialogue and shared scenarios

One of the central tasks of change agents is the creation of visioning capabilities in the organization. Gratton writes that 'the capacity to create and develop a vision of the future that is compelling and engaging [is] at the very centre of creating a human approach to organizations'.[22] But where does the vision come from?

Vision emerges from dialogue – both inner dialogue within ourselves and dialogue within the organization and with its external stakeholders. The task of the change agent is to work with others to create new meaning, for new meaning creates new realities. This is the process that Weick calls 'sensemaking'.[23] Dialogue is not chatter but rather engagement at the deepest level with ourselves and with others. Dialogue begins with cultivating awareness and with listening; it continues with responsiveness and an exchange that is a catalyst for creative change.[24]

Dialogue can change people's perceptions of themselves and of their organization. From these new perceptions a sense of collective identity and purpose emerges that can renew or transform the existing culture of the organization. If this happens, the leadership of change passes from the handful of change agents who began the change process to a much larger network within the organization. Leaders create leaders.

One of us is a member of Westpac Bank's Community Consultative Council. The CEO of Westpac, David Morgan, meets annually with twenty community leaders from not-for-profit organizations. For two and a half hours he, and some of his staff, listen as each leader in turn discusses what issues concern them when they think about the next five to ten years. The key issues raised at this meeting become an input to Westpac's corporate planning process. Measurable goals are set and reported on the next year. This is a simple and cheap environmental scanning process, and creates an ongoing dialogue with some key stakeholders who are often drawn in to contribute to the resulting action plans.

> Leadership is about 'bringing everyone along' in a balanced way, not just in their minds so they understand it, but emotionally as well, in their hearts, so they are really energized and identify with it, and they themselves take part in the leadership.
>
> (Frank Blount, former CEO, Telstra)[25]

Our own experience in working with effective change leaders at all levels of organizations is that they have a profound belief in the ability of others. This belief manifests itself through challenging others to contribute even beyond what they thought was their best and supporting them in doing it. Typically, others say of such leaders: 'You know, he (she) believed in me more than I believed in myself. Through him (her) I learned that I could accomplish much greater things than I ever thought possible.' This is true empowerment and it is part of the process of creating organizations where everyone has the opportunity to lead in developing a sustainable workplace that offers exciting and meaningful work.

However, some conflicts of interests in organizations are intractable. When this is the case, leadership becomes the art of achieving what you believe is the best possible outcome in the circumstances, even if that does not match your ideal. Negotiations and compromise may be necessary to produce small wins that can be built on later. A general rule for change agents is that if you can't go round it, over it or under it, then negotiate with it.

Identifying and dealing with resistance to change

All change agents encounter resistance to the changes they attempt to introduce. There is an extensive literature on resistance to change and how to deal with it. Much of it is written for senior executives and embodies the assumption that positive change is mainly initiated by senior executives, who encounter resistance to change from middle management or the work force. Our own experience is that senior executives are as resistant to change as anyone else and the initiative for change often comes from elsewhere in the organization. The reality is that most people resist change when others are attempting to change them; few do when they feel that they are in charge of change.

People are particularly likely to resist change when they see it as threatening their interests and when they believe that their knowledge and skills may be made irrelevant as changes take place. As we move towards sustainability there will be those whose interests are threatened and whose current knowledge and skills become obsolete. Not all resistance to change is irrational. As change agents we need to understand that change is a political process in which people's power and status are implicated. There will always be those whose identification with the old order is so strong that they will actively oppose or passively resist change towards the new. There can also be legitimate disagreements – value conflicts – about the best way to proceed in progressing sustainability: disagreements about priorities, about facts such as the potential danger of certain substances, about strategies and tactics for moving forward. As change agents we need to work to create an evolving consensus among interested parties. Active engagement of those who will be affected by the changes is often the most effective way forward. However, it does not always work. There can be delays, obfuscations, sidetracks, subversions. As in all fields of endeavour, persistence is a large part of success and persistence comes from a deep commitment to a meaningful view of the future.

Learning as we go

Quinn recalls a time when he and a student were writing a case study of a company and interviewed the CEO. The CEO recounted the story of the company's first five years as if it had been the unfolding of a clear strategic plan. This didn't match Quinn's understanding of how the changes took place and he challenged the CEO by giving his own version: Quinn saw it as a rather chaotic learning process. The CEO was somewhat taken aback by this, but then smiled and said: 'It's true, we built the bridge as we walked on it.'[26] Initiating and managing a change process, particularly in the area of sustainability where there are no standard models, will always mean building the bridge as we walk on it. Planning is important but it will be an evolving process and, despite our best efforts, the implementation will sometimes be disorganized and discontinuous. Learning as we go is the way we become skilled change agents.

Making it happen

The implementation of change for sustainability requires relentless attention to the detail of corporate responsibility. At Nike, for instance, a team of approximately 150 people are charged with corporate responsibility either solely or as a significant part of their work load. A key task is to identify risks and opportunities concerning corporate responsibility. Each leader in the team has a reporting line to a business unit and to the responsibility team. As well, sourcing managers bring corporate responsibility data into their decisions about what factories merit increases or decreases in production orders.[27]

Contributing to living networks

An important part of making change happen is networking with like-minded people. Change agents spend real time in building networks to provide information about the systems they are working in, to act as channels of influence and for support in what is an emotionally demanding endeavour. But where do we find like-minded people?

Values researcher Ray has identified three major groups in the United States whom he refers to as modernists, heartlanders and cultural creatives. The modernists embrace mainstream materialist values, try to acquire property and money, are value winners and are cynical about idealism and caring for others. The heartlanders hold conservative values, reject modernism, favour traditional gender roles and fundamentalist religion, and are volunteers who care for others. The cultural creatives reject modernism and support the values of an integral culture that seeks to integrate life on the basis of diversity. They have a well developed social consciousness, are optimistic and committed to family, community, internationalism, feminism and the environment. They are concerned about health, personal growth and spirituality. Cultural creatives share with modernists openness to change and, like heartlanders, care about community and personal relationships.[28] Ray's surveys estimate that 47 per cent of the US population are modernists, 29 per cent are heartlanders and 24 per cent are cultural creatives.

We expect that a disproportionate number of leaders in sustainable change programmes will be drawn from the ranks of the cultural creatives. Clearly, what Ray calls 'integral culture' is a value set that supports the views we have espoused in this book. Ray argues that there are about 50 million cultural creatives in the United States and that they are the leading edge of cultural change in the country. It seems that there are at least that number in Europe also.[29] We are not alone.

Other studies of changing values support these findings of a significant value shift occurring on a global scale. For example, Ronald Inglehart analysed data from the 1990–91 World Values Survey and showed a shift towards the values of an integral culture in a number of societies. He concluded that there was a global trend towards postmodern values that includes less interest in economic gain, less confidence in hierarchical institutions and a greater commitment to sustainability. The value shift also involves a search for more personal meaning and a deeper sense of purpose in life.[30]

Part of our networking can be a process of finding those who share these values so that we create the interpersonal links that are part of the flexible architecture of the sustainability movement. We can build the momentum for change most readily through networks of those who are committed to the cluster of values that support sustainability.

In an example of such networking between business leaders in response to government inaction associated with climate change six Australian CEOs (from the major companies IAG, Westpac Banking, Visy Industries, BP Australasia, Origin Energy and Swiss Re) met to form

the Business Roundtable on Climate Change. In contrast to the Business
Council of Australia, which has not been able to develop a position on
climate change, the Roundtable group argue that climate change is a
major business risk and that action is a business imperative. They have
produced research showing that it is possible for Australia to cut its
greenhouse gas emissions by 60 per cent from year 2000 levels before
2050 and still have strong economic growth. Their Roundtable report
argues 250,000 jobs could be at stake if greenhouse action is delayed.
Delay will also mean the need for much more drastic and costly action
later on, they argue. The momentum for change is likely to come from
their call for a national, market-based carbon pricing mechanism, which
they want the government to sketch out a framework for next year.[31]

Who are the leaders/change agents?

We have outlined the personal characteristics and skills of effective
change agents. But what roles do change agents occupy and how do
these roles affect the contributions they can make to the sustainability
movement? Our list follows, and then we discuss how their distinctive
contributions can make corporate sustainability a living reality.

Change agent roles

- *Internal*
  - ○ Line roles: the board of management, the CEO, the senior
    executive team, other managers and supervisors, general employees.
  - ○ Staff support roles: human resources (HR), organization
    developments (OD), industrial engineering and environmental
    specialists, life scientists and information technology (IT)
    specialists.
- *External:* politicians, bureaucrats and regulators; investors;
  professional business consultants; customers; community activists,
  concerned citizens and intellectuals; environmentalist activists; those
  who speak for future generations.

What are their distinctive roles? We now take up the issue of how the
various roles listed above can contribute to sustainability initiatives.
As outlined, we divide them into roles internal to the organization and
external to it. All these roles can make a distinctive contribution to

moving organizations towards sustainability; in collaboration, they can have an irresistible impact. We begin our discussion with roles internal to the organization.

Internal change agent roles

The internal roles consist of 'the line' and 'staff support'. The line consists of the board of management, CEO, senior executive team, other managers and supervisors and general employees.[32] The staff support roles consist of specialist professionals who provide support to those in the line. We will deal with the line roles first.

Line roles

Boards of management. Boards of management can play a crucial role in setting the operating rules for an organization. Directors have heavy legal responsibilities and may be liable to major penalties if the organization is not compliant. They also have ultimate responsibility for appointing the CEO and signing off on the firm's business strategies. The relationship between the board and the CEO appears to be critical if an organization is to act more responsibly towards its stakeholders. Research by KPMG's Corporate Citizenship and Business Ethics Unit indicates that directors of public companies see the CEO as playing the key role in setting the ethical and accountability agenda of the organization and that interaction between the board and the CEO is crucial to communicating and embedding this agenda across their organization. This interaction could include determining CEO selection criteria, corporate values and ethical performance criteria.[33]

Boards of management often lack sufficient diversity to deal effectively with the shift from sole focus on shareholder value to meeting the expectations of a wider set of stakeholders. The changes we are advocating mean that the membership of boards needs to change so that they sample the diversity of stakeholders whose interests the board must now represent. Corporate sustainability has implications for corporate governance.

Line managers include the CEO, senior executives, managers and supervisors or team leaders. Gratton views the line manager's role in the change process as being courageous enough to create broad involvement, to support the process of change, and to ensure that Human Relations is centrally important to the business.[34] The CEO and senior executive team's central task is to ensure that sustainability strategies are an integral part of business strategy and that they contribute to profitability, to customer satisfaction as well as to the welfare of other stakeholders. Their role involves communicating that corporate objectives include sustainability and outlining what this means for the integrity of organizational structures, processes, products and services. Their actions must also match policy statements rather than contradict them: it is important that they model what they are espousing, allocate resources to support the change process and ensure that measures of business unit performance include progress on sustainability goals. As strategies are implemented successfully, line managers also have the responsibility for seeing that the resulting learning is communicated across the organization so that successful sustainability innovations are adopted and adapted.

The CEO. The role of the CEO is vital in terms of both symbolic and practical leadership. It is no easy role. Elkington describes the dilemma faced by Ford Motor Company chairman William Clay Ford. Ford made a series of major sustainability initiatives, including a model citizenship report called *Connecting with Society* in which he gave his view that the popular sports utility vehicles were unsustainable given the petrol they consumed. He said that Ford aimed to be a model company for the twenty-first century, particularly in the area of sustainability. The report had only just been released when there was a recall of 6 million defective Firestone tyres that were shown to have triggered many accidents, including deaths. Ford vehicles, particularly sports utility vehicles, were the major users of the tyres. Firestone had attempted to cover up the growing history of accidents and became mired in lawsuits as a result. Firestone was the supplier but Ford's reputation was also affected. The Ford Explorer was equipped with the Firestone tyres and had been a major profit generator, so profits slumped. Addressing the 2000 Greenpeace Business Conference, William Ford said: 'This terrible situation – which goes against everything I stand for – has made us more determined than ever to operate in an open, transparent and accountable manner at all times.'[35]

The CEO of a public company faces the dilemma that many market analysts and investment funds seek short-term returns and, as yet, place far too little emphasis on the importance of the issues we have discussed in this book. The CEO who is attempting to build a sustainable and sustaining corporate culture faces a daily performance evaluation by a share market which traditionally places little value on this. As we have discussed, ethical investment funds have demonstrated consistently superior returns and the size of such funds is growing. Nevertheless the CEO must deliver in the short term and find resources to invest in the future. This is no easy task, particularly in a recession; sometimes it feels to CEOs that they are running up an escalator that is moving in the opposite direction. Nevertheless many CEOs manage to generate short-term gains by 'picking low-hanging fruit' while quietly investing in building the capabilities of the corporation to generate medium to long-term performance, including performance due to sustainability initiatives.

Hart and Quinn saw CEOs as playing four kinds of leadership roles in the change process: motivator, vision setter, analyser and taskmaster. These roles are directed respectively to people, the future, the operating system and the market. They investigated the typical roles played by CEOs and linked these roles to three measures of firm performance: short-term financial performance, growth and future positioning of the organization, and organizational effectiveness (non-financial measures of performance such as employee satisfaction, product quality and social responsibility).

Hart and Quinn found that CEOs used the taskmaster role the most but the role did not influence any of the three performance measures. The analyser role, directed at creating improved efficiency, and the vision setter role were significant predictors of business performance and organizational effectiveness, but not of short-term business performance. The motivator role was, however, a particularly strong predictor of organizational performance on all three dimensions.[36] The research results also demonstrate that those CEOs who used all four roles achieved higher levels of performance than CEOs who did not.[37] Being an effective CEO demands a varied role repertoire and the flexibility to move in and out of different roles as the needs of the situation change. These qualities of the CEO are the qualities of any organizational leader, writ large: all leaders need to be able to understand the issues (analyser), inspire others (vision setter) and help them focus their energy (motivator).

We have recognized that both incremental and transformative changes can facilitate organizational sustainability. If it is the profound transformational change associated with redesigning the organization around sustainability principles that is chosen as appropriate, then, above all, the CEO and other corporate figures must be able to face the realities of what the organization is and what it needs to change. As Debold puts it, the CEO who has the capacity for 'creative responsibility' also has the capacity to face everything and avoid nothing. Ray Anderson, chairman of the carpet manufacturer Interface, is such a leader. Through his leadership and with the advice of designers who can envision business models based on the creativity of Nature, Interface has saved A$255 million in the last decade by implementing innovative manufacturing processes aimed at eliminating hazardous wastes.[38] Another example is the drive to micro-franchising taken up by corporate leaders of organizations such as Unilever. Based on the famous example of the Grameen Bank, whose micro-finance operations have successfully assisted many thousands of poor, mostly female, clients to borrow money interest-free to establish their own business, micro-franchising targets the 'bottom of the pyramid' (BOP) section of the market. Tex Gunning, the global head of BOP strategy for Unilever, argues that his vision of Unilver micro-franchising not only leaves a smaller environmental footprint but has the capacity to end child malnutrition.[39]

Other managers, supervisors and team leaders contribute to the strategic process and actively translate the strategies into practical action plans. If they are to be effective, these plans will include achievable but challenging sustainability goals and involve the introduction of processes and systems that embody ecological and human sustainability principles. Supervisors and team leaders, in particular, are the critical front line of both incremental and transformational change. Their support and feedback are vital to a successful change programme.

At any level of the organization, leaders who recognize the importance of sustaining the diversity and interconnectedness of life forms and who value their employees and the wider community by definition must address organizational issues of gender, diversity and power. Benn *et al.* argue for a new mode of thinking about leadership that recognizes the importance of leadership for diversity in achieving change for sustainability.[40] In evidence they quote a series of empirical studies of organizations where women have achieved a critical mass as senior/leadership levels. These studies show that the presence of women in senior management roles not only adds to diversity but also facilitates more effective accessing of the creative potential of that diversity.[41]

General employees often see themselves as having more limited power than executives and managers. They certainly have more limited authority; but general employees make or break organizational strategies. A strategy that is not translated into the moment-to-moment, day-to-day operational work of the organization is like a bird without wings – it never gets off the ground.

The No. 1 in the list of 100 Best Corporate Citizens selected by *Business Ethics* magazine in 2006, Green Mountain Coffee Roaster, provides a good example of the power of employee commitment to make a difference in the sustainability strategy of the firm. According to Winston Rost, Green Mountain Coffee Roaster's director of coffee appreciation, taking a number of its 600 employees on an annual trip to coffee-growing co-operatives in Vera Cruz and Oaxaca, Mexico, has given them an appreciation of how hard the coffee growers work and has dramatically raised staff awareness of the value of the firm's long-held commitment to social and environmental issues. According to Rost, many employees now say they will never spill another bean again. As well as being a good corporate citizen, the firm is also showing economic sustainability. It saw 2005 revenue of US$161.5 million with net income of US$9 million, a 15 per cent increase over the year prior.[42]

On the list, Californian-based Hewlett-Packard is the only company that has made the top ten in the list of Best Corporate Citizens each year, mainly on the strength of its diversity and community performance. With HP also, employees are crucial to the company's success. According to HP's vice-president of global inclusion and diversity, sixty employee resource groups involving a rich mix of race, gender and sexual orientation air professional development issues and raise awareness of diversity issues. HP also has some highly innovative environmental programmes (such as developing model recycling standards which it shares with its competitors).[43]

Staff support roles

Staff support roles are usually occupied by specialists who do not have the authority held by line managers. Their impact is achieved through expertise and influence rather than authority. Human resource and OD specialists, industrial engineers, environmental specialists and IT specialists are particularly important in making change happen.

Human resource (HR) specialists are an integral part of the change planning process, including working with and to the senior executive team. They must also be active in creating and maintaining the guiding coalition that leads the change process and they need to provide technical expertise on HR issues such as performance reward systems and training and skills development needed to build the competences required to progress through the sustainability phases. The case of Carlton United Beverages, described in Chapter 3, illustrates the dependence of sustainability performance on the HR function.

Organizational development (OD) specialists are particularly important in the organizational reshaping process. Not all organizations have OD specialists or, if they have, refer to them in this way. By OD specialists we mean change agents with highly specialized skills around the process of corporate change. They are professionals with training and experience in techniques such as team building, conflict resolution, counselling and inter-group relations. They are accustomed to working with the hot human process of change as it occurs; they take emotional reactions as a normal part of any significant change process and are not fazed by them. They are accustomed to working in ambiguous situations where they have little authority and to collaborating with others to design the ongoing process of change. Working on the edge of chaos and keeping organizational change processes on track and productive is their specialty.

Industrial designers and engineers. In manufacturing and other industry sectors, specialists with an engineering or industrial design background play key roles in process design, planning and operations. Where they have a grounding in business process re-engineering (BPR) this can prove invaluable in redesigning product flows to make them more efficient and sustainable. Their grasp of the technical knowledge needed in moving to sustainability can combine with the skills of HR and OD specialists to be a winning combination. Where such specialists have a working knowledge of the principles developed by the 'cradle to cradle' design experts Bill McDonough and Michael Braunghart they can be instrumental in redesigning the firm's business model around the 'eco-effective' concept of zero waste.[44] In this model the firm owns the molecules or the building blocks of the products, which are then continually recycled according to market demand. Cars, for instance, would be returned to the manufacturer. Materials would either be composted or recycled into new models. The concept is dependent upon design for ready disassembly and the minimal use of toxic materials.[45] Designers working according to the 'biomimicry' principles developed by such experts as Janine Benyus can also radically reconceptualize the firm's business model in order to integrate sustainability.[46]

IT specialists. Information technology is an enabler of corporate success. No large, complex modern organization can afford to lag behind the leading edge of change in information technology, particularly with the rapid development of e-commerce and virtual organizations. IT specialists are vital to the construction of the computer-based systems needed for co-ordination and control of a wide variety of processes, including complex supply chains. They need to understand the imperative for building sustainable systems and the requirement for them to be both efficient and user-friendly. IT specialists can easily become lost in their world of rapidly changing technology and lose touch with the firm's business imperatives. Sustainability-oriented organizations work to overcome this. At Westpac Banking Corporation, for instance, an annual Chief Information Officer's Challenge Progamme brings in external consultants to facilitate an intensive series of workshops. A different selection of IT managers each year explore and produce recommendations on topics designed to link the IT division into the business as a whole. Each year the series produces confronting and challenging recommendations for both the IT function and the bank and each year some of the recommendations are acted upon. One of us, for instance, has been consulting Westpac on this programme since 2003 and can attest to its value in linking information technology into the wider CSR ethos of the firm.[47]

As an organization progresses through the six phases of sustainability, there is an increasing requirement for a more holistic and integrated approach to both human resources and environmental management. This means that the HR and environmental management functions, in particular, must change and eventually merge or collaborate closely with a mutual understanding of how their efforts contribute seamlessly to the emerging philosophy and practice of sustainability.

External change agent roles

In the sustainability movement, external change agents have played a major role in bringing pressure to bear on organizations to adopt more sustainable strategies. This external pressure has been at times adversarial in both the human and ecological areas of activity. While there will be a place for adversarial activists in the foreseeable future, a shift in emphasis has taken place as more organizations move beyond compliance to launch sustainability initiatives on a voluntary basis. New collaborative alliances are taking place across the boundaries of organizations and external change agents have important roles to play in these alliances. Major and minor consulting companies have also moved to set up specialized practices to provide advice on a variety of sustainability issues.

Politicians, bureaucrats and regulators. The role of politicians, bureaucrats and regulators is to create 'third wave' economies that support 'third wave' organizations. This means having the courage to challenge the narrow assumptions of 'second wave' economists who dominate departments of finance in most Western economies. It means being open to the new fields of ecological economics, industrial ecology and intellectual capital. The countries making most progress in this regard are the Netherlands, Germany, Finland and Denmark. Japan, too, has highly developed national strategies in place concerning product stewardship. These countries are already creating national policies that shift first and second wave corporations forward into the growth industries of the third wave and are developing new export industries in, for example, alternative energy generation. In Denmark, for example, the wind power industry alone generates over US$6 billion a year and employs 15,000 people. Developments like the diversification of energy sources represent significant strategic opportunities for both countries and companies.

China patently has enormous challenges in addressing the problems of regulating such a huge number of firms, many of which are SMEs in far-flung areas of a huge country. Yet some of its laws are highly advanced. Labour laws, laws controlling emissions in new cars, laws controlling traffic movement in and out of central Shanghai – all are in advance of most countries in the West. Implementing these laws is another question and one the central government is acutely aware of.

Investors control the flow of capital to corporations directly and through brokers and funds. There is no more powerful pressure for change than the withdrawal of investment from public companies or the flow of capital to them. It is vital therefore that investors support companies that are working to implement sustainability policies and withdraw investment from those that are not. Companies with sustainable policies give better returns overall than those without such policies, so, on financial grounds alone, this is a viable investment policy. Customers can exert similar pressure through shifting their buying to favour sustainable products and services. As these products and services are healthier, this is also a sensible pattern of consumer spending. Consumers are increasingly demanding openness in terms of ingredients and components in products (for example, information on genetic modification of foods). Supporting increasing transparency makes an important contribution to advancing the sustainability movement because transparency makes informed consumer choice possible.

Community activists, concerned citizens, intellectuals and scientists also have important roles in demanding transparency in company operations, assembling the best available knowledge about the impact of particular kinds of products and services (for example, chemicals), and bringing external pressure to bear on companies that avoid their responsibilities to their work forces, communities or the environment. In addition, as more companies move to an 'inclusive leadership' approach that welcomes the participation of a range of stakeholders in achieving corporate sustainability there are emerging opportunities to collaborate on new initiatives. Community activists also have a vital role in speaking for the natural environment – they are often closest to it and best able to provide a voice to protect it.

Green Mountain Coffee Roaster, for example, began to improve its environmental performance in 1989 when it formed an environmental committee and created a rainforest nut coffee to support the Rainforest Alliance, a non-profit dedicated to protecting ecosystems. The company has grown increasingly active in the countries where coffee is grown and has been a pioneer in the fair trade movement, which pays coffee growers stable, fair prices.[48]

Future generations

Finally, we have included future generations as change agents. The unborn generations are not, of course, yet present and so are unable to act for change that will serve their interests. They need spokespersons to stand for intergenerational equity. In our view, those best equipped to play this role are parents, educators, youth leaders and others who strongly identify with the children of the future and can speak for them.

Building alliances of change agents

Many change agents feel isolated and unsupported in working towards the creation of a sustainable future. Their activities often have little impact and are lost in the ongoing operations of large-scale, complex organizations. As the sustainability movement advances there are increasing opportunities to lead by forming alliances between change agents working within an organization and others outside it. Such alliances can create a pincer movement of pressure for change in the first three phases of sustainability and so build momentum for compliance and for the movement towards compliance plus. In the latter three phases they can create increasing momentum by linking initiatives in different parts of the organization and in the community – initiatives that otherwise might be struggling on their own. It is vital to keep in mind that this is a social movement that extends beyond the corporation and, like all social movements, its success demands disciplined co-operation despite inevitable differences of values and skill bases.

Constructing the sustainability agenda

In Figure 9.2 we have summarized some the challenges the change leader, whether of the SME or the large enterprise, will need to address. So what is the agenda for collaborative action between change agents if they are to address these challenges? The boxes contain summaries of the main points of the sustainability agenda we have discussed through the book. The first outlines the internal agenda, that is, the changes in the work force itself that are needed to build a relevant base of human capabilities. The next one outlines the external agenda, that is, the move towards

Figure 9.2 *Idealized leadership model*
Source: Modified from I. Rankine Kerr, 'Leadership strategies for sustainable SME operation', *Business Strategy and the Environment*, 2006, 15, 30–9.

stakeholder involvement and participation. The third box outlines the agenda for the ecological environment, that is, the changes that need to take place in the corporation so that it does not damage but restores and renews the natural world.

Human sustainability: the internal agenda

- Adopt a strategic perspective to workplace development.
- Build the corporate knowledge and skill base (intellectual and social capital) of employees – develop human potential.

  ○ Foster productive diversity in the workplace (OH&S, gender equity, participative decision making, work–life balance).
  ○ Develop the capability for continuing corporate reshaping and renewal, including visionary change leadership.

- Create communities of practice to diffuse knowledge and skills.
- Provide relevant expertise in the best way to organize work for high performance and satisfaction.
- Represent employees' concerns to management while simultaneously giving employees an increased role in organizational decision making.

Human sustainability: the external agenda

- Reinterpret strategy around a wider range of stakeholders and develop co-operative strategies with them (responsiveness).
- Add, rather than subtract, value for all relevant stakeholders.
- Build a culture of workplace learning and commitment to a 'generative society' through a declared and enacted value base.
- Initiate and sustain an ongoing dialogue with stakeholders to define key elements of social responsibility – set priorities (accountability).
- Define social goals, develop action plans to reach these goals, monitor and disclose performance against key performance indicators (transparency).
- Seek genuine feedback on performance from stakeholders – welcome and learn from criticism.
- Win, by responsible informed action, the support of all stakeholders for the organization's continued existence and growth.
- Design a production system that is an integral part of the ecology (like an earthworm).

- Conduct life-cycle assessment and a policy of resource stewardship.
- Eliminate waste and pollution, particularly by product redesign and developing an industrial ecology.
- Form active partnerships with 'green', human rights and other community groups.
- Appoint independent experts to monitor the corporation's environmental 'footprint' (environmental auditing).
- Link action on human sustainability with action on ecological sustainability to create an integrated, seamless approach to corporate sustainability.

Achieving ecological sustainability

Owning your power and changing corporate culture

Corporate culture is strategy in action.[49] Culture arises out of the collective experience of the members of an organization; it provides a framework of meaning to interpret the stream of events people encounter in the workplace so that they can make sense of their work and their role in the organization and society. Culture is a guide to action – at best a living expression of the strategic intent of the organization. The role of change leaders is to actively engage in the process of meaning making so that they are an integral and powerful part of the process of cultural redefinition that must take place in order to create sustaining organizations in a sustainable society.

In this change process, actions are often more powerful than words, though words have an important place. Symbolic events are frequently the focus for significant shifts in cultural awareness. Part of the role of the change leader is to become an actor in the unfolding drama of change towards sustainability. Paul Bate refers to cultural leadership as 'multilateral brokerage in a jungle of meaning'.[50] This emphasizes the dynamic nature of the change process, the centrality of meaning making and the change agent's function as a broker working the active dialogue of actions and words around the organization's future role. Bate rightly points out that change agents can't control cultural development – they can only 'initiate, influence and shape the direction of the emerging culture'.[51]

> The art of cultural coevolution is the art of managing dynamic complexity over time. Connecting things is relatively easy – the skill

is in finding ways for them to connect in an organized, indirect, limited, yet coherently meaningful way.

(R. D. Hames and G. Callanan, *Burying the Twentieth Century*)[52]

As change agents and change leaders we are only one source of influence in a complex changing reality. Nevertheless let us not underestimate the potential transformative power that we represent. As Korten has stated:

> The transformative power of the organism – both human and nonhuman – is the ultimate source of all that has value in the fulfillment of our own being. It includes not only the whole of the natural living capital, by which the planet's life support system is continuously regenerated, but also the human, social and institutional capital by which we utilize the wealth of the living planet to serve our needs and by which we may ideally come to lend our own distinctive capacities to further life's continuing journey.[53]

Change leadership involves owning our power and using it responsively and responsibly.

Putting the jigsaw puzzle together

We began this book with an analogy. We wrote that constructing the sustainable organization of the future is like assembling pieces of a jigsaw puzzle. We have identified a range of organizations which represent parts of the puzzle because they have already begun inventing the future. No individual or group has yet grasped the whole picture; not all the parts of the puzzle are in existence; but when we make an inventory of what this organization is doing here and what another is doing there, the bigger picture emerges. We have used the sustainability phase model as an overlay to the puzzle – we think it clusters the pieces in a way that delineates an integral part of one section of the final picture. We all have a role to play in helping put the puzzle together, in unfolding the 'implicate order'. We can lead where we are now, by fulfilling the potential of the roles we hold in the organizations of which we are a part. If we act with integrity, standing with courage for the planet, for a healthy society and for future generations, our leadership will contribute to creating a new organizational reality – the sustaining corporation that contributes to creating a fully sustainable world.

Notes

1 P. Senge, 'Foreword' to D. Chatterjee, *Living Consciously: A Pilgrimage towards Self-mastery*, Oxford: Viva Books and Butterworth-Heinemann, 1999, p. xiv.

2 I. Palmer, R. Dunford and G. Akin, *Managing Organizational Change*, New York: McGraw-Hill/Irwin, 2006.

3 S. Benn and L. Wilson, 'Insurance Australia Group: A Case Study', *Case Studies in Innovation and Excellence 2*, Sydney: School of Management, University of Technology, 2006.

4 Nike press release, 21 October 2004 'Nike names new VP of Corporate Responsibility Maria Eitel becomes President of the Nike Foundation' . Online. available at www.csrwire.com/article.cgi/3154.html (accessed 12 May 2006).

5 S. Benn and S. Low, interview with A. Sairenan, Environmental Manager, South Pacific, Hewlett-Packard, Sydney, 12 May 2006.

6 Nike 2004, Corporate Responsibility Report. Online. Available at www.nike.com/nikebiz/gc/r/fy04/docs/FY04_Nike_CR_report_pt1.pdf (accessed 10 May 2006).

7 Chatterjee, *Living Consciously*, p. 31.

8 C. Handy, *The Elephant and the Flea: Looking Backwards to the Future*, London: Hutchinson, 2001, pp. 74–5.

9 Quoted in Chatterjee, *Living Consciously*, p. 45.

10 R. E. Quinn, *Deep Change: Discovering the Leader Within*, San Francisco: Jossey-Bass, 1996, p. 9.

11 F. Luthans, K. Luthans, R. M. Hodgetts and B. C. Luthans, 'Positive approach to leadership (PAL): implications for today's organizations', *Journal of Leadership Studies*, 2002, 8 (2), 3–20; F. Luthans, 'Positive organizational behaviour: developing and managing psychological strengths for performance improvement', *Academy of Management Executive*, 2002, 16 (1), 57–72.

12 D. Dunphy, unpublished notes, The Skilled Practitioner workshop, 2001.

13 Chatterjee, *Living Consciously*, pp. 51–4.

14 From A. Einstein, *The World as I see It*, reissue edition, New York: Citadel Press, 1993, quoted in V. D. Dimitrov, 'Complexity, spirituality and ethics', in *Integrating Purpose, Vision and Practicality: Proceedings of the IV annual conference Spirituality, Leadership and Management Network*, Canberra, 6–9 December 2001, p. 22.

15 Quinn, *Deep Change*, p. 203.

16 Ibid., p. 204.

17 L. F. Buscaglia, *Living, Loving and Learning*, New York: Ballantine Books, 1982, p. 3.

18 For those who want to pursue further the idea of spiritual intelligence a useful starting point is D. Zohar and I. Marshall, *Spiritual Intelligence: The Ultimate Intelligence*, London: Bloomsbury, 2000.

19 S. Benn and L. Bone, interview with Mike Hawker, CEO, IAG, Sydney, 20 April 2005.

20 B. Hirsh and P. Sheldrake, *Inclusive Leadership: Rethinking the World of Business to Generate the Dynamics of Lasting Success*, Melbourne: Information Australia, 2001.

21 Ibid., pp. 211–12.

22 L. Gratton, *Living Strategy: Putting People at the Heart of Corporate Purpose*, London: *Financial Times*/Prentice-Hall, 2000, p. 17.

23 K. E. Weick, *Sensemaking in Organizations*, Beverly Hills, CA: Sage Publications, 1995.

24 For a more extended discussion of the nature of dialogue see E. H. Schein, *Process Consultation Revisited: Building the Helping Relationship*, Reading, MA: Addison-Wesley, 1999, pp. 201–18.

25 F. Blount, 'Changing places: Blount and Joss', *Human Resources Monthly*, 1999, December, 10–14.

26 Quinn, *Deep Change*, p. 83.

27 W. Nattrass, M. Nattrass and B. Horniman, 'New rules, new plays in the changing game of business', *Batten Briefings*, Charlottesville, VA: Darden School of Business and Batten Institute, University of Virginia, 2006, 1–7.

28 Quoted in D. C. Korten, *The Post-corporate World: Life after Capitalism*, Bloomfield, CT: Kumarian Press, 1999, p. 215.

29 'The invisible movement', *Trendspotter Newsletter* No. 2, Denmark: Novo Group Academy, October 2001, p. 4; website: www.novogroup.dk/academy; see also 'Storming the mindsets', *Future News*, 6 (2), 2001, Sydney: Futures Foundation.

30 Quoted in Korten, *The Post-corporate World*, pp. 218–19.

31 D. Snow, 'Business warms to change', *Sydney Morning Herald*, 10 April 2006. Online. Available at http://www.smh.com.au/news/environment/business-warms-to-change/2006/04/09/1144521210225.html (accessed 12 May 2006).

32 Of course, many organizations today do not have a 'line' in any simple sense – the term comes from traditional bureaucratic organizations. We use the line/staff distinction as a simple descriptive classification system.

33 A. Lagan, 'A View from the Top', Sydney: Corporate Citizenship and Business Ethics Unit, KPMG, 2006.

34 Gratton, *Living Strategy* p. 125.

35 J. Elkington, *The Chrysalis Economy: How Citizens, CEOs and Corporations can fuse Values and Value Creation*, Oxford: Capstone, 2001, pp. 118–20.

36 S. Hart and R. E. Quinn, 'Roles executives play: CEOs, behavioral complexity, and firm performance', *Human Relations*, 1993, 46, 543–75; also reviewed in Quinn, *Deep Change*, pp. 148–51.

37 This result holds true regardless of firm size or the level of competitiveness of the firm's environment.

38 E. Debold, 'New operating reality', *Executive Excellence*, 2005, 22 (11), 8.

39 S. Hart, *Capitalism at the Crossroads*: *The Unlimited Business Oportunities in Solving the World's Most Difficult Problems*, Philadelphia: Wharton School, 2005; K. Magleby, 'Microfranchises as a Solution to Global Poverty'. Online. Available at http://66.102.7.104/search?q=cache:4Uu6zT7CPTEJ:www.omidyar.net/group/poverty/file/7.35.11055472357/get/+unilever+microfranchise+tex+gunning&hl=en&gl=au&ct=clnk&cd=1 (accessed 13 May 2006).

40 S. Benn, D. Dunphy and A. Ross-Smith, 'Building Sustainable Organizations', Presentation at Academy of Management conference, Atlanta, GA, 2006.

41 C. Chesterman, A. Ross-Smith and M. Peters, 'Senior Women Executives and the Cultures of Management', Unpublished report to a major Australian financial institution. 2003, C. Chesterman, A. Ross-Smith and M. Peters, 'Changing the landscape? Women in academic leadership in Australia', *McGill Journal of Higher Education*, 2004, 38 (3), 421–36.

42 D. Roth, 'Celebrating companies that excel at serving a variety of stakeholders well', '100 best corporate citizens for 2006', *Business Ethics Magazine*, 2006, 20 (1).

43 Ibid.

44 W. McDonough and M. Braungart, *Cradle to Cradle: Remaking the Way we make Things*, New York: North Point Press, New York, 2002.

45 B. Doppelt, *Leading Change towards Sustainability*, Sheffield: Greenleaf Publishing, 2003.

46 J. Benyus, *Biomimicry: Innovation inspired by Nature*, New York: Harper Perennial, 2002.

47 See Suzanne Benn, personal communication.

48 Roth, 'Celebrating companies that excel'.

49 P. Bate, *Strategies for Cultural Change*, Oxford: Butterworth Heinemann, 1994.

50 Ibid., p. 243.

51 Ibid., p. 245.

52 R. D. Hames and G. Callanan, *Burying the Twentieth Century*, Sydney: Business & Professional Publishing, 1997, p. 35; 41 Korten, *The Post-corporate World*, p. 117.

53 Korten, *The Post-corporate World*, p. 117.

Appendix

The corporate sustainability checklist

Characteristic	Activities
	Compliance
Vision/goals	Develop an integrated, organization-wide plan for sustainability
	Implement systematic and ongoing improvement in industrial relations, OH&S, EEO, EMS and community services
Change agents	Ensure top-level commitment
Key activities	Select and develop change agents and nominate responsibilities
	Identify and regularly update the organization on the risks of non-compliance with current legislation, possible future legislation and public opinion
	Organize workshops to define compliance roles
	Clarify roles of top management, compliance officers and other stakeholders
	Assign staff responsibilities to improve existing IR, EEO, OH&S and Environmental Management Systems
	Develop staff training systems
Corporate policies/ strategies	Foster an understanding of business ethics across the organization
	Work toward a comprehensive sustainability strategy
	Foster an individual sense of responsibility for the environment and the need to be alert to potential sources of pollution and resource waste
	Minimize adverse environmental effects of all activities and take steps to minimize waste and conserve energy

Take necessary measures to prevent avoidable accidental releases of pollutants

Provide advice on the safe handling, use and disposal of the company's products

Examine product liability requirements

Take employee suggestions and feed back into account

Minimize risk using a precautionary approach

Build and sustain reputation

Build a learning platform for the organization

Stakeholder relations
: Establish positive relationships with community and government

Avoid greenwash by reporting conscientiously

Enlist NGOs as environmental and social monitors

Establish volunteer relationships

Assist public authorities in establishing well founded environmental regulations

Human capabilities
: Create OH&S, EEO, IR and community relations policies and involve employees in ongoing improvement

Implement employee training programmes for OH&S

Implement employee awareness programmes for human rights and EEO obligations

Develop human sustainability auditing and reporting capabilities

Identify human rights, OH&S and IR obligations of members of the supply chain

Establish relations with a third-party professional to conduct external audits

Ensure ongoing compliance through implementing ISO 9000

Ecological capabilities
: Implement environmental awareness programmes

Develop ecological auditing and reporting capabilities

Identify the environmental obligations of members of the supply chain

Ensure ongoing capacity to address compliance through the implementation of voluntary standards or continuous improvement systems such as ISO 900I

Tools/techniques
: Develop a Sustainability Plan which covers the management and operation of facilities and the design, manufacture and delivery of products and services

Tools/techniques (cont)	Involve employees in planning for the development of the Sustainability Plan
	Establish auditing and reporting systems
	Develop relationship with relevant regulators
	Communicate Sustainability Plan aims, objectives and benefits to employees and suppliers
	Press suppliers to be compliant through face-to-face meetings
	Ensure that contractors working on the organization's behalf apply acceptable human environmental sustainability standards
	Ensure that any transfer of technology is accompanied by the information needed to protect the environment
	Assess in advance the environmental and human sustainability implications of new processes, products and other activities
Production/service systems	Identify legislation and standards associated with all production and service systems
	Ensure assessment, monitoring and reporting systems are in place to address compliance requirements relevant to all products and services

Efficiency

Vision/goals	Generate cost savings via the pursuit of efficiencies in ecological and human sustainability areas
	Generate efficiencies by reducing costs; adding value and innovation
	Develop an organization-wide approach that seeks to shift from cost to innovation in order to capture sustainable competitive advantages
Change agents	Allocate change-agent roles to operational and line managers with relevant technical expertise
	Ensure top level commitment
	Develop change programmes that generate efficiencies in specific areas – through the use of programmes – TQM, Natural Step; EMS
	Pilot programmes and look for opportunities to widen their sphere of influence

Corporate policies/strategies	Develop a systematic approach to the management and pursuit of efficiency. Look for 'small wins' and use them to spread the project, create a more programmatic approach Create corporate incentive schemes that reward employee performance and start to build social capital De-layer through the use of teams with the aim of increasing workplace commitment/outsource non-core activities
Structures/systems	Establish assessment systems to address OHS and community issues, i.e. start to develop internal structures for external stakeholder information management Implement HRIS systems in order to track human resource performance Assess and report on social/environmental impacts beyond compliance requirements Establish environmental management systems and link into corporate-wide systems Assess product risk and other liability issues and look at building into value-adding and innovation approaches (eco-design)
Stakeholder relations	Identify key external stakeholders and engage in dialogue, symbolic activities Form alliances with suppliers and subcontractors in order to deliver on environmental criteria for product/service efficiency Focus on the customer and look to add value to products by moving features to services Build new capabilities though shared learning experiences with other organizations Seek to build human capability through collaborative arrangements with other organizations
Human capabilities	Develop increased returns from human resources; develop a systematic approach to human resource management Identify required competences in middle managers and commence competence development Focus on appropriate employee skills development (communication, systems analysis, conflict management, problem solving) Reorganize in multi-skilled teams where appropriate

Human capabilities (cont)	Establish systems for employee empowerment Calculate cost/benefit ratios for human resources
Ecological capabilities	Develop the skills required to identify and pick off low-hanging fruit Start to develop competences in eco-design, supply chain management and procurement practices Develop and use systematic tools and measurement systems
Tools/techniques	Develop and use proven programmes – TQM; the Natural Step Implement TQEM and EMS Develop corporate-wide reporting systems for knowledge sharing
Production/service systems	Minimize environmental load and life cycle impacts Ensure packaging/design impacts along the supply chain Commit to take back products at the end of their life Review all material and energy flows in physical and monetary units in order to identify efficiencies

Strategic

Vision/goals	Scan the environment (present and future) to identify (1) potential threats to the sustainability of existing products and services, (2) potential opportunities for creating innovative sustainability products/services Ensure business activities generate competitive advantages through the pursuit of sustainability Develop a vision that defines core sustainability competences and values
Change agents	Benchmark against industry best practice Encourage feedback on new ideas in order to generate strategic insights Implement interpersonal skills training with a focus on developing the change competences of the organization Develop systems of knowledge sharing among employees Work to develop close relationships with stakeholders – internal and external Work towards establishing enabling organizational structures – teams, virtual teams and networks Aim to develop long-term sustainability competences

Corporate policies/strategies	Integrate human and ecological sustainability systems to create dynamic core competences
	Align the corporate vision on sustainability with practical policies and strategies for action
	Formalize the commitment to sustainability at board level
	Develop management plans and set targets for the integration of environmental, financial, human competences, and knowledge management
	Create cross-functional sustainability integration teams
	Use TBL/Balanced Scorecard to demonstrate corporate performance
	Promote research and development into next-generation environmentally sound products and services
	Constantly undertake stakeholder analysis
Structures/systems	Develop systems for capturing and utilizing employee knowledge
	Develop systems for training, development and transfer of knowledge that focus on core competences
	Develop structures – teams, project teams, virtual teams and communities of practice – that enable the pursuit of sustainability
	Align supply chains, stakeholders and logistics systems; examine e-commerce potential
	Develop performance management systems that monitor and reward sustainability performance of business units
Stakeholder relations	Define and communicate strategic interests and potential benefits with stakeholders
	Develop codified rules for the management and co-ordination of relationships
	Develop strategic relationships with NGOs, community organizations and other corporations
	Collaborate with non-profits and other commercial organizations and build reputational capital
	Leverage partnerships for sustainability, such as communities of practice
	Develop key components of innovation competition
	Work with communities of practice to develop knowledge base – become an agent for change

Human capabilities	Support work/life balance for employees
	Provide diversity training
	Empower people by giving them the tools and motivation to innovate and express values through work
	Implement career and benefits planning
	Develop flexible workplace practices such as telecommuting or work sharing and video-conferencing; utilize new information technology to create project and virtual teams
	Ensure that good architecture provides a pleasant working and living environment
Ecological capabilities	Develop capabilities for monitoring and acting on a broad range of ecological and social information
	Develop key relations with stakeholders
	Incorporate core competences on design/technology into strategies
Tools/techniques	Use Triple Bottom Line reporting or Balanced Scorecard
	Conduct culture-building activities
	Initiate strategic competitor analysis
Production/service systems	Establish and incorporate systems of industrial ecology
	Develop industrial ecology synergies through supply chain management
	Increase focus on research and development

The sustaining corporation

Vision/goals	Review basic corporate values; create a codified set of company values
	Ensure top-level support for a strong sustainability position
	Re-examine organization values against changing external expectations by active workshopping with stakeholders
	Codify corporate values
	Broaden stakeholder analysis to include society as a whole, future generations and the natural world
Change agents	Ensure that the senior executive team deeply internalizes and acts on sustainability principles
	Build strong collaborative networks between internal and external change agents to create momentum on progressing sustainability

Corporate policies/strategies	Build on the sustainability achievements of previous stages
	Use external bodies to conduct social and environmental audits; cultivate transparency and accountability
	Communicate achievements to employees, the community and other organizations and share learning with alliance partners – build reputational capital
	Develop new market opportunities; provide customized services
	Contribute to maintaining the biosphere
Structures/systems	Develop a networked, flexible corporate structure
	Form alliances and emphasize collaboration
	Create a strong corporate culture around core sustainability values
Stakeholder relations	Develop a shared vision with non-profit organizations
	Share employee work hours with non-profit partners
	Encourage active engagement in community activities
	Be proactive in pursuing sustainability agenda with governments and other community bodies
Human capabilities	Build the personal and professional capability of the work force; build intellectual capital within the organization and in collaboration with alliance members
	Include ethical concerns in staff performance measures
	Ensure staff relations are based on potential for contributions, not status; support participative decision making
	Ensure staff recruitment policies are proactive towards minority groups; foster workforce diversity and equal opportunity
	Ensure highest standards in workplace health and safety
	Adopt family-friendly policies
	Develop higher-order employee capabilities (process skills, self-confidence, sharing)
Ecological capabilities	Contribute to ecological renewal
	Be proactive in negotiating with other corporations for the design and production of more sustainable products
	Assist smaller corporations to be more responsible by sharing knowledge and expertise
	Use life-cycle assessment to reduce packaging, eliminate waste, increase dematerialization

Tools/techniques	Consolidate and integrate the systems adapted in earlier phases
Production/service systems	Redesign products to ensure environmental safety
	Redesign supply chains to become material processing loops to eliminate waste and pollution
	Dematerialize physical products where possible to emphasize service activities

Source: B. Nattrass and M. Altomare, *The Natural Step for Business*, Gabriola Island: New Society Publishers, 1999; Social Venture Network, *Standards of Corporate Social Responsibility* at www.svn.org/organization.html accessed 18 April 2002.

Further reading

Beer, M. and Nohria, N., *Breaking the Code of Change*, Boston, MA: Harvard Business School Press, 2000.

Burnes, B., *Managing Change: A Strategic Approach to Organisational Dynamics*, 3rd edn, Edinburgh: Financial Times/Prentice-Hall, 2000.

Clarke, T. and Clegg, S., *Changing Paradigms: The Transformation of Management Knowledge for the Twenty-first Century*, London: HarperCollins Business, 2000.

Conger, J. A., Spreitzer, G. M. and Lawler, E. E. (eds), *The Leader's Change Handbook: An Essential Guide to Setting Direction and Taking Action*, San Francisco: Jossey, 1999.

Doppelt, B., *Leading Change toward Sustainability*, Sheffield: Greenleaf Publishing, 2003.

Diamond, J., *Collapse: How Societies Choose to Fail or Survive*, Victoria, Australia: Allen Lane, 2005.

Dunphy, D., Benveniste, J., Griffiths, A. and Sutton, P. (eds), *Sustainability: The Corporate Challenge of the Twenty-first Century*, Sydney: Allen & Unwin, 2000.

Elkington, J., *The Chrysalis Economy*, Oxford: Capstone, 2001.

Ehrlich, P. and Ehrlich, A., *One with Nineveh: Politics, Consumption, and the Human Future*, Washington: Shearwater Books, 2005.

Flannery, T., *The Weather Makers: The History and Future of Climate Change*, Victoria, Australia: Text Publishing, 2005.

Hamel, G., *Leading the Revolution*, Boston, MA: Harvard Business School Press, 2000.

Hart, S., 'Beyond greening: strategies for a sustainable world', *Harvard Business Review*, January–February 1997, 67–76.

Hart, S. and Milstein, M., 'Global sustainability and the creative destruction of industries', *Sloan Management Review*, 1999, 41 (1), 23–33.

Hart, S. and Milstein, M., 'Creating sustainable value', *Academy of Management Executive*, 2003, 17 (3), 56–67.

Hoffman, A., *Competitive Environmental Strategy*, Washington, DC: Island Press, 2000.

Kotter, J. P., *Leading Change*, Boston, MA: Harvard Business School Press, 1996.

Meadows, D., Randers, J. and Meadows, D., *Limits to Growth: The 30-Year Update*, White River Junction, VT: Chelsea Green, 2004.

Nadler, D. A. and Tushman, M. L., 'The organization of the future: strategic imperatives and core competencies for the twenty-first century', *Organizational Dynamics*, 28 (1), 1999, 45–60.

Nattrass, B. and Altomare, M., *The Natural Step for Business*, Gabriola Island: New Society Publishers, 1999.

Orsato, R. 'Competitive environmental strategies: when does it pay to be green?' *California Management Review*, 2006, 48 (2), 127–43.

Porter, M. E. and Kramer, M, R., 'Strategy and society: the link between competitive advantage and corporate social responsibility', *Harvard Business Review*, Dec. 2006, 78–92.

Roome, N., 'Developing environmental management strategies', *Business Strategy and the Environment*, 1992, 1 (1), 11–23.

Rowledge, L. R., Barton, R. S. and Brady, K. S., *Mapping the Journey*, Sheffield: Greenleaf Publishing, 1999.

Stace, D. and Dunphy, D., *Beyond the Boundaries: Leading and Re-creating the Successful Enterprise*, 2nd edn, Sydney: McGraw-Hill, 2001.

Starkey, R. and Welford, R. (eds), *The Earthscan Reader in Business and Sustainable Development*, London: Earthscan Publications, 2001.

Sveiby, K. F., *The New Organizational Wealth: Managing and Measuring Knowledge-based Assets*, San Francisco: Berrett-Koehler, 1997.

Szulanski, G. and Winter, S., 'Getting it right the second time', *Harvard Business Review*, January–February 2002, 62–9.

Index